W9-AAK-032

Travel Writing

2nd edition

See the world.
Sell the story.

WRITER'S DIGEST BOOKS
www.writersdigest.com

L. PEAT O'NEIL

Travel Writing, 2nd Edition. Copyright © 2006 by L. Peat O'Neil. Manufactured in the United States of America. All rights reserved. No other part of this book may be reproduced in any form or by any electronic or mechanical means including information storage and retrieval systems without permission in writing from the publisher, except by a reviewer, who may quote brief passages in a review. Published by Writer's Digest Books, an imprint of F+W Publications, Inc., 4700 East Galbraith Road, Cincinnati, Ohio 45236. (800) 289-0963. First edition.

10 09 08 07 06   6 5 4 3 2

Distributed in Canada by Fraser Direct
100 Armstrong Avenue
Georgetown, ON, Canada L7G 5S4
Tel: (905) 877-4411

Distributed in the U.K. and Europe by David & Charles
Brunel House, Newton Abbot, Devon, TQ12 4PU, England
Tel: (+44) 1626 323200, Fax: (+44) 1626 323319
E-mail: mail@davidandcharles.co.uk

Distributed in Australia by Capricorn Link
P.O. Box 704, Windsor, NSW 2756 Australia
Tel: (02) 4577-3555

Library of Congress Cataloging-in-Publication Data
O'Neil, L. Peat (Louisa Peat), 1949-
   Travel writing / by L. Peat O'Neil.– 2nd ed.
       p. cm.
   Includes index.
   ISBN-13: 978-1-58297-381-4 (pbk.: alk. paper)
   ISBN-10: 1-58297-381-4
   1. Travel writing. 2. Authorship. I. Title.
   G151.O54 2006
   808'.06691–dc22

                                        2005024166

Editor: Amy Schell
Designer: Claudean Wheeler
Production Coordinator: Robin Richie

DEDICATION

This book is dedicated
to all who preserve and care for Gaia—
Our Earth—the traveler's home.

ACKNOWLEDGMENTS

A traveling writer needs the time and freedom to roam the world, and I was fortunate to be born into a family that prized education, creativity, and travel. I thank my parents, siblings, friends, and companions for encouragement and understanding. Special gratitude goes to those who provided warm homes where I could be myself when far afield. I send great thanks to the writers, teachers, and editors who contributed comments or granted permission to include their work in this book. I appreciate and salute you all.

AUTHOR BIOGRAPHY

In addition to writing this book, L. Peat O'Neil is a co-author of *Making Waves— 50 Greatest Women in Radio and Television* (Andrews McMeel, 2001). For nearly two decades, O'Neil worked in the newsroom of *The Washington Post.* O'Neil currently teaches writing for UCLA Extension in the journalism program online and writes for many periodicals, Web sites, and newspapers.

L. Peat O'Neil's short fiction, book reviews, and essays have appeared in *Potomac Review, Pearl, Pleiades,* and *Bloomsbury Review.* O'Neil was twice selected to participate in juried short-fiction writing workshops sponsored by the Jenny McKean Moore Foundation and Poets & Writers Inc. at the George Washington University.

TABLE OF Contents

THE PROFESSIONAL
TRAVEL WRITER

On the Road • Financing the Freelance Life • Our Responsibilities as Travel Writers • The Tools of the Trade • Free Trips • Contracts • Guidebooks • Joining Organizations • How to Recycle and Resell Books • Web Sites, Blogs, and E-Zines • Self-Promotion • Sustaining Relationships with Editors • Moving Up • Publication Errors • Lectures and Workshops • Develop a Specialty • The Future of Travel • Ten Steps to Get Started • Travel Like a Travel Writer

This book is for travelers and writers. Whether you plan to publish articles about your travels or improve the descriptive power of your letters and e-mails telling about your journey, this book will help you. While the focus is on creating travel articles for publication, anyone with an urge to travel will find in these pages fresh approaches to the art of traveling. A traveler using the ideas expressed in this book will hone skills for appreciating detail and uncovering unusual experiences. The writer intent on producing travel articles will receive guidance on how to record impressions and create a stylish personal account of a journey.

Novice travel journalists as well as published writers can use this book to learn how to transform journal entries into travel articles. People who want to turn their passion for travel into a travel writing career will find advice for getting started and writing exercises for building skills. Writers from other disciplines who are interested in exploring the travel genre will learn how to keep a travel journal and construct travel articles that will sell. People who haven't decided that writing travel articles for publication is their goal will find helpful advice about what it takes to be a travel writer.

The literature of travel enthralls readers with narratives and adventures from faraway places. Travel literature is a broad field, encompassing diaries, explorers' logs, collections of letters, narratives based on geographical or archeological expeditions, literary treatments of grand tours, pilgrimage reports, and even fictional treatments of journeys. The literary merit varies. It's been that way for more than two millennia, ever since seafarers, pilgrims, explorers, and traders compiled their experiences for someone else to read.

Travel writing is part of the nonfiction category of writing, which means it is factual. Not all narrative about travel is truthful; in fact there's a tradition of travelogues written by scribes who retold other people's travel stories or made up fabulous experiences in foreign places. The public snapped up these exciting tales about places they'd never see and sights that could not be verified. Today's travel writers strive to report events truthfully, perhaps heeding the advice of Samuel Johnson, who, according to *Anecdotes of the Late Samuel Johnson* by Hester Lynch Piozzi, wrote, "The use of traveling is to regulate imagination by reality, and, instead of thinking how things may be, to see them as they are."

Though some contemporary travel writers may inflate events with drama and tweak dialogue, the implied contract with the reader is that the travel story is true and the writer participated in or witnessed the events described. You can't write a travel article if you didn't go to the place. You can't make up characters or incidents to suit the story line. Travel writing is nonfiction writing. If the writer makes up the content, the product is fiction.

There are three main types of travel writing guidebooks and how-to travel books; travel journalism, which is fact-based reporting about places and people; and travel literature, which includes essays of places and personal travel narratives.

WHY THIS BOOK?

I learned to write by keeping a journal. Many of the notebooks were written while I was on a journey, and those pages became travel articles for print and online publications. Over the years, I've shared journal writing techniques with many people during workshops. After the first edition of this book appeared in 1995, I soon found myself teaching courses in travel writing, outdoors writing, food writing, and news reporting at several different universities.

Introducing writers to their senses is my first task as a writing teacher. Too often, writers depend on elaborate description when crafting a travel narrative. They amble into the rolling bright green fields that nestle 'neath rafts of puffy white clouds—the land of cliché and purple prose. They write what they think they saw and what they think it means, rather than what was actually experienced, told straight up.

Teaching people how to write travel narratives and keep useful travel journals is really about leading people to use all their senses—to hear, smell, taste, and touch, as well as see—and to report those sensations directly. Relying on sight alone to convey a sense of place handicaps the writer. Surely, the sixth sense, intuition, also attempts to capture in words a place and its people. Vivid travel writing propels the reader through the same sensual experience of places and people that the writer holds in memory. If the writer is lucky, these interactions and anecdotes are recorded in a travel journal.

Travel writing relies on showing experiences and conveying the mood of a place, so simple descriptive writing isn't enough. The writer has to notice fully and report that information to thrust the reader into the events as they unfolded while selecting narrative elements that convey an accurate portrait of the place and its people. Since a writer can't absorb and remember everything, be everywhere, or talk to everyone, the only reliable truth is the minutiae collected through the writer's senses. I teach writers to marshal their senses when they set pen to travel notebook. Write as if you are blind, I say. Push your other senses. For those who are creating their travel narrative after the fact from memory, I lead them through visualization exercises where the writer takes a specific point of view during an episode in the journey and writes from memory. The goal is to scribble concrete details of what was heard, tasted, smelled, touched, felt. In the classroom and during online courses, I use verb-based writing exercises, pointing out the analytical remoteness of verbs that describe condition or attitude and the potency of verbs that show action and sound.

"Like no other kinds of writing," Paul Fussell writes in *Abroad*, a study of British travel writing between the world wars, "travel books exercise and exploit the fundamental intellectual and emotional figure of thought, by which the past is conceived as back and the future as forward. They manipulate the whole alliance between temporal and spatial that we use to orient ourselves in time by invoking the dimension of space."

The travel diary is the vehicle for conveying the nuances of place fixed in time. Using the daily notebook as a source for travel writing is perhaps the most reliable method of capturing the passing scene. Photographs and sketches are useful. Habitual diarists—because they are used to writing details—have an edge in capturing the telling incident, the fragment of conversation, the transcendent moment that brings the reader into the landscape.

Think of travel writing by Rebecca West, Norman Lewis, Samuel Clemens, Tobias Schneebaum, Freya Stark, Patrick Leigh Fermor, D.H. Lawrence, Lawrence Durrell, and so many others. They report the details of the journey, the people of the place, the effect of the place on the traveler, and how will continue to be, despite the traveler. To infuse literary merit in travel writing, the diarist/writer needs to root the travel experiences in wider context, acknowledging history, culture, and earlier narratives of place, while sustaining awareness of his own role as the traveler moving through the landscape. These narratives weave a story line that uses the momentum of the journey in time, though rarely in chronology. The travel writer with designs on literature cultivates a stylistic voice, aware of the mythic heroic role of the traveler without sinking into ego-fused memoir.

In this book, you'll read how to demonstrate intimacy with the subjects through anecdotes, scraps of conversation, and links to personal memory that arise during the journey, while maintaining a broader understanding of the place and its meaning. Travel writers must place themselves squarely in the narrative, while sustaining the emotional distance to show that the place exists apart from the traveler's passage. Perhaps maintaining this perspective will ensure that more travel writers are aware of the impact of travel writing, and the visitors that follow, on any particular place. These techniques and others may improve travel journalism, but will literature emerge? Perhaps, if writers are diligent in pursuing individual perspectiv and write with skill and purpose, while feeding their own minds with superior writing, more of what is called travel writing will be known as travel literature.

HOW I BEGAN

My travel career began when my younger sister and I rode the Greyhound by ourselves from Canada to Washington, D.C. after a summer vacation with our cousins on Lake Ontario. I was eight; my sister was seven. I'd been on many car and train trips before that with my parents, but this was my coming out as a responsible traveler. By thirteen I'd decided to go to Europe and worked an array of after-school jobs to save money for the trip. I learned that I could always make money for travel just by working harder and saving. Prices may have gone up, but motivation is a more significant factor than cash in achieving travel goals.

At age sixteen, I flew alone to Luxembourg on Icelandic Air with traveler's checks, a notebook, and a return ticket for the student ship, S.S. Aurelia. Three months later, after a summer of adventure, hitchhiking, hostelling, and home stays with friends of my parents, I had two full notebooks and an expanded vision of the world and my role in life. I've been traveling ever since, filling notebooks, sketching people and scenes that snare my eye, and in the process, making friends all over the globe. Writing travel articles, based on excerpts from my journals, was a logical next step. I wanted to share my stimulating personal journeys with readers. And I have high-minded ideas as well. Travel writing provides a way to communicate what I have learned by keeping my senses on alert, noticing, questioning, and listening as I move through the world. If others could understand the world better by reading what I had experienced, perhaps human unity would be improved. Writing clearly and simply was part of the plan. The Zen master Shunryu Suzuki comments on communication in *Zen Mind, Beginner's Mind*, "Without any intentional, fancy way of adjusting yourself, to express yourself as you are is the most important thing."

The thirst for travel exerts a powerful force in my life. I believe that a journey can be an art form and be instrumental in personal transformation. An appreciation for the subtle aspects of travel and human connection propel my urge to write travel articles and encourage others to share their experiences with readers. I hope that other travelers will take up pen, or keyboard, and venture to share their experiences from the road with the assistance of this book.

Travel articles are profiles of a place that include the people, landscapes, weather, flora, and fauna. The history, politics, culture, and folklore are also part of the travel story. It is a genre that offers wide latitude for communication. Some travel stories are personal essays, adding the dimension of the writer's inner life. Humor is allowed and indeed prized in travel articles. Stories about the poignancy and similarity of the human experience can be told against a travel backdrop. With such a rich tapestry of descriptive possibility in each travel story, a writer can really stretch.

ARE YOU A TRAVEL WRITER?

Does this sound like you? Do you want to be a travel writer because you enjoy life and seek unusual experiences? Your antennae are up, you write the truth, but your focus is on the act of travel and what you discover while traveling. You are responsible for being accurate and to honor standards that respect all of the world's creatures and the environment needed for survival. Travel well and write about it without adversely affecting the world in which you travel.

Despite the ambivalent hero in Anne Tyler's *The Accidental Tourist*—a novel about a travel writer who hates traveling—the fact of the matter is, you really do need to enjoy traveling, the process, the going, not just the destination. An appreciation for the act of traveling is integral to writing about it. Attitude influences writing, and if a writer isn't happy about traveling, the feeling will color the text. Robert Louis Stevenson wrote, in *Travels With a Donkey in the Cevennes* (1879), "I travel not to go anywhere, but to go. I travel for travel's sake. The great affair is to move."

An ill-disposed traveler may place too many expectations on the destination, ignoring certain experiences and arriving without an understanding of how the place is reached in space and time. A true traveler strives to know more about the process of traveling than just the abrupt change wrought by a jet landing in a new location. This is not to say that jet travel should be avoided, but we writers need to be aware that our minds and expectations might still be in Omaha while our bodies land in Osaka. Perhaps we should focus on the travel process to the extent of communicating how near or far a place is in terms of attitude and atmosphere as well as literal distance. Cultivate an appreciation for all aspects of travel; this passion for the going will ease difficulties that will surely arise.

How do you see yourself as you travel—as an ambassador, a missionary, a student, an observer? Has travel changed you? Do you expect travel to change you? Perhaps you are yearning to travel but need an excuse, like travel writing, to get you started. There are no right or wrong reasons if the intention comes from your heart and you are dedicated to it. While reading this book, you may design a plan to travel and write, but it may take three years to save enough money to pay for the trip, as it took me when I was a novice traveler. Don't give up your dream if your plans are stalled. Stick with your idea. You are the one who will make it possible.

MOVING TOWARD TRAVEL WRITING

The first step on the road to travel writing is a personal contract. Make the decision that you are going to be a professional travel writer. You enjoy traveling, of course, and you'll certainly have to like writing. If you don't have a yen to hit the high road and a knack for writing, planning to be a travel writer might not be right for you. But read on—there are plenty of suggestions for travelers who only intend to dash off blithe e-mails about the journey to family and friends. There are tips on how to keenly see what you merely observe, where to meet people, how to find the heart of a place when you are just a visitor. To really travel, you'll need purpose—interests that focus your journeys. Or be willing to surrender to the flow of travel itself, making the trip a meditation on life. Whether you decide to write about your travel experiences or not, this book should help you think about the process of travel, the catalytic role of the traveler in the world, and the impact of travel on your own psyche.

A passion for human connection and a thirst for knowledge send you out on the four winds and seven seas. Enthusiasm drives you to gather experience and record the details of daily life. Read narratives written by travelers from centuries ago. The Moroccan traveler Abu Abdallah ibn Battuta and the Japanese wanderer Basho (pen name of Matsuo Munefusa) have much to offer contemporary travelers. The places those travelers visited have changed drastically since the fourteenth and seventeenth centuries, yet we are still curious about what they saw and how they achieved their destinations. We are even more enthralled by the telling of the story, the unfolding of the process of traveling. The writer's voice, above all, creates suspense, humor, consternation, satisfaction, and wonder. Do you have that voice? Are you able to tell a story about a place you know? Are you in tune with your senses, able to report what you smell, see, hear, and touch?

You can practice travel writing skills while still at home. A travel writer who lives in a place that the whole world is clamoring to read about can stay at home and compose wise stories. Writers who live in Bogotá or San Francisco or Montreal can feed stories to editors from their hometowns. The rest of us actually have to pack and go. Even if you think your hometown isn't worth writing about, try the exercises in this book and learn how to write with a keen eye. You'll soon develop a nose for the original story that makes an aspiring travel writer a published writer.

THE PLEASURE OF TRAVEL WRITING

Travel writing can reward in obvious ways, combining work with pleasure. Though you may never know who reads your work, you should know that you've helped others plan happy trips. You've brought faraway places into the minds of people who may never have the opportunity to travel at all. The world becomes a bit closer and more tightly knit through the efforts of a keen observer of the passing scene. Consider that the travel writer has a responsibility to bring a clear-eyed view of a place and its people to audiences that may never actually travel there.

THE LITERARY TRADITION OF TRAVEL WRITING

Beyond the basics of informative, service-oriented travel writing lies the literature of travel. If you've delved into travel literature at all, you know the feeling of being carried away on the prose horse of a confident writer. For a paragraph, perhaps a chapter, we are transported. This is the work of a seasoned travel writer, to transcend, to break the barrier of print and time, to bring the reader to the place described.

Absorbing writing need not be rare. With careful honing of descriptive skills, ruthless paring of cliché, and cultivation of words that communicate sensual awareness, a serious and dedicated wordsmith can create travel articles that stand out from the mainstream.

Some of the most vigorous contemporary prose appears in the travel genre. Think of Jan Morris, Paul Theroux or Alex Shoumatoff. And a few decades back, Freya Stark, Peter Byron, and Evelyn Waugh. These and so many other thoughtful writers probed the elements and spirit of place. Admirable writing is simple writing, using the enduring riches of the English language in original ways.

When prose is elegantly written, the words are fluid enough so the reader steps into the writer's shadow. This is the goal for a travel writer—to bring the reader close, so close that the writer disappears. Readers may finish the piece feeling like the experience described actually happened to them.

Clearly this is an art. Though writers may have little in common with their most devoted readers, prose connects and dissolves boundaries. There is an element in the skilled travel writer that evokes the everyman or woman, putting the reader at ease. The unspoken thought—I've felt that, I've seen that—comes to the reader's mind.

Truly evocative writing flows from the writer's ability to open the inner self, to dig in and explore what the senses reveal. Setting down personal impressions can be a risky, vulnerable activity. But confident writers are willing to be held accountable for their perceptions. A writer's self-confidence endows the prose with an irresistible quality.

USING THIS BOOK

This book is organized to help you advance toward achieving your dream of traveling artfully and writing about your experiences. Start by reading the overview of the types of travel articles in chapter one. A working knowledge of the vocabulary of freelance travel writing and editorial terms will help you understand the rest of the book, so take a look at the glossary in the appendix.

Chapter two discusses how a travel writer's trip unfolds. That all-important tool, the travel journal, is discussed in chapter three. Chapters four, five, and six deal with constructing a travel article. Photography for travel writers is covered in chapter seven.

Check out the path for marketing travel stories in chapter eight. Strong promotional and marketing skills will make a part-time effort grow, but have no illusions that you'll be supporting yourself as a freelance travel writer unless you are already successful in a related field of writing. Read about the business of travel writing in chapter nine.

Professional travel writing has changed over the past decade. Full-time staff positions for travel writers have diminished while the competition among freelance writers has increased. Despite the fluctuations wrought by economic and political shifts, almost every country in the world relies on tourism for income. A travel writer participates in an enormous growth industry.

The field is broad and there are unlimited ways of viewing it. Anyone can write herself into the landscape of a beloved place. Personal ideas and experience distinguish one piece of writing from another. When writers put their whole selves on paper, giving of inner experience, the reader is truly rewarded. Go then, and celebrate of the art of travel in your writing.

GETTING STARTED:
TYPES OF TRAVEL ARTICLES

You've taken the initiative to follow your dreams. You're about to try your hand at travel writing, see where it leads you, and find pleasure in the path, even if the destination can't be foreseen. Writing takes discipline, curiosity, and humor. Travel writing, as you might imagine, can demand a bit more—a yen for adventure, cross-cultural awareness, a grounding in history and geography, a facility for languages, and a healthy dose of humility.

In every discipline there are standards and rules. Although travel writing can be whimsical and personal, there are certain structural conventions. Travel articles can be loosely categorized into several different types, which we'll now examine.

Shaping the narrative to a specific type of travel article helps the writer stay on topic and find appropriate markets for an article. A writer who composes travel articles that fit contemporary article categories signals professionalism and familiarity with the travel genre. Knowing the various types of travel articles serves you during the writing and marketing phases.

Once you've decided what kind of travel article you are working on you can develop the theme, selecting salient details and anecdotes to tell the story.

Let's say you've decided to write a travel article about a weekend excursion to a new recreation area, a state park or waterway.

The piece has an outdoor recreation focus. As you write the article, the colorful details that engage the reader will be different from the scenes you would show if you were writing about the excursion using a family travel story focus.

In the outdoor recreation story, you would narrate the experience in the park and include factual information about sports options for other active travelers who will read your piece. In the family travel story, you would tell how a family enjoys the recreation area, explaining how the park facilities met or did not meet the needs or expectations of children, elderly relatives, and visiting kin.

To help you understand the varieties of travel journalism, this chapter contains explanations of several types of travel articles. They are guidelines, not fossils embedded in canyon walls. The types of published travel articles may change over time—stories about sweaty adventure trekking may go out of fashion, replaced by articles on luxury do-nothing splurge travel. As you become more familiar with the travel writing genre, you'll notice that many travel stories overlap several categories. Nor is this list comprehensive, because writing is always growing and changing. Travel writing evolves as its practitioners broaden their interests and hone their skills.

While you read my descriptions of the types of travel articles, make your own evaluations. Let the descriptions be absorbed in your thinking process so that the next time you read a travel article, you can identify the characteristics. If you have written an unpublished travel article, reread it to determine where it might fit in one of the categories. Consider minor changes to the article that might place it in a defined category.

This chapter should stimulate your marketing sense, too. Knowing the categories of travel articles will make conversations and e-mails with editors flow more smoothly. When editorial guidelines state that the publication wants family-oriented destination articles, regional weekend getaways, and humorous first-person essays, you will know what is expected. Should you need to call or e-mail the publication to clarify the length or deadline, it will enhance your professionalism to understand the various editorial definitions for articles. Staying tuned, as you write, to the conventions of specific articles will improve your focus and writing skill because you have defined the parameters for a given story. Knowing the type of article you will be producing should encourage you to stay on point and cut excess material.

Each type of travel article has loosely defined conventions of style and tone. A first step in refining your skills to match a publication's editorial posture is to be aware of the various types of articles that come under the rather large heading of travel writing. As you read travel articles, be sensitive to which category the piece matches and notice the word choice, style, and voice used by the writer. You'll see that within the travel article is a particular way of getting the reader's attention and presenting the material, known as the style and tone of the writing.

Notice whether the article is in present or past tense. Is the narrative expressed in first person (I, we), second person (you), or third person (the traveler, the visitor)? As you read, you'll hear the individual character and personality in the writer's voice. You may even start to picture the face behind this voice and in your imagination develop a connection to the author. This focus on the writer's voice may only last for the duration of your reading, but for those minutes (or hours if a book), that voice becomes real to you. Analyze whether the voice is appropriate to the content of that type of travel piece. In your own writing, you'll be striving to achieve a distinct voice appropriate to the material you are sharing with readers. Thus the travel writer who wants to publish an article in a hunting magazine will use language and diction that resonates with readers who are bow and gun enthusiasts. The travel article destined for a country living magazine will have a completely different tone. We'll focus on structure, style, voice, and pace of the article in later chapters; for the moment, simply be aware of the differences in various types of publications.

Accepting the utility of knowing the types of travel articles, each with their own set of rules, was the first lesson I learned about travel writing. Years ago, I asked the travel editor at *The Washington Post* how to publish travel articles. At the time, I had worked on my university daily newspaper, sold a few freelance pieces, and successfully completed several business writing contracts. About to embark on a year's travel in Europe and North Africa, I had the idea that travel writing would suit my penchant for travel. The editor told me to "study other travel articles, well-crafted pieces in the best newspapers and magazines." I took the advice seriously and devoured the travel sections of *The New York Times, The Globe and Mail, Los Angeles Times*, and *Chicago Tribune*, as well as smaller papers like *The Baltimore Sun, The Star Tribune, The Christian Science Monitor*, and *St. Petersburg Times*. Casting farther afield, to England, I read travel articles in the *Manchester Guardian, The Independent*, and *Financial Times*. Of course, I also studied the pages of *The Washington Post*.

After analyzing quite a few newspaper travel articles paragraph by paragraph, I noted whether a piece was told in first or third person; whether it was a personal experience essay or an objective description of a specific place; or if it was a collection of short informational paragraphs about a related topic without a narrative. Reading so many different stories, I began to internalize my analysis of the skeleton of the travel story. I figured the words would flow much easier if I knew where I was headed in my writing.

From newspaper travel articles, I branched out and studied travel-themed narratives in magazines and literary journals. In any article related to travel, I analyzed structure, pace, and the writer's voice. If an article pleased me, I combed the article for the author's tricks: how the writer conveyed humor, how facts were deftly slipped into paragraphs, how characters came alive with just a few sentences of dialogue. The travel articles I couldn't finish because the writing sagged were nonetheless instructive. I went back and marked the point where my attention stumbled and tried to determine why the narrative lost momentum. Of course, I also continued to read travel books and articles for pleasure, but analyzing articles to expose structure and technique became a habit.

Dip into the animated pages of respected travel authors like Freya Stark, Peter Fleming, Robert Byron, Delva Murphy, Norman Lewis, Pico Iyer, Bruce Chatwin, Paul Theroux, Jan Morris—and you'll find that their narratives usually contain far more than personal experiences. Necessary information is carried within the prose seamlessly so the reader learns many of the practical facts through the author's personal experiences. The writing is tightly trimmed and polished. Their experience permits them the luxury of digression, dialogue, reminiscence, and musing.

Expand your personal library and include travel narratives from great writers—Henry James, Mark Twain, Edith Wharton, Gustave Flaubert, Ernest Hemingway, Virginia Woolf. Oh, you didn't know they wrote travel pieces? Just about every author you can name wrote travel narratives at one point in their careers.

You'll probably want to begin collecting travel magazines and the travel sections of newspapers. Look beyond magazines specifically dedicated to travel. Ask friends and colleagues to share their magazines with you. Use the Internet to scout new publications and visit the periodicals department of the public library. Browse out-of-date travel magazines at yard sales for ideas. I usually find travel books at used bookstores and flea markets. Read them to develop your sensitivity to discern lively writing and pedantic writing. We're not talking about guidebooks here—look for travel literature.

I know you've been waiting to read about the types of travel articles. Let's dive in and see what types of travel narratives are popular. I've heard writers criticize travel writing because it employs a formula. True, novices need to practice travel writing within the structure in order to have the skills to crack the shell. Like figure skaters, beginning writers must do their "school figures," retracing the same form time and time again. Writers vary the subject and choice of words, but writing to fit the rules of length and cover the expected content without letting the structure over-power the writing does take skill. Mystery novels, romances, and thrillers have their own formulas, but after lots of practice, a writer internalizes the structure and the story flows following the appropriate outline.

DESTINATION

Destination articles are designed to hook readers' interest and send them to a travel-booking Web site or travel agent. Taking the broad view, hitting all the worthwhile tourist spots, a writer working on a destination piece pays attention to telling an attractive story spiced with useful facts. The writer's presence is muted but perceivable. Usually, some of the piece is written in the first person. The writer confides why the trip was taken so the reader can identify the purpose. For example, consider an opening like "Determined to subvert a looming midlife crisis that provokes usually sensible men to purchase expensive red sports cars, I booked a week of racetrack driving lessons at the Ferrari factory in Maranello, Italy."

The lead explains why the writer is taking the trip, where he's going, and injects a dose of humor. In such a destination piece, the writer would narrate what happened during the driving course, sketch some of the characters such as instructors and other students, explore the region and its history within the scope of the story theme, and perhaps include a couple of other related activities. The story is told by occasionally using the writer's voice, the mighty I, but most of the information in conveyed in narrative form. The story guides readers to decide whether they want to go to this place and should also serve as an armchair tour.

Destination articles explore the place within the structure of the story themes—in this case themes include car racing, driving lessons, Italy's race car industry—within the geographical region of northern Italy, which offers historical landmarks, natural charm, social history, and more. Typically, destination articles for the reading public in the United States and Canada focus on reliable tourist routes like Florida, California, Hawaii, Prince Edward Island, New York City, Great Britain, Europe, the Caribbean. But articles about lesser-known destinations such as the Yukon, Tasmania, Patagonia, or Madagascar are just as worthy. In fact, travel editors need a certain number of articles each year that focus on regions or activities overlooked by mainstream travel writers. Still, you'll need to write about the well-trodden places as well as fresh travel destinations.

Let's analyze a popular destination, Florida. Newspaper travel sections routinely devote a section to travel in Florida every year. Magazines feature Florida regularly, as a family destination, an outdoor wonderland for fishing and boating, or as a honeymoon destination. Consider this question: Why is Florida such a popular destination? It can't be the weather, because from May to October, Florida is hell's vestibule. There must be something else attracting so many visitors. The Disney expo-parks near Orlando? The space shuttle launching complex at Cape Canaveral? The Everglades' alligators and palm trees? Fast-paced Miami? The climate has a lot to do with Florida's winter appeal, but I think the real reason is the state's diversity. In addition to its growing population, Florida has been home to a variety of cultures for centuries. Your job, as a travel writer, is to discover a new destination story about Florida, a unique approach to a multifaceted place.

SPECIAL INTEREST

The special interest travel article deals with specific activities as they relate to travel. Food, shopping, golf, gardens, art, antiques, and baseball—any topic set in a specific location. The purpose of the piece is to inform readers how they can learn more about their hobby or personal avocation or pursue it while on vacation. The railroad buff, doll collector, vintage car restorer, orchid grower, and many more have magazines devoted to their hobby. Usually people who are passionate about a leisure-time pursuit are eager to learn more about it, even if they're already semi-experts. A travel story focused on these interests should find a berth in the respective magazine that focuses on each leisure pursuit.

Writers of special interest articles need to be familiar with the subject—credibility suffers if a writer discusses golf courses and has never swung an iron. There, you see, I could be making a golfing gaffe by writing "swung an iron." Be wary of inventing phrases unless you know the subject. Perhaps, with tenacious research, a credible piece could be written with only a passing acquaintance of the subject, but I'll bet the article would sound stiff and lack a personal touch. One way to write a special interest piece if you aren't versed in the topic is to take the novice's point of view. For example, the lead might go: "I don't know a thing about golf; so how did I come to be swatting balls across the clipped green grass of St. Andrew's?"

JOURNEY

Different from destination pieces, journey articles emphasize the way you get there. Scenic drives, vintage railroad, tramp steamer, bicycle, courier flight, footpath—the story focus is on the mode of travel. Think of times past when the going was good, the grand age of travel when steamships were standard, airplane seats were comfortable, attentive service the norm. The journey travel article attempts to recreate that mood, unwinding a story as the journey progresses so the destination is less important to the story focus than the means of travel. Advice will creep into the piece, but the romance of the journey is the main attraction, the focus of the prose and description. History will likely figure in several paragraphs, and there is always room for humor.

Stories about particular types of transportation are important to armchair travelers who are fascinated by trains, planes, boats, etc. and may never actually travel. The writer's impressions and feelings serve as the reader-writer bonding point. Travel articles that focus on the journey are also attractive to the general traveling public who use these articles for specific trip planning.

The journey article needs a strong personal narrative story line and useful facts. In the November 2004 issue of *Smithsonian* magazine, an article by Andrew Curry details photographer Aaron

Huey's 152-day walk from California to New York. It's not a very long article; excerpts from Huey's journal and his photographs comprise the essence. When the journey involves doing the same thing every day, crafting a compelling article is more about editing than including everything.

Perhaps you are a devoted railway rider and yearn to take a cross-country train trip. In this era of air travel, long-distance rail travel is somewhat unusual. Paul Theroux's 1970s train ride from Boston to Patagonia, which he chronicled in *The Old Patagonian Express*, probably isn't possible in 2006. If you undertook such a story, you would discuss the history of long-distance rail travel in North America, the amenities past and present, the scenery along the way, and perhaps include comments or anecdotes from railway employees and other riders. Narrative about points of interest along the journey and thumbnail sketches of people encountered make the journey come alive. The start and finish of the trip bracket the narrative on the act of travel.

THE ROUNDUP

No, it's not a preview of rodeos or a story about dude ranches or farm stays. In the roundup travel article, the writer collects information on a half dozen or so different places with a common thread drawing them together. A paragraph or two introduces the theme that binds the elements together. Ideally, the lead sets the tone and hints at two or three of the individual items.

Some newspaper travel sections publish roundups of brief stories by many travel writers about bad journeys. The roundups sport cute summary titles like "Holidays From Hell," "Turkey Trips," "Vicious Vacations." Other publications publish travel vignettes with a romantic theme around Valentine's Day. Bear this in mind if you have a story about a rotten travel experience or a travel anecdote steeped in romance. When you make marketing inquiries, ask about contributing to the annual roundup features. Here are a few topics for roundup articles:

- museums and churches in Rome that are open to the public all day
- modestly priced family restaurants (not fast-food chains) in New York City that are open on Sunday
- Colorado microbreweries offering tours and samples
- Las Vegas hotels that welcome pets
- Irish country house hotels with facilities for wedding parties

HISTORICAL OR HOLIDAY PEG

Tied to an anniversary, holiday, or historical event, the holiday peg story depends on a date. But beware—many editors avoid holiday peg stories because they see it as a hackneyed method of structuring a travel or lifestyle section. Other editors follow the predictable cycle and accept holiday peg stories as soon as they can get them. For the writer, this means approaching an editor with a holiday story well in advance. In fact, a few months after the event is a good time to pitch a story for the following year. Such a conversation might go something like this: "I just read your President's Day travel feature on 'Ford's Theater and the House Where Abe Lincoln Died.' For next President's Day, would you be interested in a travel story about tracing Lincoln's visits to Civil War battlefields? I had in mind a 'footsteps of the President' story line. Perhaps we could illustrate the piece with historic photographs that are in the public domain." Obviously, you would have prepared your phone script and be ready to answer specific questions.

Periodic events such as the Olympics, World Cup, World Expos, or the annual naming of the European City of Culture are natural pegs for travel stories. Major travel magnets such as these will draw lots of tourists, and travel editors know to provide a range of stories to satisfy this market. Many publications assign their staff writers to handle travel stories in conjunction with news-related coverage. If the staff writers are swamped with work, however, the freelancer has a potential opportunity. So, even if you are turned down early because a staff writer may be doing travel stories related to the major event, as long as the editor has expressed an interest in your work, try again closer to the event. If the editor has flatly rejected your ideas and previously published work, don't annoy the editor by calling or e-mailing again and again. Try another publication. Research will pay off here. You need to know where these events will be held for the next several years so you can sell stories pegged to the events, destination and side trip pieces. Search the Web or visit a reference library to determine future sites for Olympics or other international events.

Instead of writing a destination piece about where the Olympic Games will be held next—a story that most publications will assign to their staff writers—you could construct a side trip travel piece or a travel service article related to the Olympic Games site.

The holiday peg story can overlap other types of travel stories. Think of a New Year's holiday food and travel story or an outdoor recreation story focused on Thanksgiving. Indeed, it's possible to write travel stories focused on an important world cultural or recreational event in every one of the categories summarized in this chapter.

Hook the winter year-end holidays by writing about traveling in a sleigh, or consider playing with opposites. I sold a story about "Christmas in a Muslim Land" to the *St. Petersburg Times* travel section. Later, this story of cultural contrasts netted a positive response from an online editor at *National Geographic*.

SIDE TRIP

Its name clues you in: a side trip from a major destination. The side trip travel story spins off the well-traveled route, revealing a new facet of a popular attraction. Smart travel writers know that there are some destinations that are always going to be featured: European capitals, major U.S. tourist centers like California, Florida, and New England, the Caribbean, and the Pacific Rim. Side trip stories enable an editor to create a focused issue with several stories about the same general area. Side trip articles serve the leisure and business visitor who is pressed for time. Usually, side trip excursions can be done in a day or less. Details about transportation, days of closure, hours of opening, admission fees, etc. are significant. Readers don't want to take the time to travel away from their primary destination only to find out the nearby attraction is closed for the day.

Here are a few samples of side trip stories: "Woodlawn and Oatlands: Historic Plantations Near the Nation's Capital"; "Tibetan Buddhist Retreat on Staten Island"; "Chartes: Day Trip From Paris"; "Escape Los Angeles on Catalina Island."

OUTDOORS OR RECREATION

The outdoors and recreation travel story is much like a special interest story except it takes place outdoors. It resembles a destination piece and could be a side trip, but it always takes place outdoors. The outdoors travel story overlaps with the other categories in terms of structure but usually involves physical challenge and an element of adventure.

The market for travel stories about outdoor activities is growing and covers all demographic groups. Guided biking adventures, water and mountain sports, recreation for handicapped people, family sport, retirement camping, ecotourism, luxury walking tours where participants stay in chateau hotels, the list goes on. If there is one area to pay attention to in addition to food and travel, it is soft adventure and sport-related travel. Soft adventure usually refers to a packaged adventure tour involving physical activity—hiking, mountain bike riding, horseback riding, rafting—led by an experienced guide. A travel writer with an interest in an outdoor activity can specialize and corner a niche. Paragliding, rock climbing, snowboarding, windsurfing, scuba diving, sea-kayaking, walking, hunting, fishing, bird-watching—whatever level of outdoor challenge you choose to write about, the criteria are that you know the vocabulary, do it yourself at least once, and it be outdoors.

The great thing about being a travel writer is that even if you have never done an activity before, you can try it out at an interesting location and write about the experience! Readers will understand; they are often first-timers, too. Your going out in advance and writing about how to tackle a new outdoor activity helps them take that long-awaited bicycle tour in Provence, that first scuba plunge in the Cayman Islands, that first family camping trip in the Great Smoky Mountains in Tennessee.

During recent years, "ecotourism" and "ethnic tourism" have entered the travel lexicon. The concept of sustainable tourism embraces a range of principles that include leaving minimal impact on natural areas, supporting indigenous businesses and travel services rather than European or U.S.-based tour operators, participating in local conservation or cultural efforts, learning about the people and finding ways to share experiences with them. In practice, many tour operators label travel products "ecotours" that aren't. Before using the phrase, a travel writer should become familiar with the principles that guide environmentally responsible tourism.

Similarly, ethnic or heritage tourism purports to lead people to places historically associated with certain ethnic groups—Native American first peoples, the Amish, Shakers, African-Americans, Creoles, and others. Investigate whether the tourism promoters or tour operators are exploiting the ethnic groups or whether revenues flow back into the community.

NEWS PEG

Two sobering aspects of the modern world—civil conflict and terrorism—usually mean that if a place is in the news, it should be avoided. Travel editors know that people don't want to spend their vacations in war zones and advertisers don't want their message to appear next to grim stories. Writers, on the other hand, seem to flock to troubled areas in search of award-winning stories about refugees and the fortitude of human character. I'll bet some of those writers are stashing away notes for travel pieces they'll write in the future. I guess they figure that just because a place is torn up and terrorized doesn't mean a travel story won't sell, eventually—they just need to wait a few years. Change is inevitable.

Consider Vietnam, barren and bombed, a pawn of raging political forces. Once a battlefield, it has been reopened to tourism and commerce. Getting there first when a country resumes normalcy will enhance a travel piece. Writers who pioneered contemporary writing about Eastern European countries created a rewarding niche for themselves.

When peace accords flourish in the Middle East once again, savvy travel writers will book flights to Syria, Jordan, and Lebanon, fascinating countries long off the tourist route. Read the news with an eye for forthcoming political shuffles and economic shifts. You don't have to be a fortune-teller, just an attentive observer of the world scene. Which country is angling to trade with whom? Are hostilities between political factions shifting from combat to the peace table? Where are infrastructure investments flowing?

The journalism aspect of this kind of story means that the writer will have to be diligent about balanced sources. If the tourist board of a nation-state just emerging from a war/racial disturbance/health crisis waxes long that all is well, send in the visitors, you better also talk to people who don't have a vested interest in the resumption of the tourist trade. Of course, your own observations, what you see and experience in the newly opened area, go the longest way in telling a vibrant travel story.

Can you envision these sample titles in print? "Down a Lazy River: Rafting the Tigris to Baghdad," "Traces of Ancient Greece in Libya: A Tour of the Mediterranean Coast," or "Red Sea Resorts."

HUMOR

Could there ever be too much humor in the world? Editors are hard-pressed to find funny material. Travel writers with a flair for humor are rare and are particularly prized by travel editors. Like a stand-up comic, the writer of a humorous travel article uses personal experiences for the story line. Inevitably, the butt of the joke will be the writer. We all know that elements of humor depend on the audience and the skill of the storyteller. The anecdote that sends one person into gales of laughter might not amuse the next time it is told. What sparks the reading public's funny bone changes over time, but there are some universal witticisms—misadventure, simple human error, things or people that are out of place. We tend to see humor in a situation when a person's response, actions, or words are inappropriate but still achieve a satisfactory outcome—the inadvertent success of a befuddled adult, a child's unintended wise phrases, animal behavior that seems almost human, misspelled words in signs.

The humorous travel article might be about a single event or a collection of lighthearted incidents. Examples could be an essay about a writer's penchant for mispronouncing foreign words or misadventures related to faulty map reading that led to more intriguing experiences than the original destination offered.

Readers will recognize their own foibles and create an identity bond. They'll absorb the author's travel-related mistakes and learn what not to do, perhaps even feel a tad smug at the hapless writer's errors. Confronting prejudices and misunderstandings can be funny, if we the writers are willing to be honest and humble about our mistakes and illuminate the larger issues through humor.

Humorous pieces with a light touch are always welcome on an editor's desk. Strive for the giggle; avoid clichés. The shopworn joke isn't really funny. Before the spell check and proofread, the piece should be scrutinized for offensive language and bigotry of all varieties. If you don't know your prejudices, find a neutral person to read your manuscript. We all have our blind spots and what might seem funny to one person may outrage another. One person's view of a normal joke may be taken as arrogant or racist by another person. Maintain standards of good taste in your writing; editors tend to stay on the careful side.

TRAVEL ADVICE OR SERVICE ARTICLE

Saving money, packing lightly, staying healthy, shopping in crafts markets, international business etiquette, overcoming language barriers. Travel tips for wheelchair users, what to do if your rental car is broken into, the best computer equipment for working while on the road. All these topics and dozens like them form the basis for travel advice articles. Basic research for these pieces can be done online and by e-mail. Add a few quotes from telephone or e-mail interviews with appropriate experts, salt well with personal anecdotes to introduce the topic at the beginning of the article, and voila, you have a travel advice story ready to sell. Well, not quite. You'd better be sure that the experts really are qualified, the source material is fresh, and your anecdotes are startlingly unique. If you're relying on Web-based research, use Web sites that are updated daily or weekly. A travel advice piece about lost luggage, for example, had better be extremely funny, because the theme is commonplace, "done to death," as editors say. Remember that travel advice articles or columns that cover transportation and hotel discounts or Internet travel bargains are staff-written. Editors rarely rely on freelance writers for this type of intense, detail-oriented reporting.

Look for anecdotes and quotes from other travelers to communicate the scene. Using quotes shifts the focus from you while conveying information and ambience. Don't take anything for granted. Lessons you learn in your travels can become the nucleus for travel advice articles. Your chagrin becomes the genesis of a story. Experiences like running out of gas in the desert, missing transport connections, or being stopped by a traffic cop in another country are part of real travel and the sort of anecdotes to include. The trip where nothing goes wrong isn't a learning experience.

Students often ask whether tedious travel experiences could generate a travel story about a journey that's all about poor flight service, delays, luggage gone missing, and so forth. The answer is probably not. These events are commonplace. Even if all possible negative experiences happen to you on a particular trip, who cares except you, your loved ones and, if you're lucky, the customer relations departments of the transportation companies involved in the debacle. What would make a salable story is a travel advice report on how to avoid problems during journeys or how to resolve difficulties in the traveler's favor.

Travel advice pieces can usually be resold to different markets, especially outside of the traditional travel publications. For example, an advice piece on "sandwich generation travel"—families who travel with young children and grandparents—could be pitched to magazines for parents, senior citizen's publications, and the general travel market.

FOOD AND TRAVEL

Articles combining culinary pursuits and travel are strong contenders in today's travel writing market. The food-related article is evergreen because human interest in food is timeless. Food and travel articles aren't restaurant reviews, generally speaking. Usually, this type of culinary travel story explores the cultural traditions attached to eating, cooking, and celebrating with food in a particular region or country.

Lucky the travel writer who goes to a region knowing about prized local ingredients or has an introduction to the local bread baker. This writer already has a path to follow and contacts to call. But one of the pleasures of food and travel writing is that you can start with no information; just follow your nose. Aromas will lead you to an innovative kitchen and the chef within just might share the names of a local olive oil press, chili grower, curry blender, or wine cellar. Ask questions that provoke more detailed stories. Ask for recipes if the opportunity arises. Note the chef's name, where he or she trained and has worked before—perhaps you'll construct an interview for one of the restaurant trade magazines.

If you plan to write about food, you better learn the basics of cooking. Experience will equip you to tell a good meal from a bad one and pinpoint where in the preparation the chef went wrong. Read *Larousse Gastronomique*, the massive French encyclopedia of food, and culinary historians on the world's cuisines. No one can ever know everything about food or cease to learn more. Constantly evolving, reinventing, and resurrecting itself, the world of food offers great opportunity for travel writers. Story ideas for food oriented travel articles include: "Wild Rice Harvesting in Minnesota," "Hawaii's Coffee Plantations," "Cuban Food Zones in Florida," "Where Do Chefs Eat in Rome?"

PERSONAL EXPERIENCE ESSAY

Classic travel writing that endures as literature often is in the form of the personal essay. Told in the first person, the personal travel essay is the one article that only you can write. Even if the travel subject has been examined hundreds of times, the writer's sensibility applied to the topic makes it unique. Told against the backdrop of memory, the writer's perceptions and experiences are the basis of the essay. Delve into universal themes told through specific examples that support or debunk the premise.

Far and away the most difficult genre to compose, this type of travel writing demands supple facility with the flow of words and an ability to use comparisons, allusions, metaphors, and irony with skill. The writer draws on all experience rather than impressions rooted solely in a particular location. Skilled essay writers usually have something to say beyond simple description. A strong point of view forms the track along which all the descriptive elements ride.

A personal experience travel essay is a collection of personal truths or evolving discoveries about events experienced in a place or during a journey. It is not meant as a psychological investigation of your inner motives and reactions, although touches of personal insight are useful and help the reader find a human connection. One of the strongest appeals of a personal experience essay lies in that identification with the writer, the sense that yes, the reader could have had the same experiences, felt the same way. How you care about the things that happen to you needs to be expressed in the essay; your opinion matters.

Here's what it isn't: The travel essay is not a series of diary entries about how you felt about your travel. You don't want to be like that eager student who thought that travel writing was just stringing together events related to a particular trip. All strong travel writing requires insight and perspective, but especially in the essay, you need to have thought and read about the theme in order to develop content worth writing.

For example, in a personal experience travel essay, you may be revisiting alone a romantic island where you once spent an idyllic week with a loved one. You'll notice differences—perhaps the gilded lens through which you viewed the place during a previous visit has chipped and faded—or maybe the palm-shaded one-hammock beach is now obscured by walled villas or high-rise hotels. Whatever you notice will be affected by time and your feelings. There is an edge between soppy personal reminiscences and clever, self-aware comparisons that have broad appeal. Guess which one sells to editors?

In travel articles that explore personal experiences, readers won't be able to check whether or not the set of anecdotes really happened or not, so establish reader trust early in the narrative. If the experiences were so surprising and fabulous that the essay reads like fiction, it may be wise to explain circumstances more fully in your narrative. A litany of nasty complaints isn't quite believable, either. Ideal essay writing strives for balance and uses fact grounding from neutral sources to support your thesis or prove your point.

The quality of a deft personal experience travel article, and thus a publishable one, lies in the selection of details, the authority of the voice, and the elegance of the prose. You may want to postpone an attempt at writing a personal travel essay until you have successfully handled fundamental travel writing assignments such as service articles, destination pieces, a few interviews, and weekend getaway stories. How you proceed depends on your goals. If you want to publish your travel writing, stick to the other types of travel articles that are discussed in this chapter and work toward writing personal essays after your writing facility has matured. If you just want to write and aren't aiming for immediate publication, there is no harm in striving to write the most difficult type of travel piece from the start. However, as with learning any complex skill, steadily increasing the difficulty while you progress produces enduring benefit.

exercises

EXERCISE 1: What is your favorite destination? Why? Explain the appeal of the place. Reach beyond cliché attractions like "pretty beaches" or "great shopping." The idea is to forego the commonplace and discover the unusual. The reasons might be climate, history, landscape, architecture, cultural diversity, food, or some other quality or special characteristic. Write specific statements. "Nice people, spectacular scenery, friendly atmosphere" are bland generalizations and inadequate for salable travel articles.

EXERCISE 2: To help you get started, imagine a recent travel experience and write:

I see _____

I hear _____

I smell _____

I walk _____

I taste _____

Fill in the blanks with specific adjectives and nouns or prepositional phrases to finish the sentences.

EXERCISE 3: Using the starting phrases on the next page, continue writing descriptive, sense-oriented sentences about your own experiences. The sentences do not need to relate to each other or be about the same place, although they could if you so choose. If you can't think of a personal travel experience to fit the opening written below, imagine a scene from a place you visit regularly. Use active verbs and avoid pronouns. Active verbs show action rather than state conditions. For example, "stroll" is an active verb. You see someone doing an action in your mind's eye. "Consider" is a verb stating condition and does not show action. As you work on these sentences, each could open a paragraph if you want to continue your thoughts. Coax out the details of that special travel destination you know so well. You could even write about your own neighborhood!

The streets _____
Stately trees shade _____
Buildings constructed of _____
Light cascades _____
The backdrop of sunset _____
Night noises _____
Flies buzzed _____
A guide in period costume _____
In the vegetable market vendors _____
The people here _____
Stone monuments _____

Did you notice that the second set of exercises does not use the pronouns "I" or "we" to open the sentences? Practice narrative descriptive writing where you, the writer, are invisible. Use verbs that display what your senses experience. This type of sentence construction is an important part of developing your skill as a travel raconteur.

EXERCISE 4: Make a list of your own special interests, hobbies, and areas of expertise. If you subscribe to newsletters or magazines related to these interests, study them. Are there any travel stories? Could there be? Next to each special interest on your list, write down a possible travel article related to it. Be creative; special interests can be so familiar that we don't think of them as special. Do you have a pet? Do you make crafts or knit? Tend a garden? Do you play a sport or follow sports teams regularly? Do you run or practice yoga or meditate? There are travel stories in all these activities.

EXERCISE 5: What is your favorite mode of transportation and why? List some journeys that appeal to you. For example: the drive down Baja California in Mexico, a ride on the Amtrak train from New York to Florida, the inland sea passage along British Columbia to Alaska, a gambling cruise on the Mississippi. List a few memorable journeys you've taken when experiencing the transport, the getting there, was more important than plans on arrival.

EXERCISE 6: Using your own interests and experiences gleaned in your hometown or during trips, jot down a dozen roundup story ideas. Then flip through your collection of magazines and travel sections and note the subjects of roundup stories. Evaluate your list of roundup ideas: Are they original? Why would an editor want to use them? Is there a logical regional connection?

EXERCISE 7: Write down six holiday peg or event-related story ideas. If you write: "Winter Olympic Games, Mother's Day, Christmas, July Fourth" you aren't being specific or developing the idea. Create complex story ideas that focus on the holiday in unusual ways. For example, for July Fourth, how about a story on visiting a factory that makes American flags or fireworks? For Mother's Day, examine how another country or culture honors mothers or find the town where it was first celebrated. For the New Year's holidays, visit an ice hotel or ice bar (Canada, Iceland, and other countries offer these novelties).

EXERCISE 8: Write down three primary travel destinations that you know about—your hometown or a nearby city and other places where you have lived or visited frequently. For each destination, write down six side trip story ideas. Break boundaries! Think of where to take children, where elderly people might be comfortable, where your skateboarding nephew would visit, the poor art student, the conference attendee with only two hours of free time, the sports fan.

EXERCISE 9: Quick, what countries are in combat? Were they tourist destinations before the current troubles? Or bring the focus close to home: Are there tourist destinations in the United States, Canada, or Mexico that have fallen out of favor because of lack of public transport, crime, air or water pollution, or other unforeseen disasters? Which areas, recently engaged in war, civil unrest, or environmental problems, have become accessible to visitors again?

EXERCISE 10: Consider the times when you laughed at your mistakes. Are any of them related to travel? Have friends told you odd and amusing stories from their travels? For example, did you ever mispronounce a city name and receive wrong information? I know someone who wanted to go to Dulles, an airport near Washington, D.C., but the reservations clerk quoted flights to Dallas, Texas. Jot down a few sentences about those funny occasions.

EXERCISE 11: List a few travel-related topics on which you could offer advice. Perhaps you've taken a pet on a long flight or bought a car overseas to import upon returning home. Select topics of general interest to travelers. Then, list a few travel advice topics that you would like to know more about. Nothing drives research like a personal interest in the topic!

EXERCISE 12: Remember the best meal you ate? Where was it and what made the meal special? Did you wonder where the ingredients came from? Focus on following the path of regional food—the taste, texture, and combination of sauces, spices, and ingredients. Look into the history of the food, what farms produce the ingredients, and how the ingredients reach the market or restaurant.

EXERCISE 13: As part of the self-education process, read anthologies of travel essays or seek literary travel writing in small press journals. Take note of the scenes and characters used to illustrate the writer's experiences. Develop your own appreciation for the passing scene by practicing active looking and listening.

HOW A TRAVEL
WRITER PLANS TRAVEL

All the world offers a potential travel story, but how to choose? Dedicated travelers won't have any trouble selecting a destination from the "list"—whether written down or imagined. Personal desire motivates selecting a destination to write about. After all, if you want to be there, you have a better chance of communicating experiences with enthusiasm. A lackluster travel story derives from a writer's boredom. You'll also use savvy marketing judgment in planning your travels.

Do you have that list of places you want to visit? If not, take a few minutes to jot down ten destinations or journeys that you intend to experience within the next five years. Don't think about the cost, child-care arrangements, your day job, security, or financial commitments. Open your imagination and scan the world map to discover your special trips. Write down why you want to visit these places, what influences your hope to go there. Perhaps you've read a book about the region. Search your memory for places that have personal significance. This list is your dream sheet. Use it to focus your travel plans, research, and marketing. You can always add to it as your career as a travel writer unfolds. The list is a reminder for you to focus your travel goals. Later, in the marketing chapter, we'll cover another aspect of your goal as a travel writer, achieving publication.

As you select a destination, consider what will make your story unique and how you will shape the story. Bear in mind current travel trends. For example, if you see a travel article in a national magazine about Oregon's wine country and notice another piece about Portland's innovative chefs and your frequent flyer statement contains a promotion for new air routes to the Pacific Northwest region, you may have spotted a regional travel marketing focus. Let's say you flip through a magazine at the dentist's office and a travel article features walking tours in Tuscany. Later, you see walking vacations promoted in a fitness magazine. There's a spot on the TV news about walking for health and the Sunday travel section reports on group walking tours for senior citizens. Get it? The travel trend is walking vacations.

How do you get on the front end of the information curve for travel trends? How do you create story ideas that anticipate social trends while satisfying your personal interests and abilities? Realizing that walking vacations are hot after you've seen two or three articles means you aren't going to be able to sell a similar story to those publications. And possibly other publications have already assigned similar walking vacation stories. While a case can be made for pitching story ideas to editors of smaller publications using story ideas you've seen in nationally circulated publications as leverage to encourage your target editor to approve a similar assignment, you aren't developing your skill at crafting story ideas. You are picking up the scent from other writers who've trod the path.

Leading-edge travel writers do their own story idea research. Talk to travel agents and tour promoters, travel industry public relations specialists, and journalists. Explore online travel forums. Study travel magazines published in other countries. Examine data compiled by visitor's bureaus on who travels to various cities around the world. Ask your friends and business associates where they are traveling for leisure and business.

Destinations become trendy for seemingly frivolous reasons, but there are ways of discovering the next desirable travel destination. A travel writer should be attentive to trends in other industries—design, food, entertainment, and fitness. This is part of the process of deducing where travelers are heading and what travel stories they want to read. Stretch your own horizons. Consult fresh information sources—newspapers from Singapore, financial magazines from South Africa, lifestyle Web sites in India. Though it would be useful to read other languages, you can explore the globe in English using the Web. Even if a Web site is written in a language you don't know, there are browser tools to handle rough translations into your preferred language.

Broaden your research to track social and entertainment trends that might not be familiar to you. Leisure travel is a discretionary expense, so it tends to track other lifestyle industries, particularly entertainment. Has a movie made in a certain location been released, like The Lord of the Rings series shot in New Zealand? Was a bestselling novel set in Kentucky? Were the Canadian Maritime provinces featured in a television drama series? Film locations may sway people to visit a particular destination, and people who don't plan on visiting the film set still want to read about the place. A movie about the Alamo may not rack up box-office returns, but the fact that the Alamo was central to a movie sparks interest in a travel article about the historic site. Once again, be ready to construct story ideas before the film or television series is released. If you're interested in writing travel stories related to entertainment trends, you'll need to read trade and business publications—*Variety, Advertising Age*, and *Financial Times*. At the very least, editors will recognize the tie-in and you'll have a reliable hook to sell those destinations.

Culinary enthusiasms inspire travel articles. When Southwestern cuisine hit the expense account palates a few years back, travel articles about New Mexico and Arizona cropped up in national magazines. What will be the next culinary big bang?

The anniversaries of various wars fostered a wave of battleground tourism. Archeological discoveries, ethnic heritage, and environmental issues also influence people's travel choices and editors' needs.

STORY IDEA DEVELOPMENT

To sell travel articles you need well-crafted story ideas. Review writers guidelines from travel magazines, in-flight and general interest publications, and invariably you'll see that editors are look-ing for fresh and unusual story ideas. You can usually find writ-ers guidelines on a publication's Web site or request by mail directly from the editorial office. Trouble is, some travel writers overlook the research phase in story idea development. Your "unusual idea" may have appeared in print recently. Pay attention to idea trends, read back copies of the publication you're targeting, either on the Web if stories are archived or in the library. While you're at it, review travel publications from other states and countries. Consider how you will develop story ideas for international as well as U.S.-based publications. We'll also look at this process further in chap-ter eight and examine realistic markets for your story ideas.

Fresh story ideas for travel feature articles are difficult to craft. It's not enough for you to base your story idea on the cruise you've signed up for or wherever you feel like traveling. You have to consider other elements in the publishing equation—what edi-tors will publish and what readers want to know. As a writer, you have to consider how to target specific publications for each story idea or completed article. For now, let's discuss how to evaluate trends and build story ideas that appeal to editors.

Questions to ask yourself as you muse about the topics you want to write about:

- What is the focus?
- What topics or events does the story cover?
- Why would an audience care about this destination or story slant?
- Who needs the information?
- What is the appropriate time to market a story about this place?

Before you approach an editor, remember the points an editor needs to know. These are typical questions running through the editor's mind:

- What's the story about?
- Is there a focus?
- Why is it timely?
- Is the story evergreen or is there a date or event hook?

- How will this author develop the story?
- Is this writer capable of completing the project on time?
- Who will the writer interview and where will the writer travel?
- If the writer has already completed the travel research, what did she learn and why is it interesting enough to write about?
- Who is the audience?
- What is the angle or slant?
- How long will the story be?
- Are there photos available?

Think about these questions as you toss around plans for travel articles. The story idea process serves your publishing goals if you think of the downstream product and where it might fit for publication.

IDEAS AND MARKET FLOW

While your own travel dreams are always worth pursuing, travel writers aiming for the fast track to publication will hone their story ideas to the needs of current market flow. What does that mean? You'll improve publication opportunities if articles explore places where people are likely to visit and the content fits with other articles recently published in a given magazine or newspaper.

Ideas that might have been attractive to travel editors in 2000, such as adventure trekking in Central Asia or renting a houseboat in the lake zone of Kashmir, probably aren't going to attract a tourist base in 2006. If you don't know why, you haven't been reading the newspapers. Similarly, if the Caribbean or Pacific Oceans have been whacked by typhoons or hurricanes, a travel article researched prior to the damage will need updates and perhaps a different focus. If the disaster was of epic proportions, such as the Indian Ocean tsunami of 2004, it may be years before tourism infrastructure is restored.

Pay attention to economic issues such as the value of the U.S. or Canadian dollar to other currencies. Perhaps the high value of the euro or yen will keep leisure travelers in North America, or send them to South America, where dollars tend to have greater purchasing power. An important step in crafting your ideas to meet current travel trends is being aware of current events, in North America and around the world.

Another key step in creating story ideas that are irresistible to editors involves attentively reading several issues of the publication where you intend to send your work. What are urban newspaper travel sections publishing? What articles do you see in regional travel magazines? Are the articles about driving tours close to home? Are the stories about family travel or cruises? Perhaps the stories have an educational slant or explore regional and ethic heritage. While you are building your portfolio, create story ideas that mimic current travel trends but have unique story angles.

Before approaching a publication, always examine several back issues. To make this research applicable to the ideas you've already sketched out, consider slanting your existing ideas to match themes in the publication you are targeting. If the magazine favors spa retreats, include a spa in your wine-tasting story plan. If a famous opera singer once owned the country inn you visit, dig up classical music magazines and slant the story to that audience. If the newspaper's leisure section regularly runs a local road trip column, cut your article and shape it into a day trip story with an emphasis on driving.

If you're like me, you might resist the notion of tailoring your story ideas to resemble published work in a specific newspaper or magazine. Fair enough. We writers rely on a self-image of creativity and originality. You can still be creative while working within the parameters of publishing success. Especially during periods when the cyclical travel business turns downward and travel advertising wanes, causing publishing space for travel articles to diminish, writers need to be creative in different ways. Apply your creative spark to crafting the story slant. Be creative about packaging and marketing your work.

When you're stuck with a pile of stories that aren't selling, reslant the content to match current editorial needs. Target the story to a particular audience sector—for example, instead of writing a general article about spring break in Cancun, Mexico, shape the story to appeal to a particular group—windsurfers, microbrew enthusiasts, salsa dancers, scuba divers, or amateur metal prospectors.

Some freelance writers may think this is elementary, that matching story ideas to the market is an obvious step toward selling your writing. But editors tell me that they regularly receive stories from so-called travel writers who simply write up their vacation experiences and then cast about blindly hoping to find an interested editor. These writers don't think about story slant or investigate opportune story ideas before traveling let alone match the story idea to a particular publication.

I trust you are aware the travel industry is cyclical, with regular swings up and down depending on economic, political, and security factors. When travel-related industries thrive and travel advertising flourishes, a writer enjoys easy sales. Writers need to understand contemporary market flow, bearing in mind economic conditions impact available space for print, broadcast, or Internet publication.

The news isn't all bad. Savvy writers approach the marketplace on many fronts, sending work to Internet-based publications, small low-paying literary journals, newspapers, regional magazines, and international publications. If you are keen on success, you're going to have to put more energy into marketing, planning stories with markets in mind, seeking new places to publish, and investing time in the query process.

Here's how I would research the idea-market process. I've recently traveled to Iceland. As a preliminary step, I've researched the Library of Congress electronic periodicals database to note which publications have run travel articles about Iceland in the past five years. (You could use Nexis or other fee-based news databases, or a Web search using Google or another browser.)

I jot down names of English-language publications where articles have appeared and take note of the slant by reading the headline, abstract, or first paragraph. While I don't have a particular story idea in mind yet, I do have notes from the trip and a general story concept. Most of the articles that my research turns up about Iceland deal with variations of the "ice and fire" theme—glaciers, hot springs, and volcanoes. Others stories focus on Reykjavik's club scene and the "land of endless summer nights" theme. Obvious topics, all. Those are the same topics that Iceland uses to promote itself in advertising. Are writers and editors simply imitating Iceland's tourism press releases?

My next step is to see which airlines fly to Iceland from major urban centers in North America. I'll examine tourist data from the Iceland national tourist office to determine where their visitors come from. Are most of their visitors from London, a mere three hours away? Or do tourists arrive from Boston, one of the major hubs for Iceland's national airline? I have more research ahead of me: Which Europeans visit? Scandinavians? While I was there, I noticed a tour bus of people from the Philippine Islands. What were they doing in Iceland, I wondered?

And I still don't have a story idea in mind yet, because I need to shape my story idea to the current market flow. Perhaps most visitors to Iceland come from warm climates—people in search of radically different landscapes. Or perhaps the country's national airline has opened new routes with direct connections to California, Canada, or Florida?

Another step in my story idea shaping process will be to ask colleagues and friends to tell me their impressions about Iceland. Even if they've never been to the northerly island, they probably have a notion of the country. It helps me in my writing process to understand what average folks—non-travel writers—know about the place. When I mentioned Iceland to a well-traveled British friend, he pointed out that the late Victorian author and artist William Morris had visited Iceland and was enthralled by the place. I realized that could be a useful fact to incorporate in my story idea construction.

Finally, I might examine the list of places that have published something on Iceland and see if I can develop a pattern. Why, for example, have urban papers in the southern United States virtually ignored Iceland?

The point in this process of building story ideas is to look beyond the obvious, strive to find ideas that are completely different than what's already been published on the topic, and please yourself.

SOURCES FOR IDEAS

It's useful to examine where you are finding story ideas. Do you simply wait for press releases from the travel industry and react to the prepackaged concepts? Do you explore favorite regions and wait for inspiration? Do you have a tried-and-true path through Web site research that yields travel trends? Do you page through recent travel magazines and create ideas based on the places editors seem to be featuring?

Do you write about what interests you or what the marketplace is buying? Ask yourself what you care about. If you're after publication in particular magazines or newspapers, analyze those publications for their consumer appeal. If you just want to write and the appeal of a byline is greater than the paycheck, follow your dream and write.

What do you hope to achieve in your route to publication? Realistic goals are easier to achieve. Setting publication goals with magazines far beyond your current writing ability might spur you onward, but it discourages most of us to have our work continually rejected. Better to aspire on several tracks—a glossy national magazine, an Internet-based publication, a midsized urban newspaper, a local newsletter, a literary journal, and a mainstream regional magazine. Pursue all tracks and you'll be surprised at the returns.

Aspiring travel writers who only query the national well-known publications limit their chances of ever seeing their work in print. Travel writers who limit their scope to local publications miss the bigger paychecks and publications with national or international readers. Follow all the paths to publication at the same time. Surprise yourself!

Good judgment should shape your travel decisions. Visiting international trouble spots doesn't make good marketing sense. Besides the inherent danger, there is the fact that travel editors aren't interested in stories from places that are falling apart politically. Putting yourself in the line of fire in order to research a travel story is just plain stupid. If you've just gone to a place where unrest is brewing or a disaster suddenly occurs, consider reworking the story with a current events angle and approach a news editor. Travel editors are reluctant to dedicate space to stories about places people are afraid to visit or can't get to easily. Advertisers don't promote places that aren't safe for tourists. Stay current with global news and think of events in terms of business and leisure travel. After you read a news story, ask yourself: Will people be encouraged to travel here because of this event or will they stay away? If they stay away, where will they go instead of this place? What place is similar to the troubled area, is accessible, and can handle the influx of tourists?

Seasonal timeliness is crucial. Coordinate travel destinations with your marketing schedule. Know how far in advance an editor lines up seasonal stories. Summer travel is planned by consumers months in advance; editors of the "slick" magazines assign and purchase stories more than six months in advance of cover date. (These publications are known as "slicks" because of their paper sheen and glossy photography; you also need to be a pretty slick writer and marketer to land in them.) There are exceptions, but a lead of time of four to nine months is not unusual for major newspapers and smaller monthly magazines.

PREPARE TO GO

Research your destination; support your story idea with information. Rather than tote around heavy guidebooks, I use Internet research wherever I am or carry photocopies of data that might be useful. Bear in mind that the Web doesn't contain all the information you may need, and in any event, a trip to the library or your own reference shelf might be more efficient. Weeding through four thousand Web hits related to a research topic is not an effective use of your time. Those who use digital notebooks and cell phones with Web access might rely on those tools for on-site research.

Take the time to call the tourist office or visitor's bureau of the destination country or city. Many countries sponsor tourist offices in major North American cities. Countries without tourist bureaus funnel inquiries through the Embassy's commercial counselor. Within the United States, Canada, and Mexico, states, provinces, and many cities have tourist bureaus that will provide brochures, maps, and information. I recommend leaving most of this research material at home.

PACKING PRACTICUM

How you pack and what you bring will affect the quality of your travel experience. Bruce Northam, a versatile travel writer and editor based in New York City, advises, "My first rule for travel is: The first thing you pack is yourself. Pack a mission with good intentions and the stories write themselves." For a novice travel writer, there's a little more preparation involved, but the essence of Northam's comment is significant. Invest in your dreams, educate yourself, and trust yourself. A journey I yearn to take has me leaving everything but passport and funds at home, taking nothing but the clothes on my back. The story would be about traveling really light!

Here are some tips I've learned during decades of travel. When I set out on my first solo trip in 1966, I used an extra-large suitcase, a copious zippered tote bag, and a purse with a shoulder strap. Inside were clothes for three months; I anticipated a range of experiences from the Salzburg Music Festival to tramping around farms. I had toiletries, books, a travel iron, a jar of peanut butter, and many pairs of shoes. I was only sixteen and didn't yet know that you could find everything you need in Europe.

Now we're halfway through the first decade of the twenty-first century and I know better. Part of the fun of travel is exploring: Go to the local market after you arrive and shop for necessities.

Whatever you think you need, you can probably find it wherever you go and possibly net a shopping anecdote for your article. But if you're staying above the tree line in the mountains of Kyrgyzstan, you'd better have sufficient toilet paper and plastic bags for packing out personal waste—there's no convenience store at fifteen thousand feet.

Travel experience hones packing technique. Find a bag that fits your stature. It's difficult to be a travel writer and a packhorse. Do you have a hand free to write notes or fend off aggressors? Can you gallop for that airport departure gate or that bus pulling away from the curb? Don't travel with a cumbersome duffle bag that slams against your leg or a poorly designed rolling bag that tilts off its undersized wheels. Where do you plan to stow your luggage as you squeeze into the bench seat of the jitney that runs from the airport or bus station to your lodging? The ideal bag should be sturdy, small enough to tote or wheel down an aircraft aisle and light enough to hoist overhead or hold on your lap in a tight spot. Check zippers or latches with the bag stuffed beyond capacity: Do they separate? Do straps and handles cut into your palms or drag on your shoulder?

Don't surrender valuable weight to the bag itself—avoid heavy leather bags and complicated duffel-backpack combos. Color and material is up to you, but waterproof nylon canvas is usually durable. Determine whether the bag really is waterproof—leave it under the shower or out in the rain packed with dirty laundry for twenty minutes and examine the results. Bring along a big thick plastic bag to line the luggage and protect clothes.

Wherever you go, you'll want to blend into the local scene, and an expensive suitcase or matched set of luggage screams "tourist target." Rough up your baggage; create smudges and scratches on the surface. I slap duct tape or tie cord on my bags to make them look old and to distinguish them on the luggage carousel. For me, carrying a purse or briefcase in addition to luggage can be difficult and invites robbery. When traveling, I stash cash and valuable papers in my shoes or a money belt. Divide your valuables; keep a small amount of cash in your pocket for easy access. Avoid pulling out a wallet or money belt in public.

Airport security rules now dictate that we have to keep our bags with us at all times. Since I rarely check my bag, everything I need is close at hand—there's no need for a handbag or briefcase. If my bag is checked somewhere, I just remove irreplaceable items (camera, documents, computer, notebook, etc.) and put them in a nylon bag stashed inside the larger bag until needed. Some travel writers use a small sports duffel bag in subdued tones or carry a small suitcase to make a businesslike presentation. Bright colors like pink or orange help identify luggage, and I personally think odd-colored bags discourage thieves because the bag would be easy to spot during pursuit.

Real travel freedom is never waiting at the baggage carousel. Garment bags are the standard for many American business travelers, but they are awkward to carry for any distance and as your travel writing career takes you to the antipodes, you'll be flying on aircraft without storage compartments or riding on buses with the bag under your feet or strapped outside on the roof rack.

Keep track of your belongings. If you're carrying three items, take note that you have the three bags before moving to the next point in your day's journey. Know where your documents and valuables are stored and check their security after every transit—before you leave and after you arrive. Then, if anything is missing, you'll have a better estimate where and when the loss or theft occurred. Common spots for losing documents, credit cards, or money are at purchase points or identification checks. Don't leave the ticket counter, duty-free store, or immigration checkpoint until you have mindfully returned the items to your habitual storage place. You don't want to waste your most valuable resource—your time—hunting down or reporting lost possessions. Resist the urge to hurry because the line behind you is long or because you feel pressured in a challenging environment. On days or nights when you'll be in transit, allow extra time and use any waiting intervals to catch up on your notes.

WHAT TO TAKE

Define the activities and climate where you're headed and make a list of what you think you'll need. During the days before departure, accumulate the items in one place, perhaps on a spare bed or a bookshelf. Look at this pile of belongings. Do you want to carry them every day for the duration of your research trip? Then cut the pile down. Consider whether any of these clothes or accessories can be bought at the destination or used and given away. Leave behind anything you can't afford to lose, such as jewelry, sentimental photos, or expensive electronics.

When you're on the road, send your excess gear home or give it away. During a two-month jaunt through Asia that covered chilly and tropical latitudes, I carried only an expandable shoulder bag and a small soft knapsack, about the size of a daypack. As I journeyed and acquired brochures, filled notebooks, and painted pictures, I mailed packages home, along with heavy clothes not needed in temperate Indonesia.

Some travelers take their oldest gear and give it away as they travel. This idea can backfire: One travel writer I know who bicycled the length of Japan, much of it during the rainy season, left his tattered, rotting sneakers in a traditional inn, beside the trash can. In the morning, the manager chased after the cyclist, waving the disintegrating shoes, yelling that he'd left valuable personal items behind. My friend accepted the sneakers with a polite bow, honoring local customs, and found a public trash can for disposal.

Dress for the climate where you'll travel. Bear in mind that during the northern hemisphere summer, the southern hemisphere experiences cooler months. Remember that mountainous areas always provoke extremes—heat, precipitation, and chill. Investigate when rainy seasons occur. Don't confuse the dress code of a country's resorts and beaches with urban centers. On Mexico's Riviera you'll wear shorts and sandals but not in the capital city.

A selection of knit tops and easy-care slacks or skirts is the nucleus of a traveler's wardrobe. Knits weather the pressures of packing; so do some silk garments and many synthetic fibers if you can stand them next to your skin. Cotton and linen wrinkle, but some loose clothes are intended to be worn rumpled. Coordinate the pieces, adding distinctive accessories—a vest, scarves, an unusual shirt, a belt, or bright tie. On a long trip, the clothing should tolerate hand washing. During my solo walk across France through the Pyrenees in 2001, I wore the same quick-dry clothes every day, washing them out nightly.

Test all ensembles before packing. Are quick-dry pants still wet in the morning if you wash them out at 10 P.M.? Do the clothes stay wrinkle free? Are they easy to clean? Are the colors neutral? Do the garments fit you? Will you sweat or feel too chilly in them? I hope you know the theory of dressing in lightweight layers so you can peel off or add extra garments as you move through different temperatures—air-conditioned buildings to steamy streets.

Roll or fold the clothes to fit the bag. Some people use tissue paper in the folding lines of business clothes. Clothes and undergarments can be compacted inside sealing plastic bags. Stuff socks into shoes and enclose shoes in plastic bags. Heaviest items go on the bottom; work up to the lightest. If you are checking your luggage during air travel, keep a change of clothes and nighttime essentials with you. Or travel light and just use one bag to take with you in the aircraft cabin. Use sample-size toiletries or buy everything on arrival. It makes no sense to carry a twelve-ounce tube of toothpaste on a one-week trip.

Handy items to have along include duct tape, large safety pins, nylon cord, extra plastic bags, a sewing kit, disinfectant, a set of cutlery, and a water purifier. Take one book unless you are going to a remote area. And you'll have your journal with you as well, I hope. Oscar Wilde famously wrote, "I never travel without my diary. One should always have something sensational to read in the train."

DRESSING THE PART

Consider the purpose of your trip and the destination. If you are staying at the Ritz Hotel in London, you probably could show up with your clothes in a paper bag and be greeted with aplomb. However, in the range of lodgings between rustic dormitories and five-star hotels with unflappable desk clerks, there are places where you may feel uncomfortable if you are underdressed. Baggy jeans worn with underwear peeking above the waistline is not appropriate dress for a travel writer unless you are covering a skateboarding event. May I suggest that we travel writers do nothing to further the regrettable image that North Americans have for wearing gym clothes and sneakers for all occasions?

Being mindful of dress customs in other cultures is part of the travel writer's pre-trip research. If the men in Manila don't wear shorts and tank tops, except on the beach, you'd be wise to keep your profile similar. If the women in the country you're visiting cover their derrieres with pants and a long tunic, adjust your wardrobe to imitate their style. Don't forget that dress codes vary by region and city here in the United States, too. As a travel writer on the move, you're not expected to dress upscale every day and evening, but I'd recommend having one ensemble for chic events. I recall a surprise invitation in 1997 to a fancy hotel reception honoring a newspaper in Jakarta and though I had a suitable dress, my footwear consisted of flip-flops and hiking boots. I snuck out and bought inexpensive flats so I would be dressed correctly at the reception. You're a working professional; that means being able to meet anyone at any time.

PERSONAL COMFORTS

When I travel, certain amenities are always with me: a bottle of water, high-protein snacks, fruit, a small pillow, earplugs, and an eye cover so I can sleep anywhere. There was a time when I stashed a Swiss Army knife in my carry-on bag, but those days have passed. A hooded sweatshirt completes the long-haul flight kit. The hood blocks light and sound while providing warmth around my neck. After a neat brandy or scotch, sleep comes at the usual hour and I manage to snooze, if not slumber deeply, the entire trip.

Keep in mind that you can place advance orders for vegetarian and other special meals on most airlines. I supplement meals offered by airlines with my own fruit and snacks because I don't like processed food. If you have special dietary needs, provision yourself for the journey. If you've ever traveled on long-distance trains, you know it's the custom to carry a bag of food, bottles of water and wine, fruit and bread. While you don't have to carry a load of groceries along on a flight, being self-sufficient gives you an edge on circumstances such as weather delays, runway waits, cancelled flights, and other unpleasant transit problems.

The stresses of travel, noise, jet lag, and long hours on the road will probably cut into your sleep routine. If you skip time zones, circadian rhythms of sleeping and wakefulness will be altered. Circadian rhythms are twenty-four-hour cycles of body temperature, hormone and plasma levels, and other biological factors. Sunlight affects these cycles. Analysts advise spending time outdoors in daylight as soon as you can after arriving at your first destination. If it's daylight when you arrive, go outside, not to bed. If it's dark, go to sleep and try to resume your usual cycles of rest and activity timed to daylight where you are.

Sleep will sustain you during difficult times and help you regain equilibrium. Try to start out on your journey well rested and alert. Whether you drive or fly, ride the train or bus, you'll be taxing your reserves of patience and equanimity just by being away from home and your chosen routines. Adjusting your body to the new time zone can be jump-started prior to departure by modifying sleep and waking times to fit the destination. Reset your watch to the destination time zone as soon as you enter the aircraft. Health professionals recommend avoiding stimulants like alcohol, coffee, cola, and tea during flights. Drink lots of water, not carbonated beverages that can aggravate the digestive system. Exposure to daylight is key to adjusting to the new time zone. Move around outdoors in the daylight as soon as possible at the destination. Even if the sky is overcast or it's raining, spend time outdoors.

Try maintaining your usual bedtime routines while traveling—that can help you feel comfortable. Ask the hotel to provide a quiet room away from elevators and street noise. Specify nonsmoking rooms if you don't smoke; arrange for two wake-up calls in case you miss one. Bring family pictures, a favorite small pillow, or a coffee mug to make the temporary environment seem more familiar. Stretching and exercise will improve physical well-being. Pay special attention to your physical condition during the first couple of days; head to bed in the evening when you are tired and sleep until you awaken naturally. Take care of yourself so you won't waste valuable travel time being sick.

SAFETY AND SECURITY

Much has been written about the problems travelers encounter in airport security checks. Do yourself and other travelers a big favor and remove knives, scissors, and other sharp tools. Anticipate the security checkpoints. Pay attention to regulations concerning use of cell phones and other electronic devices in airports, arrival areas, and on board. Some airport screening checkpoints will take away water bottles and other open beverages. Be gracious and follow the rules. Select your shoes carefully. Footgear with metal shanks, clothing embossed with metal studs, metal support devices, and medical implants probably will set off the security screening alarms. Review FAA, TSA, and IATA security rules before you fly.

Too many high-profile terrorist incidents have affected travel patterns during the past fifteen years. It's useful to remember, though, that there have been terrorist attacks all around the globe for many decades. The chances of a traveler dying because of an act of terrorism are pretty slim; the risk factor is beneath notice. You're far more likely, statistically speaking, to have a car accident on the way to the airport or slip and fall in the hotel bathroom or on a broken sidewalk. Stay alert, mind your back, blend into the local scene, and keep track of your belongings.

Don't let political strife ruin your travel plans, but take prudent steps to research the immediate realities of the places you want to visit. Do not rely on stale information and stereotypical warnings. With so much information available on the Internet, you can read local newspapers in advance, assess whether there is political unrest, and uncover specific guidance about storms and environmental problems. Arm yourself with information.

THE TRIP BEGINS

Your bags are packed. The airport van is on its way. Notebook and maps stashed in your carry-on bag; documents, tickets, and funds are secured. Does your heart beat a little faster knowing you are about to embark on a thrilling adventure? Exotic cities, engaging people, and curious sights lie ahead. Or have you traveled so much that you take it in stride, just one more stamp on the passport? I hope your passion for travel hasn't faded, no matter how often you've set forth. Let yourself revel in the anticipation. That's part of the appeal of travel. Prime your curiosity; the adventure is about to begin.

Oh, wait—there's more. You're also embarking on a double life—seeing the world for readers and for yourself. The path you are starting involves some effort, alertness, and finely honed perceptions of the passing scene. You are traveling as a travel writer!

Too often the lure of the perceived glamour of travel writing obscures the real work involved. Yes, gathering information in the field is more fun than tapping a computer keyboard or hanging wallboard. Remember that travel writing involves work, self-discipline, stamina, and organizational skills. Dash your illusions of a lifestyle enjoyed in luxury hotels and the first-class section.

At least at the beginning of your career you'll be paying your own way and hoarding tips on budget travel. The average travel writer preparing a story for a regional travel magazine drives to a motel, tours the destination, and snaps pictures, all the while asking questions of the guide and writing down information. That night, our freelance writer transcribes the notes, transfers digital photos to the laptop and types a first draft, falling into a fitful sleep on an unfamiliar bed. Next day, more of the same or the writer hurries home to finish the piece for an impatient editor. Okay, I admit it, that's an extreme scenario—usually you'll have more time to finish the article.

Novice travel writers should be aware that the process of seeing the world as a travel writer is more demanding than traveling for personal pleasure. Rarely is it glamorous. And by the time you're invited on first-class familiarization (fam) trips, you'll be writing for editors who won't publish stories that derive from free trips. Read more about free travel in chapter nine.

THE TRAVEL WRITER'S DAY

Vacation trip or travel writer's trip? Though vacation time can be structured to permit research for travel articles, working travel writers aren't vacationing—the word means to leave or vacate the usual routine. When a travel writer travels, she is involved, following leads, asking questions, interviewing people, and writing or recording notes. A travel writer's workday probably unfolds like a regular workday. Rise early, breakfast well, move into work mode, and leave time for a break. After lunch and a brief interview with the chef or restaurant manager, the travel writer again opens his notebook and pursues unusual experiences. Perhaps there will be a chance meeting with a colorful local or a scheduled tour arranged by the tourist office. Mindful of when museums and monuments are open, the writer has compiled a personal checklist of when to visit specific landmarks. Most important, though, will be time allowed for serendipity and discovery. You're there to write about people in their place. Engage people in conversation; ask questions that spark discussion. Even if you don't speak the language precisely, make contact and seek information.

Let me share a story about serendipity and travel. In 1991, I planned a two-month journey to New Zealand and mentioned my plans to an editor at *The Washington Post*. He exclaimed that he would be in the same part of the world, around the same time, on a three-week sea cruise to ports in Australia and New Zealand. We laughed that it would be remarkable if we met, considering that neither of us knew the other's itinerary and considerable distances would be covered. I had no idea where I would be on any given day. My travel style is to block out the time, plan a few specific activities and locations, and follow my nose as the trip unfolds. I wagered him that we would meet, so great is my confidence in the serendipity factor in travel.

Weeks into my trip, I was walking down a street in Queenstown, New Zealand, looking for a beer and dinner after spending the day hiking in the highlands. Lo and behold, there was my friend heading toward me. He'd just arrived in Queenstown on the ship that evening and was leaving in the morning. The window of opportunity for us to cross paths was less than six hours and yet it happened without planning. What's the lesson? Trust the forces of nature. Be alert, pay attention to your surroundings, and use your eyes. You might see someone you know on this small planet of ours!

During that same trip, I sat beside a businessman on an inter-island flight. Glancing at his reading material, I noticed a newsletter about meat exports. Prior to my departure, a Washington editor had asked me to write a story about trade with New Zealand. Did I miss this opportunity to meet a potential source for the article? Of course not. I introduced myself, apologized for reading over his shoulder, and a friendly discussion of New Zealand's meat exports ensued. A few weeks later, I interviewed this export manager for the trade story. Paying attention pays off!

Cultivate an appreciation for chance by intentionally getting lost on foot—during daylight—in a nearby city you do not know. Stay lost for a while, noticing where you go, what you see, and how you feel. Look around, not so much for an exit to the experience of being lost but to intensify your perception of place. Do this because your mind will be more alert once you realize you are not on familiar ground. If you can suspend the need to find your way out for the moment, you'll exercise internal antennae. Use this chance to improve dormant powers of perception that will serve your quest to see and describe new places and experiences.

I hope you don't have the impression that travel writing can be left entirely to chance. Nor is a research trip all work. There has to be some time for reflection and absorption. After all, with stimulating experiences happening to you and so much fresh information coming in, your mind needs some stretch time to consider what you've seen and heard. And you wouldn't have embarked on the travel writer route if you didn't expect to mix work and pleasure to some extent. Just keep the professional commitment in mind.

TIME FOR REFLECTION, LEARNING TO NOTICE

When I need time to reflect on what I've seen, to process information, I take a long walk without my notebook and let thoughts flow. If anything really important comes to mind, I can write it later. The idea is to release myself from the pressures of having to notice and write. Usually, a couple of hours "off duty" provides vista for a fresh start. Some of my most interesting travel encounters have happened while I was just wandering without a particular objective. Trust that you'll find enough material to write about so you can take time away from your plans and gain insight and inspiration from the place and the people where you are. As Shunryu Suzuki writes in *Zen Mind, Beginner's Mind*, "When you do something, if you fix your mind on the activity with some confidence, the quality of your state of mind is the activity itself. When you are concentrated on the quality of your being, you are prepared for the activity." Make time to focus on yourself and how you are feeling as a traveler. Consider how you are pleasing or challenging yourself in this location and sparks and action will emerge.

Concentrate on being yourself in the place where you are, noticing all that is going on around you. Put your energy into your senses so your eyes, ears, nose, skin, mouth, and mind take in all ambient information. Prepare yourself to be an attentive observer and you will be fully engaged in the activity itself.

This technique works particularly well if you are trying to write travel stories about a place you know well. In the beginning of your career, you will probably be writing travel stories for local and regional publications. Roam around your hometown and discover what you never knew was there. Fully participating in the immediate environment should reveal a random spectrum of experiences. After your walk, write down what you saw; teach your-self how to be a full-time observer. Don't let your rambling thoughts, memories, and associations dominate your perceptions. Pay attention to the sensory information you gather as you move around. Travel writing contains more than what you see; remember to listen, smell, touch, taste, and feel. For the moment, don't rank the sensory information; just notice and record in your mind and in the journal. A familiar street will never be the same again if you are really engaged in the present.

Honing a quality of alertness will serve you in many ways. You'll learn to sense difficulty and potential danger; you'll learn how to ask the questions that will get you the information you need when you need it; you'll spot the extraordinary; you'll be ready when opportunity manifests; and you'll be living in the moment.

Learning how to look is fundamental for travel writing. Train yourself to notice in a fresh, thorough way by pretending you are a spy, a movie director, or some other role that encourages you to really look at what your eyes register, from the orange candy wrapper on the street to the constantly burning street lamp to the single pink rose blooming in January in an untended garden, and so on, around and up and over and down the street. Record the middle ground, the distance, and details close at hand. Develop your storytelling skills and curiosity by making up stories about what you see. Practice storytelling with fiction to improve your nonfiction writing prowess. What questions would you ask and of whom? Use your home ground to train your sense perception. Then go ahead and visit places farther away, finding ever more challenging places.

ORGANIZING TRAVEL TIME

All of us confront the challenge of organizing time to pursue the projects we elect to do. When you are traveling, much of your time seems to be wasted en route. Don't fret; use long journeys to work on manuscript drafts or expand your travel journal entries. Focus your thoughts on the work and the miles fly. I carry printouts of articles and edit or work on a laptop computer. Many airports have wireless zones, and don't forget humble electrical outlets if your computer's battery life is low. Even driving trips can be useful; have a tape recorder ready to capture ideas. I've tried using dictation software while driving, but the sound was distorted in the car and much of the text turned to gibberish. If you have a well-charged PDA and a fold-out keyboard, you could work almost anywhere. Freelance writers who hope to make a professional-level career must be focused and organized.

ONE TRIP: THREE STORIES

Different stories can be constructed from one visit to a particular destination. You'll need to derive two, three, or more stories from each trip if you expect to cover your expenses or make a modest profit. Factors that limit multiple stories include insufficient research material and lack of personal stamina. It's downright difficult to write a story when you've returned home without the necessary notes. As for stamina, I think the easiest way to maintain morale on the job is to invest a high level of personal interest in the project, wherever you go. Keep focused on the task and have some reason for the trip beyond just going there to write about it. Investigate a hobby, visit a school, seek out a local artisan, find the farm where vegetables are grown, watch a favorite sport—the topic matters less than the fact that it gives you, the travel writer, a focus.

Budgeting time for various targeted research forays will depend on the proposed articles. Let's say you've decided to write about a winter getaway destination—a ski resort in the West or a tax-haven gambling zone on a Caribbean island. You hope to cover your expenses by producing three travel stories. One story might be a roundup of ski destinations. Another might focus on family travel options with the ski focus: how to keep the kids amused while the adults try snowboarding, or write an evaluation of children's ski classes. And the third might cover the history of the ski resort area, relying on celebrity name-dropping to advance the story.

If you're using an island destination, stories could focus on shopping for crafts market bargains or outdoor adventures such as parasailing and snorkeling. A third article might fill a special interest niche, like Caribbean gardens or food. Of these three potential stories, the one that will require the most time is probably the outdoor action-adventure episode. If the story line uses the beginner's point of view, you'll have to attend the classes, interview other participants and teachers, and actually go out and windsurf, snorkel, or snowboard. Even if you have mastered the techniques of a sport already, you'll need to explore several venues geared to the skilled sports enthusiast as well as discuss options for the tourist who is trying the sport for the first time. That kind of research chews up your time.

To manage your travel research, determine which pursuit needs the most time and do it first. For any family travel story, you'll either have to bring your own or pay close attention to what other families are doing. Develop a list of questions that cover family needs: Does the restaurant have high chairs? Are baby-sitters available at the hotel? Is the swimming pool, ski slope, or toboggan run supervised? Where are the entertainment attractions for adolescents and how much are children's tickets? Interview other guests.

Research the shopping stories as you move around. Gather prices, store addresses and hours and design information as you pass by stores, museum gift boutiques, and markets. Ask local contacts where to find quality goods and where residents browse for bargains. If you don't write this information down as you walk around, it's unlikely you'll be able to recover it later. Post-trip research by phone or Internet may be an option, but it's faster to grab the information as you go. Facts about duty-free shopping, export and import taxes, customs forms, certificates to export works of art, and the like are useful to readers.

INTERESTING THEMES SELL STORIES

Editors want travel articles with original story lines, narratives built on engaging experiences focused on specific topics. Editors don't want rambling travelogues and plodding chronological reports. Successful travel writers tackle several of their personal interests during a trip and explore new topics to keep their curiosity level elevated. A novice travel writer might be more successful choosing an avocation or hobby as a focal point for the travel story. If you play an instrument, for example, seek out local musicians or instrument makers or composers as a starting point for your travel article. Visit the local concert hall or jazz lounge. When a person likes what they write about, enthusiasm for the subject comes across to the reader. By the way, knowledge and enthusiasm also help convince editors that your article is unique. When you get to the point of marketing your story, the interest that shines in your voice, e-mail, or letter makes your story more attractive than a well-researched but flat piece of writing. Travel for its own sake is fine, but the writer who pursues a private passion while traveling brings more to the story. That's what Bruce Northam meant when he advised, "Pack yourself first."

NOW YOU'RE THERE

Look around, check out the neighborhood near the hotel or house where you are staying, study the map, and plan efficient ways of visiting significant landmarks or monuments. Coordinate outdoor tours with the weather. Raining every morning? You may have to postpone the walk in the park and head for the nearest museum, library, mosque, or market. But you don't always have to change plans because of the weather. Indeed, experiencing the mood of a locale in all kinds of weather is a way to heighten your appreciation for the place. How do local people react to the weather?

If there is a concierge at the hotel, introduce yourself and mention your special interests, but be discreet about describing yourself as a travel writer. Perhaps you are reviewing the hotel; you may not want your true purpose known at all, as the management may lavish special treatment designed to impress. Maintain your own agenda, but be sensitive to interesting alternatives that may arise.

I recall one of those interesting alternatives: I was staying at a campground near Carthage in Tunisia and noticed a crowd of people bustling inside a community recreation center, setting up a platform for a band. I asked a bystander what was happening. He said that his relatives would be celebrating a wedding that evening and promptly invited me and my companion. And we went, discovering a noisy and joyful scene rich with wailing music and singing, spinning costumed dancers, and tables crowded with delicacies. Everyone drank fruit juice, cola, or tea. The bride sat on a throne-sized chair at one end of the stage, robed and heavily veiled, with women in ornamented gowns standing around her. The groom watched the celebrations from a chair on the other side of the stage. He wore a dark suit and was surrounded by male companions. We didn't stay until the end, but we heard the music nearly all night long. Just think, if I hadn't satisfied my curiosity by asking what was going on when I first noticed the preparations, we'd never have been invited to the wedding party and instead probably would have been annoyed by the all-night revelry.

When your first day as a travel writer has ended and it's time to rest, reflect on all the fascinating sights and encounters you've experienced during the day. Take time to record your impressions in your journal. The sun's long transit is over and tomorrow promises a world of adventure and opportunity.

WHAT TO LOOK FOR

Finding local culture and activities at your destination isn't difficult if you think in terms of equivalent sites at home. Find out where people congregate: around markets and shopping areas, in cafés and restaurants, plazas and parks, schools and places of worship, at laundries and bakeries, bars and city hall. In rural areas, the center of town might be a crossroads where the bus stops or mail is delivered. Find out where people eat breakfast and join the crowd.

Develop a feel for local society by watching what happens among the people. Are women huddled at one fountain and the men around another? Do children play freely or do they stay right by their parents? Are all ages and genders and economic groups present in the public areas? Do you see beggars or musicians busking in the streets? Are you the only obvious visitor? Test your observations with a reliable source, a personal or professional contact who can verify where the various economic and ethnic groups live, work, and play. Find out where the rough part of town is and also where working people eat and shop. Visit a university or school. Go to a sports arena or playing field. Go to a church and stick your head into a clinic, kindergarten, or hospital. Be nosy in a polite way.

FIND OUT WHAT'S HAPPENING

Open your eyes and look carefully. Listen. Posters, flyers, local newspapers, and radio may announce festivals, celebrations, concerts, dances, theater, and parades. Ask people what's going on next weekend. Encourage them to tell you a story about their place. Ask shopkeepers where they go to have fun, ask the barber where to eat, dance or gamble. Even in the smallest village, there will be a store, café or taxi stand where people congregate to share food, stories, and entertainment. As a travel writer, you want to participate in all aspects of daily life to give a human face to the places you write about.

Practice this kind of research while you are still at home. Instead of skimming over the events listings in the local paper, consider which ones merit a travel article. The Civil War reenactment, the sheepdog trials at the ranch, the annual St. Lucia's Day candle lighting could lead to interesting travel stories. Look for posters and banners announcing dances, auctions, or sports events. Train your eyes to notice what often fades into the background.

Practice plucking out the details; look for what seems out of place, different, or in contrast. Scan a street scene and then pan your eyes slowly. Memorize what you see in a mental video camera so you can replay what you've seen, remembering that memory is always a kind of fiction and is never absolutely exact.

APPROACHING STRANGERS

You may have been advised early in life not to talk to strangers, but a travel writer must talk to strangers. Hone your instinct for picking the right strangers for conversation. In many parts of the world, the news is passed by word of mouth. Hesitate to ask and you miss the story. Bars and cafés are informal community centers in many places. We're not talking about the glittery coffee bar or dim cocktail lounge at the American-style hotel but the local tavern or tea shop where people—often only men in some parts of the world—huddle like conspirators and talk about politics, their kids, the crops, and the weather. Despite different gender customs in various countries, I've found that a modestly dressed traveling woman is treated carefully. Ask for information politely and you'll be treated in kind.

In North America, the local meeting place might be a fast-food restaurant, diner, or café. Cashiers and service staff at truck stops sometimes know what is happening in the region. Poke through the thrift shop or the hardware store and pose your questions. Get a haircut from a small-town barber or use the computers at the local library to access the Internet and quiz the librarians about local lore. Use every encounter as leverage for information.

STAYING SAFE ON THE ROAD

Of all the places I've traveled, the United States is statistically the most dangerous, primarily because of the prevalence of guns. And, in all my travels, it's the only place where I have been physically attacked. (I fought off a knife-wielding rapist in Florida, suffering knife wounds to my hands. He was caught later that day.) Yet most of us know that except in the stress-primed urban blender, chances are slight that we'll catch a stray bullet or be attacked by a mugger or rapist. Travel through small towns and rural areas and the likelihood of trouble decreases even more.

Succumbing to fear can ruin a trip. Know your limits and strengths; if you are frightened of going out alone, travel with a friend or change your fear by learning self-defense techniques. I've practiced kickboxing and karate for years, even though statistically there's little chance I'd be attacked twice in a lifetime. Let the hotel desk clerk know you are going out and when you are likely to return. Take on protective coloration by dressing like the local folks. If women wear loose pants or a long skirt and cover their heads with a scarf in public, you might consider doing the same or an approximation. Do the men bare their legs and arms, or are they all wearing trousers and long-sleeved shirts, even in hot weather? You may think that in the age of the global village and CNN how you dress makes no difference; however, I make these suggestions based on conversations with people I've met around the world and on the advice of cross-cultural educators. Wearing clothes that somewhat resemble the garments of the local population is visual evidence that you have respect for them and have noticed how they dress and act. Your appearance then becomes part of the unspoken dialogue, and if your garments seem familiar, this gives you introductory leverage and, I believe, a degree of protection.

There are no set rules on how to start conversations with strangers. Here are my guidelines: Watch the group dynamics, find a physical opening if there is a group, make eye contact, smile, say a word or two of greeting, and wait and listen a while longer. When there's an opening, state your question. Ask for advice or information. Don't rush. While this is an interruption and you may feel you shouldn't take their time, most people like to help. They may be curious about you and ask questions. Answer briefly. If you speak too rapidly, you may not be understood or may be perceived as being aggressive. Keep your volume and emotions in check; don't be intimidated and don't get angry or loud if no one responds immediately or helps you. There may be reasons for their lack of communication. Tough as it may be at first, the ability to approach strangers anywhere in the world is a useful skill for a travel writer, and it could be a survival skill. The more often you practice asking questions, the better you will handle unfamiliar situations.

Bear in mind that you'll need to ask a complete range of questions about whatever information you seek. Sometimes people don't volunteer the one answer you need. There will be false starts;

you may be given incorrect information because the person you asked doesn't want to appear unprepared. Saving face is important in many cultures and any answer is deemed better than saying the person doesn't know the answer. You may ask the wrong person and have to try several times to get the information you need. People may give you an answer that is partially right but mostly wrong because they want to give you some kind of answer. In some places, you'll need to ask the same question of several people and make a guess as to which one is right. Soon, though, you'll find that you have developed an innate sense for who knows what is going on and how to approach with easy grace. My rule is to ask three likely people the same question, especially concerning street directions.

Do you believe that most of the world's people have good intentions? They aren't "out to get you." Try to cultivate an attitude of neutrality and acceptance rather than suspicion and hesitation. In my travels abroad and in North America, I've found almost everybody kind and helpful. The French aren't all rude and Central Americans aren't trying to cheat you. Southerners aren't really slow. Don't subscribe to lame cultural and ethnic stereotypes promoted in movies and television situation comedies. Base your responses and opinions on specific experiences, not stereotypes and clichés.

By talking to strangers, I've met wonderful people and built enduring friendships in many states, provinces, and countries. Some of the friendships started when I asked directions. I've crossed North America by land nearly a dozen times and have received singular hospitality here, too. Perhaps the way we are treated depends on the way we approach others.

FINDING A STORY

In the international arena, the same kinds of sources—posters, radio and television programs, local newspapers, and Web sites—yield potential material for your travel story. Language might present a hurdle, but if you have a pocket dictionary or some familiarity with the language you ought to be able to figure out the specifics. Stymied by a poster? Ask someone on the street or at a nearby shop to interpret. School children are often a good source for translating assistance because they are probably studying English.

When I was exploring Spain and Portugal during a leisurely two-month driving tour, my willingness to ask questions paid off. We crossed the border into Portugal and found a grand commotion in the streets of Elvas. This town is just a border outpost, yet the streets were crowded and the public squares bristling with energy. We poked around and discovered a huge carnival and fairground. Cowboys in leather chaps milled around. Bronze-skinned men hoisted tents and tacked strings of lights between poles. Pink posters stapled to telephone poles showed a bull's head and some large Roman numbers. After a conversation with an older Portuguese couple who were settled into their campsite with TV, lawn chairs and a full-size kitchen stove, I pieced together the story. The town was famous for its bull festival and farm fair. Though not widely known to tourists, people from all over the Iberian Peninsula flocked to this fiesta. When I checked the guidebooks later, all mentioned the bullfights during this May festival. We just happened upon it.

Another serendipitous event occurred while I was with an adventure group trip in the Russian Far East. Overhearing one of the guides discussing a native festival that he planned to attend after the tour was over, I asked for more information. The festival would be held in a remote village way off the beaten track, which in Siberia truly means inaccessible. A group of young villagers and a few dedicated old-timers who remembered the tribe's rituals that were forbidden during the Soviet era would be celebrating the Ahahahalala harvest festival of the nomadic Koriak tribes of eastern Siberia. Cultural anthropologists from Germany and the United States would participate and record this revival of a traditional celebration long dormant. And, sure, I could tag along if I paid my own way and didn't cause any trouble. Who could resist such a unique opportunity? The unexpected detour resulted in an adventure travel story in a major newspaper, a chapter in a travel anthology, and a story for a Web-based travel publication about world festivals.

USING WEB SITES AND GUIDEBOOKS

Like most travelers, you probably choose the top tourist attractions selected from guidebooks, Web sites, and brochures published by tourist boards and culled information from friends or colleagues. Evaluate these popular venues with a keen eye. Is the climb up the Statue of Liberty really worth suffering the stuffy heat inside? Are the lines painfully long, as I found at the Taj Mahal, and will you need to find an alternative entry to share with your readers? Is the museum or monument so overrun with visitors that you can't see anything, as often happens at Washington, D.C.'s Air and Space Museum? Most important, are you visiting these places because you think you should or because you are really interested? Engaging travel writing is not about hotels and museums, meals and sunsets; it's about real people and how they live.

To taste the flavor of a place, put yourself in a variety of situations. While you will start with a focus on your own interests, you'll also have to explore sites of interest to a wider audience. You may enjoy wrestling matches and detest botanical gardens, but your readers may want to know about both. While you shouldn't attempt to create a story about a topic in which you have feeble interest, check out other activities to mention in your travel articles. Search beyond the guidebooks and read literature and history for story ideas. In chapter six, there's discussion about facts and what to read before a trip to stimulate your curiosity.

TRAVELING INCOGNITO

There will be times when a travel writer wants a protective identity. Objective reporting is easier when the hotel or restaurant staff don't know you're a travel writer. If you don't reveal what you are writing in your notebook, or for whom, you maintain neutrality. Once the word is out that you are a travel writer, special services may ensue. Nice for you, but those niceties are not likely to be forthcoming for your prospective readers. Table service may be swift and gracious for you but curt and disinterested for your readers. Privacy and invisibility allow the writer to ask questions and probe.

On a junket, which is a free trip offered to travel writers and editors or other people working in the travel industry, it is difficult, if not impossible, to maintain a low profile. In the eyes of the travel promoters, the writers are on the job 24/7. Before accepting free group promotional tours, ask yourself: Is this the kind of trip I want? Will I be able to pursue my travel interests and develop real stories? Will I be herded around and rely on what is dished out? For me, the answer is clear. I've never had a great time on a junket. Problems beyond my control dampened the experience or the group dynamics dominated the daily scene. Junkets and fam trips occasionally offer networking opportunities, but traveling on your own itinerary and following personal interests propel the best journeys and make the richest travel writing. There's more discussion of press junkets and free travel in chapter nine.

FINDING THE OUT-OF-THE-WAY STORY

Sometimes travel writers just have to rely on instinct. Practiced voyagers have a sixth sense about direction, nosing out hidden corners of a city, discovering a remarkable restaurant, happening upon the organist rehearsing at the cathedral, visiting the beach as the triathlon begins, approaching the proper stranger who just happens to speak English and teach at the university.

Instinct develops after years of practice. If you don't have much travel experience, better stick to the tried and proven, testing yourself slowly with small forays off the beaten track. We're not talking about taking life-threatening risks into the outback—just explore places where there are no historic monuments, no famous churches. You might need to get out of the car and walk or bicycle and spend time exploring. As with any set of skills, making mistakes will broaden experience and ripen instinct. Let serendipity happen. An editor at *The Washington Post* told me, "Every travel story has been done already; we just have to experience it differently and tell it better." Here are some suggestions for sniffing out unusual stories:

- Pay attention to what is happening around you. Can you trace that distant sound of music? Are musicians practicing for a party?
- Why are all the drivers blowing their car horns and waving flags out the window?
- What do the posters on every lamppost say?
- Is that crowd at the edge of town gathered for a circus, a crafts festival, or a cattle auction?
- What do the banners on the statues say?
- Why are all the museums closed on a certain day?
- Do police stop cars routinely or is there a problem?
- Why are the streets deserted?

Set out on bicycle or foot to the dusty, forgotten places off the beaten track for the story that no one else will find. Change your mode of transportation: If the place you are exploring is near a body of water, rent a boat or ask a fisherman to take you on a tour. Go to the train or bus station if you arrived by plane or car and take a short excursion to a nearby village. If you're in a city, find out all the ways people arrive. Pause for a moment at a rail or bus station or metro and notice whether they are carrying briefcases, shopping bundles, or books—perhaps there is a special market nearby not marked on the map or in your guidebook. Your readers will need this information in the travel article.

Hang out at the college or university. Read bulletin boards and strike up conversations with students. If you are in another country, people may be pleased to practice English. If you are in North America, explore the youth beat at clubs and colleges.

Remember to spend time in ethnic neighborhoods that are often the most vibrant in urban culture. Go behind the scenes. Arrange a backstage tour at a theater. Tour a museum with a guide or a volunteer docent who can talk about how exhibits are planned and the provenance of the collection. Ask to meet an artist or craftsperson. Talk to gardeners, guards, waiters; they may have been working there for decades and have stories to tell. Find out where the sports teams practice; can visitors watch?

Visit a monastery, cemetery, archeological dig, old hospital, or local historical society. If you find someone to talk to on-site, so much the better. If not, take notes and pictures; look up the history of the place later on. Sometimes, you'll just learn some interesting facts about an old building and the research won't be useful for your article, but more often than not, you'll discover new material for travel articles.

Look into people's daily lives. Attend a religious service or a trial. Visit the local library. Ask a school principal if you can tour a school. Go to the market at dawn when the farmers are arriving and the restaurant staff are buying. Talk to a seamstress or a cab driver and ask where they eat lunch. Then go there.

Why poke your nose into all these aspects of a place when all you plan to do is write about your visit to the museum, the civic monument, the trendy chic restaurant, and the fishing wharf? Because just about every travel story has been done already; you have to find a fresh angle, a new twist that sets your story apart. A different perspective and an unusual voice is what a travel editor is looking for.

Read the local newspapers. Even if they are in a language you don't understand, a picture might spark your curiosity or you can ask someone to translate for you. While visiting Hilo, Hawaii, I picked up a copy of the local free paper and scoured the listings for events that might be fun for my friend, her young teenage son, and me. We had to pass up the evening's jazz and theater offerings, but a costume parade celebrating Mardi Gras was scheduled at dusk. We never would have known about it without checking the local rag.

ENGAGING LOCAL CONTACTS

A sure way to gain a true picture of a place is to meet a family and share a meal with them. While this might seem impossible if you have no friends in the place you will be visiting, there are ways to network to find contacts. Many countries sponsor "Meet the People" programs where visitors are matched to local residents of similar age, education, and professional status. The hosts invite the visitor to share a meal or tea, depending on the culture. Basic personal information is exchanged before the meeting. The smart visitor has photos of family and hometown to show the hosts.

Before you depart, join one of exchange programs such as Servas and seek contacts who have agreed to meet visitors. Another networking technique is to identify counterparts to your club, hobby, school, sports, or professional association. Do this when you are traveling within the United States and overseas. People who live in the place you are writing about will usually know more than you. Developing contacts after you arrive at the destination is an option, but it is much easier to arrange meetings in advance. Everybody has commitments these days and your hosts may not have time for you if they don't know you are coming. International sports and hobbies groups are a source for overseas contacts. The Sister Cities program may yield a foreign contact if your hometown or a nearby city participates. Use Internet searches for sister city programs and contact the appropriate national tourist board or community organization for specifics. Check with the chamber of commerce or city government public relations department for information.

Ask work colleagues if they know anyone where you are planning to go. Perhaps they can set up an appointment for you. Make the phone call prior to your trip or just after you arrive so there will be time to arrange a convenient meeting time. If you are invited for a meal, always bring a small business gift to your host or hostess. Encourage your new acquaintances in the place you are visiting to help gather information. It will certainly be easier for them to listen to the local radio or television broadcasts for information on interesting events if you are in a country where the language is not your own. Ask them to explain the local scene. If you know a festival or holiday is coming up, ask how the locals celebrate and get specifics on places and times. Perhaps you will receive an invitation to participate. Offer to help with preparations.

We've all had the experience when well-meaning friends hear about our travel plans and give us dozens of addresses and phone numbers of their good friends, business acquaintances, and other contacts, urging us to give them a call because "they just love visitors." Sometimes that works out; sometimes it's an etiquette nightmare. They're saddled with a stranger and you'd rather be alone. Once you're a travel writer, though, those local contacts become valuable. Any name "in country" has potential worth.

E-mail or phone these local contacts when you arrive and explain your story idea. It's been my experience that people are proud of their hometown or region and are thrilled to share their special places with a visitor. Meet for coffee or a stroll through a public area. You can ask questions and glean advice about local cuisine, shopping tips, or unique neighborhoods. Your contacts offer a speed course on local lore, behavior, and customs. Take their suggestions about safety, money, and other issues of personal comfort seriously. If you hit it off, plans can take shape for a longer tour or a meal with the family.

Meeting a family can be one of the most interesting and memorable international travel experiences you'll have. Here's your chance to talk to older relatives, let the students practice their English, or watch a meal being prepared. Wherever you are in the world, eating or drinking together bonds people and cements friendships. In Fiji, I met a teenage girl at the beach who had the same first name as I do—Louisa—although she spelled it differently. She enthusiastically invited me to share dinner with her family and stay the night. At their home, I saw that the family had to scrape together the ingredients for dinner, borrowing eggs from one neighbor and greens from another's garden. A chair was brought for me, the westerner, while everyone else sat on woven mats on the floor. I was instructed to take my food, and then everyone else would eat. At first this made me uncomfortable, to be treated as an honored guest, but once I realized that their hospitality rituals required me to fulfill a certain role, I did as I was told.

I've been welcomed to farm tables crowded with abundant food produced by the household. There have been lean times when I brought the bread and fruit left-over from my lunch or a chocolate bar to augment a meal, sharing what I had in the same spirit my hosts were offering. Along the way, I've downed tripe, salmon's eyes, bear knuckles, and an array of noxious beverages. Even though some of the food I've been offered hasn't been to my liking, I've at least tasted everything with a smile and been honest when I couldn't continue. Although it has been difficult to eat when I suspected I was taxing the family larder, I have learned that when people offer hospitality sincerely, it is an honor that should not be refused. Whether in the United States or the wider world community, the interplay of sharing a meal or refreshments is fundamental to understanding people and culture. A travel writer who is serious about learning regional qualities will meet and eat with local people.

Always offer a gift to the host or hostess—special treats or flowers or something brought from home for just such an occasion, such as music CDs and tapes, souvenir T-shirts, or regional crafts. While some countries may foster political rhetoric contrary to the government of the United States, people generally welcome souvenirs that evoke American connections—sports team gear, pop music memorabilia, and bumper stickers. I'd advise against distributing souvenirs with religious or political connotations. Years ago, guidebooks suggested that travelers distribute hard candy or souvenirs such as flag pins or key chains, but cheap items with global distribution hardly convey a special connection. Still, anything that has a personal imprint could be given as a remembrance. A good rule to follow is to consider how you would feel if someone gave you the same item.

Do you have photos of your family and home or postcards depicting your city? Bring them along. Everyone likes to see photos that root you, the traveler, in a particular place. Sharing them makes you less the stranger passing through and more like the people you are visiting—you too have a house and relatives, a pet or garden.

STAY-AT-HOME TRAVEL WRITING

Not all travel stories take the writer far away. In fact, a logical place for a beginning travel writer to write about would be places close to home. Finding a unique story close to home is a useful assignment for a novice to get started. Your job is to seek subjects for travel articles, if not in the town where you live, then in a nearby city, the state or provincial capital, or within the region.

Most of us care about our home ground. The trick, of course, is to select familiar subjects nearby that will engage a wider audience. Pick topics that haven't been covered by other writers. Market research is the key. All through this book, I discuss how you figure out what editors and readers want, but remember your own interests should motivate your travel, even if you can't go far afield.

Start the process by thumbing through small local papers, newspaper travel sections, and all the nearby regional and state or city magazines. Take notes on the types of articles you see. Many of these free tabloids and regional periodicals carry sections on recreation and regularly include travel stories. Check to see if they are written by staff or freelance contributors. Special interest magazines offer publishing opportunities for novice freelancers with a travel article written close to home. Your residence becomes a type of credential—who better than a local person would know the best aspects of travel in the region?

The unique qualities of a place close to home may not be immediately clear to an inexperienced writer. Someone may live in the heart of a dynamic city and not be able to think of story ideas that haven't been done already. But even in suburban towns and rural counties, there are stories galore for writers who have investigated the market and plumbed their memories.

For example, one of my dearest childhood memories is going to the public library. On first blush, I can't think of any reason why a visitor would care about my neighborhood library. Or can I? Two of the libraries in the local county system were housed in charming old bungalows. One has been declared an historic landmark and is devoted exclusively to children's literature. Children's reading and storytelling programs are held there. The other was torn down, the one I used to visit as a child. Aha! The story unfolds. My personal memory and public interest do intersect. Visitors from out of town might well be curious about the children's library that's been named an historic site. Families might want to attend the story hours for children. My travel article could start with my memories, explore the historical background of the children's library, and explain the significance of the library and its collection. During research, I might broaden the story by discussing historically significant buildings in that neighborhood. The point is that a travel story lurks behind the simplest personal memories; it's up to us, with our traveler's understanding of human interests and our keen observation skills, to endow the familiar with universal appeal.

exercises

EXERCISE 1: Create a travel article idea close to home. Here are the kinds of questions to ask yourself:

- Is there a nearby college campus with historic buildings?
- Does the community have a park featuring a nature center or wildlife preserve?
- Have any famous people lived in the area?
- Are there historic homes open to visitors?
- Perhaps you know of a shopping district for local crafts or antiques. What is the history of that statue in front of the civic center?
- Why are all the Italian restaurants in a certain neighborhood?
- What is it about the river that attracts all the kayakers in spring?
- Why is the sports stadium or art gallery named after a certain family?

EXERCISE 2: No point in trying to write about a place if you don't have a feeling for it—you need a reaction, opinion, or observation. Probe your suitcase of memory and pull out the names of local places that have personal meanings. Jot down a word or two saying why. Now put yourself in the shoes of a visitor: What about the place would interest a stranger, a person with no history invested in the location? Find points where your reasons for caring about the place and a visitor's interest intersect. That is the place to begin the story. Make a list of all the local places you want to visit or revisit that have potential as travel articles.

EXERCISE 3: What creature comforts do you need when you are away from home? List a dozen (or more) aspects of daily life that you consider important. For example: daily hot showers, three large meals a day, air conditioning, reading in bed before sleep, freshly brewed coffee, etc. Now, refer to your list and think about how deeply you would be troubled if you had to forego any of these habits or comforts. Make a list that reflects the absolute minimum of comfort you could handle away from home. Could you still maintain neutrality and persist in travel research if you were unhappy or under stress?

EXERCISE 4: Make a packing list for a five-day trip to a tropical island. Imagine that you will be sightseeing in cities and the countryside, taking pictures to illustrate your article, learning a new sport, going to restaurants and nightclubs, shopping for crafts, sunbathing on the beach. You know the temperature is stable and warm, but the nights are cool. Do you have more than twelve individual garments on the list (not counting underwear)? Can you edit the list to nine pieces or less? Hint: Think double duty for each item you put on the list.

EXERCISE 5: Let's do a hands-on exercise about developing story ideas. Make two columns—stories you want to write and stories you know a certain publication will publish. List your ideas under the appropriate columns.

EXERCISE 6: As you brainstorm about possible story ideas, prepare a written query or phone script to present your story idea to a specific editor. Try composing this query while you're developing the story idea; save early impressions and enthusiasm about the story for the subsequent pitch to editors.

THE TRAVEL JOURNAL

Whether it's called a diary, notebook, or journal, a written record of immediate impressions is the travel writer's most valuable tool. The travel journal holds your written notes on general observations and specific experiences. Some writers use electronic tools to facilitate note taking during travel—digital or tape recorders, PDAs, laptop computers, and pen-sized scanners offer options for recording your immediate impressions of places, situations, and people. Though I use all these tools, I remain among the many writers who still rely primarily on notepad and pen when out in the field.

At first it may be difficult to train yourself to write down what you see, but over time the process will become quite natural. You will turn to your tape recorder or travel journal to report what you've experienced as you would confide in a trusted friend. You'll stop to craft a clever e-mail and launch it at an Internet café or wireless zone, remembering to send a copy to yourself as an electronic travel diary. If you're carrying a laptop or PDA with folding keyboard, you'll be able to type your impressions each day. There are cell phones such as the BlackBerry and Treo with miniature keys and sufficient data storage that a very patient writer might be able to use for travel notes, but most of us need full-size keyboards for efficient note taking.

I can't imagine taking a journey without a notebook to log my thoughts, and usually I have an electronic tool or two along for expeditious reporting. Writing up the day's events in a journal helps me relive them.

The reason you'll be keeping a travel journal is to have enough information about what happened during your travels to craft an engaging article. The diary entries or e-mails that you sent yourself will be fresh if you report them diligently. Using these descriptions that pulse with the energy of the moment, you'll later have material for travel articles that will sell. The more you write down, the better your travel articles will be—not because you'll use every experience you write about, but because you'll hone your writing and observation skills during the process.

Jot down the colors, sounds, and smells you encounter. Create word sketches of people and scenes. There may be a sign you'll want to copy verbatim or a menu description to help recall a particular meal. At the notebook stage, your writer's eye is like a magpie collecting elements that shine, cramming the journal pages with description. Just as an artist always has a sketchpad close at hand, the travel writer needs a journal to record intriguing scenes, descriptions of people, perhaps even drawings.

Consider using a system of sending yourself copies of your best e-mails describing experiences from your travels. Remember to report necessary specifics about the places you are writing about—such as addresses, hours of opening, and prices.

The word *journal* comes from the French word *jour*, or day. The travel journal is a record of each day's events, experiences, highlights, and observations. You may decide to write several times during the day or sum up your experiences at the end of the day. The goal is to fill pages with bold description and sensual detail. When you read your travel journal entries, you should be able to follow your path again, seeing the glorious or depressing scenes, hearing the cacophony, and smelling the aromas. Your journal is private, not for publication, so write freely without constraint or self-editing. Grammar, vocabulary, and sentence structure are secondary considerations at this point in the writing process. However, travel writers who send e-mails as a daily record of their travels will, of course, check their work before sending it to other people.

While there is a place in the travel journal for introspection and analysis of personal feelings and the perceived meaning of events that might occur during travel, that type of rumination is typical of traditional diary keeping. The travel notebook goes further. In the wanderer's diary, the writer sets down details of incidents great and small that paint a panorama of a place that will later become the "main character" in the travel article. A writer planning to craft a juicy profile of a person requires interview material from diverse sources to capture the essence of a personality. Similarly, the travel writer collects more material than is really needed to have a wide range of descriptive anecdotes and colorful scenes to draw from during the intense writing phase after the trip is over. A diarist writing at home may not notice the physical details of the passing scene or consider the routines of daily life worthy of comment and looks inward, paying attention to intimate feelings or relationships. The travel journal writer primarily relies on the senses to record the cascade of daily impressions and looks outward, focusing on people, scenes, and situations.

No matter what record-keeping system you are using, remember to back up your work. Your travel notebook is your intellectual property and the basis for all future travel articles. If you're relying on digital tools, send a copy of the text to yourself by e-mail. If you're creating travelogue e-mails to friends or family as a foundation for future travel articles, remember to create a backup copy on server storage offered by e-mail providers. Written notebooks can be lost or water damaged if you're caught in the rain, as most travelers are from time to time. Photocopy your written journal and fax or mail copies to your home address.

The travel notebook also serves as a place to note transportation schedules, entry hours and fees, contact information for new friends, and books recommended by other travelers. The notebook can be helpful during communication. When I am uncertain about the local language, I ask hotel staff or a bilingual friend to write in my notebook the address where I am going and where I am staying in the native language. This was handy when I was traveling in China: I would show the addresses written in my notebook to a cab driver or passerby for help with directions.

There will be times when whole conversations are conducted through pictographs. Traveling in the antipodes of Indonesia, I found few English speakers, so I would draw pictures of buses, boats, food, and other necessities in my notebook to facilitate my progress. Later, while writing articles, these cartoon oddities reminded me of half-forgotten incidents.

WHAT KIND OF NOTEBOOK?

Lined or unlined, palm sized, spiral-bound or hardcover, the notebook should be portable, not so large or heavy that you succumb to the temptation of leaving it behind when you prowl about gathering material but large enough so you can comment at length. The paper should be durable, dense enough to withstand rain, sweat or spilled beverages. I use hardcover bound artist's sketchbooks with heavyweight unlined paper. Leather-bound travel diaries of the sort that people give as bon voyage gifts are lovely to hold but are impractical for interviews. Legal-sized pads are good for organizing material and taking research notes in the library but too cumbersome to carry on the road. You may need to try out several options before you find the notebook style and size that work best for you. Write your name, address, and phone number inside the cover; this unique notebook is valuable. Store your travel journal in a reclosable plastic bag to protect it. Select a serviceable, inexpensive pen that permits rapid handwriting with waterproof ink. The best notes in the world aren't much good if you can't read them, so take the time to write clearly. During interviews, ensure comments are written as the person said them so you can use quote marks around verbatim statements in your finished article. Print the interviewee's name and a contact phone number or e-mail address close to the text that relates to his words. Then, if you are confounded trying to remember who said what, you'll be able to do a follow-up interview.

Rather than discussing the ever-changing array of brands and types of electronic tools such as notebook computers, PDAs, cell phones, digital recorders, and scanners, I ask that you keep in mind that these tools will improve or will be replaced by more efficient portable devices. Whatever information you might glean from this book, there might be more useful options available in the future.

WRITING A TRAVEL JOURNAL ENTRY

Some people write as they go, noting incidents as they happen. Other writers, and I fall into this group, absorb the scene for a few hours, then pause and write what they've seen or felt. The intervals of observation vary, of course. At a festival of indigenous peoples I attended in Kovran, a hamlet on the Sea of Okhotsk in the Russian Far East, I wrote an impression every few minutes, then stopped writing to give my full attention to the dances and drumming. I resumed writing again after the performances ended. The process continued: watch for a while, then pause and report. On the few occasions when I've tried to write down events while also trying to absorb what is happening, I suspect I lost the deeper experience. Visual memory faded quickly because I wasn't fully there, concentrating on the moment.

Each person has different capacities for processing experiences and information. I favor a Zen approach—experience the moment and develop a strong visual and aural memory. I think we remember best what we experience deeply. For me, writing continuously while trying to capture events going on around me results in a diluted impression. Perhaps the key is to be alert to interludes when notes can be taken without losing full attention to the unfolding scene.

On the other hand, I've been with other travel writers on press junkets while they diligently recorded the facts as a guide delivered them. When they sit down at the computer later, those writers have concrete information for story construction. But do they have experiences to share? Facts can be obtained afterwards, especially with the ever-expanding databank on the Internet. Experiences can't be fully recreated. I'd rather try to concentrate on what actually happened while it was happening and then meet one-to-one with a guide or museum caretaker after a tour and ask questions.

While I'd like to think that every fact could be recovered through research, the truth is some questions can only be answered on-site. The Internet is a resource without parallel, but much of what is offered on the Web must be fact checked again.

Experience comes but once, while you're in it. Focus on the present, develop a prodigious memory, and write what is happening. Some information can be researched later, but the intimate, firsthand details you seek are best obtained on-site and in the moment. You may develop a personal notation system for flagging questions as they arise so you can get answers before you leave the site.

This is the way I do it: On guided tours, or any situation where I'm taking notes from spoken information, I listen attentively, jotting notes about what I notice and what I hear. I record the highlights that interest me and facts that would be necessary in any travel article about the place. I figure what appeals to me will be sufficient to craft an article. If I have a question, I draw a box around the note then pursue an answer on-site. Sometimes that isn't possible, but when I do subsequently maneuver into a conversation with a guide or curator, the box around the note reminds me I had a question. My memory is sharp enough that I can remember what the question was within a short time frame. If I wait until days or weeks later when I'm back home at my desk, there's the frustrating possibility that I won't remember what the follow-up questions were. Whenever possible, seek answers to your questions on-site, at once.

One drawback of tours organized for travel writers is the constant refrain of facts buzzing like frayed tunes on faulty headphones in the background. Participants dutifully scribble notes, filling their reporter's books with data they'll never use in an article because it is just too dull. Or maybe they do use avalanches of facts in their stories, which might be why they remain unpublished. Some people fill digital recorders with droned statistics about per capita income, crop yields, demographics of tourists, and the number of hotel rooms. Later all that bland information that the tourist bureau deems important will have to be sorted through, uploaded, or transcribed, just in case a really titillating fact snuck into the lecture. Where is the unique travel experience? Where are the local people? How can an interesting story be told using only facts? Might as well rewrite a page from the tourism promoter's press kit or cull data from guidebooks and construct an article that reads like a high school term paper. Have the courage to create your own travel experiences and the self-confidence to write what really happens, not what some marketing executive thinks other travelers should know about a place.

In time, you will develop a personal sense of what experiences to record in the travel journal or travelogue drafts you send yourself by e-mail. At first, you will probably write more material than you need. As you write in the journal, keep in mind the purpose of your trip, your interest, or the quest that has sent you forth.

If you are using the e-mail-to-friends method of note taking while you're on the road, remember that the tendency for most people who write e-mails about their travels is to be gushy and long-winded, omitting specific details, relying on complaints and contrasts to attempt to convey differences in various locations. This type of superficial travel impression won't provide material for travel articles destined for publication. Take the time to use your senses—smell, taste, touch, hearing, and sight—as you report specific scenes and encounters with memorable people. Even when you use electronic reporting methods, keep a small notebook handy for writing up-to-the-moment information.

Here is an entry from the travel journal I kept during an off-season trip to Italy. I didn't have an assignment from a publication, but I was deeply interested in the Etruscan culture and knew that editors have a perennial need for stories from Tuscany. Trouble is, Tuscany is hardly an undiscovered area, so I knew a salable story needed a personal twist. Dry historical detail on the remains of Etruscan civilization would smother my story. A travel story larded with history is a surefire no-sale. To make the Etruscan ruins story contemporary and gripping, I planned to focus on atmosphere and my unique experiences.

The journal entries concentrated on what I saw, heard, and smelled. My writing also records the imaginary tangents, an important ingredient in travel writing with a history theme, where the writer's musing, mixed with fact, gives the article buoyancy and dimension in the present.

> Inside the large tomb [Tomba dei Vasigreci 6 b.c.] at Ceveteri—round on outside, cut into compartments inside. Did they preserve the dead bodies or let dust become them. Worms and slugs—could they penetrate these tombs or did the bodies lie as if asleep until plundered for their jewels. Roman wealth as grave robbers. Did the Etruscans come here while alive to get the feel of the tomb? And I, stepping up into the light have veils of rebirth shaken from my shoulders like the cobwebs on the tomb ceiling covered my eyes. You can hear birds outside and in the ones by the road that aren't part of the pay-to-see section. Cars are heard and vibrations from airplanes too. This tufa rock carries vibration well.
>
> Inside another there are also three smaller chambers with beds and in the large room, chairs on either side of the entrance, facing the rooms of the dead. Everything feels slightly tilted so the head parts of the dead rooms are visible to the people in the chair. I can see four places inside the rooms at once, plus the four couches outside.

Enclosed in brackets, the fact written in the first line was added after the journal entry, culled from a guidebook and noted in the margin later that day. The writing is rough and often I slip from the active voice, but in the journal, the goal isn't flawless prose but words or phrases that convey atmosphere and evocative detail. In final form the story hung on my fascination with tombs and grave sites and, naturally, it ran on Halloween. This diary entry mutated into the following paragraphs, which appeared in the *St. Petersburg Times*:

> Inside one tomb I sat in the stone chairs that are on each side of the doorway. From that position, one could see the carved stone beds provided for the dead.
>
> The notables were laid out in full regalia on these stone couches, whole families together in the large rooms. Weapons, jewels, and household goods for the afterworld were distributed among them, but these items have been removed for museum display or plundered for the international antiquities commerce.
>
> I peeked inside another tomb, cut in a rock wall and with its neighbors, resembling a row of townhouses, each with its own oblong door. Inside, there were three small rooms with niches for stone beds. Oddly, though one would think the sound wouldn't carry through the stone city, inside certain tombs I could hear chirping birds, cars, and airplanes....
>
> Ultimately, my visit to the necropolis at Cerveteri created more questions than answers for me. Why are some of the tombs round on the outside and divided into square compartments inside? I wondered if the Etruscans preserved the dead bodies or let dust overcome them. Were the tombs sealed as the Egyptians did? Their funeral rituals—equipping the dead with household goods for the afterlife—somewhat resemble the Etruscans.
>
> Did Etruscan families come here and visit their dead, sitting on the chairs at the entrances, becoming familiar with the tomb they would later occupy?

Much of the finished article follows the text in the journal. What I recorded from sense perception found a place in the final piece. Passive voice became active voice: "cars are heard" became "I could hear." The questions raised during my visit remained questions in the article, designed to provoke curiosity in readers. When people who've read this piece visit the Etruscan tombs, perhaps they will have similar musings. Even if a reader never visits this archeological site, the story entertains the armchair traveler.

For other sections of the article I looked at photos taken that day at the necropolis and concentrated on visual memories that could be transformed into words. Reading over my notes, I found useful commentary about the weather, fruit trees in bloom, a chill wind, and the isolation of the archeological site. During the trip, I read D.H. Lawrence's book about his journey through Italy, *Sea and Sardinia*, and referred to his observations during a visit to Cerveteri in my article.

Sure, I could have written more in my travel journal that day, but the visit was so overwhelming that my mind was filled with questions. I had poked around on my own in deserted areas of the site, descending ancient steps and peering into dank grass-topped tombs. As you progress in your reading and investigative travels, you may discover that, like me, you'll need time to process certain experiences. That evening, I talked about the necropolis with a friend who lives in Rome and has been to Cerveteri many times. I jotted down comments from our discussion and further thoughts and questions raised by our conversation.

The travel journal, then, becomes more than an on-the-site report. My journal material about Cerveteri included quirky personal questions raised by the visit, dialogue with myself, fragments of conversation with guards and other knowledgeable people, research notes taken from signs and guidebooks, titles of books to consult. Recalling such a variety of information afterward might be impossible; try to record as much as possible while you are on-site and concentrate on refining your powers of description.

What happens when the travel notebook is thin, the entries sparse and cryptic, composed mostly of isolated facts? You'll be in trouble when you sit down later hoping to write the article. I learned this after a visit to Terme di Saturnia, a spa in Tuscany. I was so busy enjoying the heated pool and herbal facials that I neglected my journal. When an editor called me looking for a travel piece for an upcoming issue, I had to scramble to construct a story from my Saturnia notes that were fat with facts provided by the medical director but lean on description, portraits of people, and details of the spa experience. For structure, I chose an upbeat format of ten lessons for spa life explained through capsulated experiences. Compare the brief journal entries with paragraphs in the published article that appeared in *Washington International*.

> A.M.—table flatware. classic and white dishes. 17th & 18th c. portraits. armoires. old oil paintings. white walls. breakfast in robes or exercise togs. street clothes to leave. castle in village of Saturnia on hill mist rising from pool. A few energetic bathers paddle in the turquoise water. Italian celebrities. Romans. Swiss. U.S.—Beverly Sassoon, Wim Wenders. nobility.

Those notes became:

> Next morning, I dressed casually for breakfast, but everyone else was tucked into terry robes and slippers. Talk about overdressed; I was the only person in the room with shoes on. Lesson two: Despite the silver plate, napkins, and seventeenth-century paintings on the walls, comfortable informality is the rule at Saturnia.
>
> You probably won't recognize the Italian celebrities who swing up from Rome, and this isn't the kind of place you'll ever see Howard Stern. Saturnia protects its celebrity guests and won't reveal who has been there recently. Those look-alike robes and baggy exercise togs provide anonymity for a reason. Lesson three: If you see celebrities, ignore them.
>
> A few intrepid souls paddled through the winter chill in the warm turquoise water. After breakfast, I joined them, happily soaking ... until I looked at my hands and the silver rings I wear. They were blackened and tarnished by the sulfur. Lesson four: Don't wear jewelry in the water.

A few brief words in the journal formed the foundation for three paragraphs. One sentence in the journal—"A few energetic bathers paddle in the turquoise water"—found its way nearly intact into the paragraph about wearing my silver jewelry in the sulfurous water.

I remembered that the cryptic entry "Italian celebrities. Romans. Swiss. U.S.—Beverly Sassoon, Wim Wenders, nobility" derived from the assistant manager's comments about famous people who had visited the spa even while she steadfastly protected the privacy of current guests. Howard Stern's name was added because he was prominent in the news at the time this article went to press.

Over the years, I've learned how important it is for a travel writer to talk to other people, ask questions, and observe. And jot down all the notes you can.

Here's a diary entry from a trip to Panama that provided the foundation for two stories so far; one ran in *The Washington Post* in 2002 and the other on National Geographic's news Web site a year later.

> Smithsonian tour—disorganized. No on-site guide at boat launch. Dock serves as dredging operation for canal—only help is from people used to the routine. No phone line or responsible person. Spray, freshwater. Edges of islands draped in green—palmetto, brilliant shades of velvet, spikes of leafless trees occasionally. A palm at water level. No mangroves. After apx. 30 min STRI moves into view. Absence of bird except kits and pelicans overhead. Perhaps cause of noisy launch. Scattered rafts, buoys and a derelict boat or two. Best facility for tropical research in the world. For a scientist "The big big laboratory, the forest, is just a few meters from here," says Claudio, the guide. 1540 hectares protect forest, total nature monument—5400 hectares. Any effect to canal watershed affects Barro Colorado. El Nino—Gatun Lake lowest level of Canal. Gatun largest manmade lake. Dead trees left over from 1998 El Nino? On island: puma moving here because of outside pressures. World rsch center—students working here. for a Biologist, this is known as Panama, not for Noriega, Canal and military. SI offers course to Panamanian students to do rsch here. Places to live for rschers. Howler monkeys yowl in background like lion's den and send leaves and palm fronds falling.

Howl for territory control and informant … Facility built 1923-1930 "My Tropical ___" Frank Chapman—scientist who foresaw importance of research. Tropical Bees research—nocturnal species solitary or social. Inefficient registration—not enuf time in woods—too expensive at $70.

Based on these notes, a published paragraph from *The Washington Post* column went like this:

During canal construction, engineers created Gatun Lake, where ships now nose toward the oceans. You can visit the Smithsonian Tropical Research Institute on Barro Colorado, an island in the lake where scientists have been studying tropical biology since the 1920s. The $70 fee includes lunch and boat transit from Gamboa Locks …

As you can see, not much material from the journal entry appears in that published article. My annoyance with the management about poor directions to the dock and launch weren't reflected in the finished article because ultimately I realized the error was mine. I hadn't read the brochure correctly and had arrived for the launch at the wrong time. It would be inappropriate to pass along my complaints, though the brochure could be improved for clarity. In such a case as this, the travel writer has the duty to evaluate personal experience carefully and revise negative impressions to a neutral position if the problem isn't systemic.

For the article that ran on *National Geographic*'s news Web site, the same notes expanded with further research and e-mail interviews with scientists.

Once a mountain top where howler monkeys roamed, the lush island of Barro Colorado in the middle of the Panama Canal is now populated by scientists at work for the Smithsonian Institution's Tropical Research Institute (STRI). The tropical forest on the island is one of the most intensively studied preserves on the planet. The island's 3,700 acres (1,500 hectares) of tropical rainforest are a biological reserve that also includes five surrounding peninsulas on the Panama mainland … Though thousands of tankers and cruise ships nose through the Panama Canal, which divides North and South America and connects the Atlantic and Pacific Oceans, only the launch that shuttles scientists and a few visitors docks at Barro Colorado.

Additional research for the *National Geographic* news Web site article included quotes from scientists about specific research projects, because that's the publication's focus. The broader travel article for *The Washington Post* didn't have space for all the facts I had gathered during the island tour or later conversations and visits to museums. However, I did need to verify prices, phone numbers, and supporting details about hotels, taxis, and restaurants. We can now find this type of information on the Internet, but it's also a good idea to retain brochures provided by the tourism office.

When you compare the journal notes written on-site with the published paragraphs, note how information is transformed from rough jottings to sentences that segue and maintain focus. Notice how many of the notes aren't used at all. Perhaps I'll put them in another article.

WHAT TO WRITE

Part of the travel writer's judgment is knowing what to write in the journal and what to leave to memory or later research. This is a personal decision, based on a judicious appraisal of available time. I've been recording trips in notebooks and honing visual recall for several decades and here are some tips: Develop an ability to memorize scenes and experiences. Test yourself. What do you see, what did you hear? Describe people in a sentence. Capture accents and gestures. Record colors and texture. While it is tempting to concentrate on writing the facts in your journal, remember to report the passing scene. If you are confident in the strength of your visual and sensual memory, you may leave some of the color commentary to memory.

There are writers who need just a word to remind them of an experience. Others save objects that are encoded with memories. I collect local newspapers, postcards, souvenir programs, sales receipts and tickets, even bus transfers. All of them remind me of the trip unfolding. If there is an opportunity, I save leaves, shells, seeds, and flowers. I sketch, write down names of people I talk to, jot down street signs, phrases from menus or advertisements. These disparate items serve as precise substance in your article so you can identify the brand name of the beer or the hot sauce you liked, the street where you encountered the helpful policeman, or the color of the wildflowers that carpet the pasture.

Processing information before writing can make for a richer construction, but I caution novice travel writers against waiting. Write down as soon as possible what you've experienced. The habit of writing at least twice a day in the travel journal, perhaps at lunch and dinner, will yield the quantity and quality of information and anecdotes you need for a successful path in travel writing. Neglect the journal and you decrease your options for writing interesting stories that can be sold to several markets.

Over time, your writing will evolve and mature. Phrases and sensations ripening in the mind for a day or more won't lose their power. When you have a few years of regular travel writing behind you, experiences can be mulled over before writing, although the travel journal will always be the primary tool for productivity.

People in the habit of jotting thoughts and observations in a diary have trained themselves to explore their thoughts. Anyone who is planning on becoming a travel writer and doesn't have the predisposition to journal writing will have to be extra vigilant to write regularly during the trip to ensure that enough material is recorded to craft a salable travel article.

The writer who already has journals or notebooks from previous journeys is rich with potential material to mine for the first few travel stories. The writer who hasn't kept a journal until now can start recording story gold. In writing workshops, people sometimes ask me whether notes from past trips can be transformed into travel articles that will sell. Ascertain whether the information is still current. If your notes are from a trip to a place that has recently undergone significant political, geophysical, or cultural changes, it's a safe bet you couldn't base a travel article on those old notes. However, if your notes are lively, ripe with engaging people, and include anecdotes and unique events, and you've checked the facts related to those notes, perhaps you can craft an evergreen travel story based on your experiences at that time, in that place. Your flair as a writer and ability to focus on a particular theme will determine whether the notes from past trips can become articles in print.

FROM JOURNAL TO FIRST DRAFT

Read the written notes taken on-site to recover the dynamic immediacy of the passing scene. The journal on your desk serves as a resource for your brainstorm of travel memories. Or perhaps you're working with long e-mails sent to family or friends from the road. For me, the entire diary serves as a first draft, although I may prune parts and use them in other travel articles with a different market focus. As we shall see in the examples that follow, some sentences from the travel journal can be directly inserted in travel articles. Other passages must be substantially rewritten to preserve continuity and style.

The next chapter covers the structure and pace of a travel article. For readers who are itching to get started and already have a travel journal, it's time to make a typed transcription of your journal, upload from your PDA, or collect e-mail text files from various sources. This will be your first draft.

Organize the travel journal entries on your computer. Skip the personal passages that explore your private moods and musings. With the define, cut, and paste keys for whatever word processing program you use, arrange related entries. This preliminary phase of typing and organizing material is easiest on a computer.

If you are using a typewriter, try this organizational technique. Type travel journal entries onto separate sheets of paper, a paragraph or two per page. Leave lots of blank space. Sort the sheets of paper or cut and paste paragraphs so related events are to-

gether. With this technique, the writer who uses a typewriter
should still come away from the transcription phase with a working draft.

At this point, I'd advise against creating a chronological log of
your experiences. Travelogues—place-by-place inventories of what
you did and where you went—are not travel articles. Read chapter four first, and do some of the writing exercises so when you do
start constructing the article, you'll have an idea which highlights from the journal or notes will tell the story in the format of
contemporary travel journalism.

Of course, some readers won't or can't wait to get started shaping the travel piece. If you are compelled to tinker with the draft
of raw travel journal entries now, remember that memorable travel writing has the same ingredients as any stimulating prose: descriptions that summon the senses, alert the mind, and trigger
memory. Details that show the place and people. Facts effortlessly woven into the textual fabric. Beyond that, travel writing
strives to put the reader on location. What turns of phrase, bits
of dialogue, or remembered experience will evoke the spirit of a
place? Consult any writing book on prose style and the advice is
the same: Use simple construction, vivid description, active voice,
and mighty verbs.

For insight on how untouched journal entries—or long e-mails
sent home during the journey—become part of finished travel articles, examine these excerpts from travel journals and the related paragraphs in published travel articles.

Freelance writer Chad Neighbor, based in Scotland, jots down
the barest of entries in his travel notebook to serve as memory
helpers. His diary entry about a stay in a cottage near a Scottish
loch reads:

> Tich-na-Coille. 150 ft from loch on part of promontr set off by
> burnlet. basic but thick walls up to 2 ft set tapering in rms up-
> stairs. w-to-w carpets, well equipped, modern furniture but
> practical, gd dining table. fire already laid (by previous occ)
> no wood but good coal. many repeat vis sometimes neg. over

> 10 years of photos on walls from 1 of them. helpful comments from other occ on, walks, restaurants, attractions, wildlife, etc. bats. post bus goes by door. black wd of rannach across rd capercaillie. schiehallion. coal fires (no logs) comments on what's lacking (washmach). fortingall yews.

These notes show a writer who uses a word or two to summon the scene to mind. This system of note taking probably wouldn't contain enough information for a beginning travel writer. However, peeking into another writer's notebook gives an idea of the many ways that details can be recorded. While Chad Neighbor's notes seem to skim the surface, he does have lots of material. For example, place names that are difficult to spell were carefully written out, although missing some capital letters because of his hasty style. Many common words were abbreviated. Scene-setting details were carried directly from the notebook to the article that ran in *The Washington Post* Travel Section.

> The attractions of these superbly located cottages are only too obvious. The scenery tends to be first rate and, in our case, the 150-foot stroll to a private beach (even if wind and water made it far too cold for swimming by non-huskies) was irresistible...
>
> Another quite different bonus of Forestry Commission and National Trust cottages is their logbooks, compiled by many years' worth of visitors. These are a valuable resource for new arrivals dying to discover the best local tearoom or spot for spying a kingfisher. We followed the advice to visit Scotland's smallest distillery at Edradour near Pitlockry—a fascinating detour.
>
> But the diaries also offer an absorbing chronicle. Some people have been spending certain weeks at certain cottages for ten years or more and feel almost as if they're part owners. Indeed the excellent photos of Tigh-na-Coille and surroundings were taken, mounted, and hung by a regular visitor there who thought the walls were a bit bare.
>
> One of the most entertaining aspects of the entries was the

complaints, visitors being clearly divided between those who expect all the modern conveniences and then some, and those who do not. There were complaints about the lack of a television, a microwave, a washing machine and, poor soul, a double boiler...

You may notice that Chad Neighbor writes a line about the logs and coal for the fire twice in the notes. He saves this information for the end of the article, using it as physical and psychological closure while creating strong internal structure for the story. The last thing he does during the trip is lay the fire for the next visitors, the scene he found when he arrived.

One of the tests of a good vacation, of course, is how you feel when you leave your temporary abode. After our week on Loch Rannoch I felt relaxed, refreshed, and more appreciative of one of Scotland's most spectacular areas.

And, after laying the last fire in the fireplace (a tradition to welcome the next arrivals) and making our last chug down the driveway, I also felt sad to be leaving.

New York-based travel writer Ann Jones shares her travel journal entry that became the lead and opening paragraphs for "Horse-Packing in Kookaburra Land," which appeared in *Diversion*, February 1991.

March 18: Drove Sydney—Tumut (6 hrs) thru central highlands of NSW—all rolling brownish grass & sheep & dusty eucalyptus—storm at Guilbourn—sandstone at Berrima—Tumut in a valley of green willow & poplar along a river—wide streets—tin roofed bungalows—dinner at Returned Soldiers League Club—Chinese buffet.

This shorthand impression of her entry to Tumut became the opening for the finished piece.

In Tumut the hot place to eat is upstairs at the Returned Soldiers' League. The restaurant is a cavernous hall with all the warmth and ambience of an American Legion post, and the food is plain—the kind my grandmother called "filling"—but the price is right. Saturday night they lay on something a little special, like a Chinese buffet. That goes over big with the locals, since there's not a whole lot of Chinese food available, as far as I could tell, in the hinterlands of New South Wales, Australia's south-eastern corner.

... I'd left Sydney that morning, heading southeast, for a leisurely six-hour drive to Tumut. The highway ascended a series of rising valleys to grassy tableland that seemed to belong only to me and the sheep—thousands upon thousands of them.

It was March, the end of Australia's summer, and the dry grass, the dusty sheep and the road were all the same color, actually no color at all. Then, below me, appeared a big stand of green poplars along the Tumut River, and the road wound down among tidy tin-roofed bungalows, steepled churches and plain faced business establishments set wide along broad avenues laid out for the grander city Tumut once intended to become.

Notice the author's effort to relate the faraway place to familiar: "ambience of an American Legion post ... the kind my grandmother would call 'filling.'" The sketchy notes in the travel journal expand when Jones uses them to summon memory to embellish the experience for the final rendering in the travel article. The note about "brownish grass & sheep & dusty eucalyptus" becomes more refined: "the dry grass, the dusty sheep, and the road were all the same color, actually no color at all."

Ann Jones says she takes notes for her travel articles in three ways: "As I go, I jot quick notes, especially facts and people's memorable remarks, in a standard reporter's notebook that is always with me. At day's end or when time permits, I try to make a longer entry in a journal, summarizing the day, including descriptive details and noting issues and themes raised by the day's events and conversations. [The excerpts included here are from her day's-end travel journals.] I also often carry a pocket tape recorder to make quick notes to myself, conduct interviews, and record the noises of the place, especially animal and bird sounds and local music.

I rarely listen to the notes or interviews, but I often replay the noises to bring back the feel of the place I'm writing about."

When I started using travel journal entries as the foundation for travel articles, the writing was rather formal and composed, as the following entries from a trip to Barcelona demonstrate. During the years since then, I've learned that it is easier to extract a first draft from travel journal entries that are focused on the details, atmosphere, and scene. Rather than striving for artful sentence structure in the journal entry, craft specific descriptions that are rooted in sensual perception. Compare the choppy description in the travel journal entries for the Etruscan article discussed earlier in this chapter with these highly structured notes on Barcelona that eventually formed the basis for a destination article with a special focus on the architecture of Gaudi.

> Today we hunted Gaudi's buildings. Beginning with the Holy Family Cathedral, still unfinished, and ending at Park Guell, a marvelous fantasy land high above the city where clean air is able to be breathed. The cathedral proved a wonder, high towers, a sand castle in pre-stressed cement. It may take another 50 years to achieve Gaudi's vision, certainly work is not progressing rapidly.
>
> The candy-colored towers are visible several blocks away. An amusement park perhaps, or a children's playground. No, Templo Sagrada Familia, the Holy Family Church between Calle de Provenza and Calle de Mallorca (north east of the Diagonal) at their intersection with Calle de Cerde. Still under construction after 100 years, this cathedral evokes the gothic spires and buttresses of churches of the Middle Ages, yet it is constructed with the humorous, even mocking, combination of materials that marks all of Gaudi's efforts. Fantastic/marvelous forms, part nightmare, part joyous fantasy, crawl upwards to the four spires on each end of the cathedral. There is also harmony, however, the spires may look like a sandcastle melting under the onslaught of the sea, but the design is wonderfully proportioned, superbly designed, and completely in tune with human sensibility.

The effect of entering a building you do not realize is unfinished is remarkable. You wonder if this is what a war zone feels like. We pursued his work in downtown area, marching perhaps longer than desirable. Got a bus up to the park which relieved our legs. There we bought post cards, attempted a watercolor (stiff, amateurish), and watched school children play. The pure air was instantly remarkable and cleared my eyes and headache. We rested up, then walked the Gothic quarter before dinner.

The published piece opened with visual drama and walked the reader through the building:

Jutting above Barcelona's skyline, the rosy-colored towers could be the turrets of a transplanted Disneyland castle. Or a fantastic suspension device from a children's playground. Or the scaffolding of a movie set. Surely not a cathedral. But the sparkling pink towers do rise from a cathedral—La Sagrada Familiar, the Church of the Sacred Family, architect Antonio Gaudi's unfinished masterpiece.

...Visitors enter the church through a vestibule that resembles many other commercially successful places of worship: admission is charged; signs in four languages advertise a multimedia documentary about the building for an additional fee; a sales clerk offers souvenirs and postcards; the visitor's registry has comments in a dozen languages.

But beyond the vestibule, the similarity disappears. The nave, the choir, in fact the entire heart of the cathedral is an open-air construction site. Great blocks of pre-cast concrete, stacks of tiles and numbered pieces are laid about, not unlike Lego pieces, waiting to be fit together. A closer look at the four landmark towers reveals they are not pink but gray concrete cones that culminate in mosaic glitter. It is the light, filtered through Barcelona's air pollutants, that makes the towers appear pastel.

An elevator whisked us and other visitors to a bridge connecting the two center towers ... figures from a dream menagerie—reptiles, amphibians, mammals—crawled up the

> cathedral's facade, part nightmare, part hilarious fantasy: A tortoise at the base of a column stretched its mouth in a gasp, a lizard curled back on itself, dragons stared....

Note how many of travel journal phrases appear verbatim in the finished piece. The general statements have sharper focus, showing instead of telling. The detached tone has become more personal and shows the reader what is unfolding. Comparing the building materials to Lego blocks continues the playground fantasyland theme established in the opening sentences. The structured journal entry mentions the improved air quality in the elevated areas of the city as it affects the writer, putting the writer at the center of attention; the published article describes the colorful effects of the air pollution and focuses the reader on the cathedral while conveying the same information about bad air in a more interesting way.

ARTFUL WRITING

Travel writers should be striving to communicate elegantly. We are the filters through which experience passes on a path to the reader. Our job is to describe accurately what we see and feel, not just reprocess factual information that is important to economists, trade brokers, or the tourist industry. As your experience grows, you'll make choices about which trips to take and whether you'll pay for them yourself, seek expense assistance from a publication, or rely on free junkets. There's more about trips offered to travel writers in chapter nine.

During a familiarization tour to Curaçao, I kept my usual travel journal, writing down my experiences and observations. I didn't worry whether I wrote down all the facts the guide was spouting, knowing this work could be dispatched handily online. I focused on what my senses told me.

Take a look at the journal entry written during and immediately after a visit to caves:

> Hato Caves. tunnels going off into rooms beyond. ribs of limestone. domes on ceiling. delicate columns inspired as Gaudi. path

built about 4 years ago. humid inside—water seeking lowest point. Iron ore on walls. Cathedral area pock marked vault wishing well. Bat chamber—skunky smell—be quiet so they can sleep. Wear sneakers; watch head. Religious fantasy faces in the stone. In cafe: Unico music box locally made, maybe guide will play contratempo. hand crank, 150 years old. 45 hammers. 8 tunes on each cylinder. still made by 2 people on Curaçao, 1 person on Aruba. gentle old rhythms of time gone by. sounds of guitars plucked or piano. Cacti grow like bushes. Near airport—wind generated electricity—new project backup power.

The journal notes became this segment of a travel article that was published in the *Toronto Star*:

Another kind of underworld is experienced at Hato Caves, a series of cool natural caverns near the airport. The tour guide embroiders the quasi-historical spiel with Amerindian legends and religious fantasy. In the bat room, visitors maintain silence so the nocturnal creatures can sleep.

Out in the bright sunlight, there's a souvenir shop/snack bar and a peaceful terrace. Turn the hand crank on the authentic Unico music box and the forty-five hammers plink out a medley of island tunes. (Some music boxes are as old as 150 years.) The mellow brown wooden box is as big as a modern jukebox. Gentle rhythms of time gone by conjure up a room of two-steppers and waltzers.

Using just the material in these few pages of my notebook, the story could have gone in several directions: the geology of the caves, interviews with the artisans still making music boxes, the wind generation project and how it affects tourism, or the varieties of cacti.

The entries were hastily scribbled phrases that would remind me during the writing phase of what the caves felt like inside. I skipped or compressed details such as how many years it takes for a stalagmite to form. That was my decision, to pre-edit notes by not writing down everything I heard so I could concentrate on the experience of being inside the cave. I knew it would be easy to research data online about the age of the cave and the lifespan of a stalagmite.

However, another writer with a different story slant could turn that bit of information into a travel story. Some editors expect travel articles to contain the basic scientific facts about natural phenomena like caves, volcanoes, rivers, or deserts. Other editors would jump at the chance to publish articles that reported hitherto unknown sightings of the Madonna in a cave niche. Know the requirements for potential markets before traveling; it will help you select details during journal writing.

You may be wondering how you can know your markets if you are just beginning to explore the possibilities of travel writing. One way is to read several issues of the publication you plan to write for. Look at online editions of travel publications: Do articles focus on facts or people-oriented stories? You can also make preliminary market research calls. Chapter eight, on marketing, delves into these points. For now, though, a reasonable guide for your note taking might be to consider that your strongest potential markets are related to subjects that interest you. That way, you'll be motivated to pursue the story to a conclusion.

It's true that at the beginning, the urge to write about everything will propel your pen. Take a step back, though. You know you can't write about everything you see and hear. And you certainly won't be able to use all those pages of notes in one story. Focus on what interests you. Have purpose; your experiences drive the story line. If the information gathering sustains your attention, when the piece is finished, the reader will stick with the story. Packing in the facts for facts' sake won't make a great travel article.

exercises

EXERCISE 1: Build a list of verbs that relate to the place you plan to write about. Forget the blank piece of paper or the cursor taunting you. Just plunge in with a list of verbs, then nouns, then adjectives and adverbs. Brainstorm about the place, history, landscape, and people—whatever comes to mind. Think action! Use a pen and notepad or bash your thoughts into the keyboard. Save this list of words; it may be useful when you are searching for a specific image.

EXERCISE 2: Take inventory of materials you've gathered—ticket stubs, photos, receipts, menus, e-mails, or postcards sent home. These artifacts could help in the construction of a travel article or trigger memories that will improve your story. Using any of these artifacts, write a paragraph or two about what you remember about the scene, the meal, the journey, or item purchased. If you have lots of memorabilia, keep the items close at hand to spur memories as you write. Fill your notebook with the feelings and mind pictures stimulated by the postcards or photos. Keep going until you have exhausted your memory bank. You'll be surprised at the wealth of material you have.

EXERCISE 3: Learn to write a useful journal entry by strolling around your hometown. Take time during a lunch hour, on the weekend, or after work. In your notebook, jot down many words and phrases—bright, active, sensual words—to describe the people you see, places you visit. Don't think about grammar, spelling, punctuation, or sentence structure. Leave a few lines or some blank space between each entry. Teach yourself to take the time to record your impressions and the details of the passing scene.

EXERCISE 4: Practice making the transition from raw journal entries to useful sentences and paragraphs. In the blank space between the notes you took about people and scenes in your hometown, use the jotted descriptions and observations to construct complete descriptive sentences. To develop muscular sentences using a variety of structures, try to avoid using the pronoun "I" and start sentences without using "The." Find powerful verbs that create images of interaction in the reader's mind.

EXERCISE 5: Use the phrases and sentences to write a letter. Pretend you are writing a letter describing the place to a blind friend or someone from another culture. Try the exercise again, but this time, write the letter to someone who formerly lived here and whom you want to come back and visit. Explore historical possibilities by writing this letter to a famous person who has influenced the town in the past.

EXERCISE 6: Writers stymied by writer's block often fritter away creative time by writing e-mails or letters. You can bypass inaction by writing productively. Write a long e-mail to a friend describing a recent day trip or excursion and instead of sending it, use the correspondence as an article draft. The letter should bubble with your impressions, interactions with people you've met, and notes on what you saw, heard, or tasted. When you are satisfied that you've told everything, go back over the letter and be an editor. Cross out any references that only the friend would understand—personal jokes, asides, names of people the two of you know, etc. What remains could become a first draft of a travel article. Be creative; use strong verbs and picturesque words. Describe people in one sentence, notice their accents and gestures, and report the scenes you observe during your day. Collect e-mails you've sent a trusted friend during your journey and, after cutting the personal and commonplace narrative, create a first draft from the communications. Of course, as with all correspondence, you should secure the permission of the person who received the e-mails or letters from you.

STRUCTURE AND PACE

Travel writing is one of the oldest forms of narrative nonfiction. People have been telling tales of their travels for as long as we've had voices. Writing those journeys down as historical record or for entertainment doubtless goes back to the earliest methods of writing. As a travel writer, you're joining a tradition that goes back to our nomadic past.

"Travel writing is, I think, coeval with writing itself," wrote novelist and critic Nicholas Delbanco in *Harper's Magazine*, September 2004. Pursuing his point from the scribes of Babylon to Hindu epics, Homer's *The Odyssey* and Chaucer's *The Canterbury Tales*, Delbanco reminds us that tales of mythic journeys and spiritual pilgrimages, as well as the explorer's journal, share travel as subject.

Travel articles have the double role of conveying hard facts and transporting readers through vigorous description. Alas, we're unlikely to experience the curiosities that Marco Polo encountered, or the sense of natural wonder Henry David Thoreau conveyed during his walking tours, or the turbulent adventures that Isabelle Eberhardt dodged while skirting the Sahara on camel. One task these and all travel writers share, though, is organizing their notes for presentation to the reading public.

In this chapter we'll delve into methods for structuring the article. Techniques for using journal entries for detail and story line will be discussed, and we'll explore ways of communicating facts without digressing from the story focus. We'll also work on finding a dynamic lead and building story momentum to a satisfying conclusion.

While you're writing a long draft version of your travel story, using your travel journals or what you've recovered from memory, it's time to organize the article and keep the story line flowing so readers (and editors) will stay interested. We want to show the story like a movie, not tell it.

That means you'll need to arm yourself with action words that express reality as you experienced it; words that also engage the passive reader who wasn't along for the excitement. Compile a list of verbs that express energy, activity, smell, taste, and sound. Add fresh verbs to the list as you read them or hear smart conversationalists using them. Be aware of the difference between verbs that describe condition (what you think about something, or the effect of an action) and verbs that show action (verbs that present something happening in your mind's eye).

What does it mean to show instead of tell? I use a verb exercise in writing classes that you can use, too. Write a short paragraph, a scene from a recent trip, or copy a passage from your existing travel journal. Set it aside and we'll work on it soon.

Showing the story involves using active voice and verbs that show activity rather than what you think about the activities. I know that's a tall order for a beginner to accomplish in early attempts, but keep the phrase "Show it, don't tell it" in the forefront of your mind as you write. Print the phrase on a post-it note or index card and keep it on your desk or taped to the computer screen. Hew to the principle of the phrase and you really will learn to write with sense-driven verbs. And that is what travel writing is all about— showing scenes that the reader can feel viscerally.

Should you find yourself stumped for the next sentence, look to the "Show It" card, imagine a scene in your mind, and paint the sounds, smells, tastes, and sights in words. If you concentrate on writing descriptions that create pictures in a reader's mind, you will be writing toward your goal.

There are phrases and images that are especially useful to travel writers. Here are a few ideas for description:

- Establishing size: "The football field sized yacht could outrace a whale."
- Comparisons: "The Alpine cabin was as narrow as a school bus, but not bright yellow."
- Linking events in your story to establish an era: "While George Washington shivered with the Continental Army at Valley Forge, Corsica's most famous son, eight-year-old Napoleon Bonaparte, was playing soldier in his father's orchard."

Let's return to the verb exercise. Using the paragraph you wrote or extracted from your travel journal, circle all the verbs and verb forms—participles, infinitives, and all tenses. Now, make a separate list of these verbs. Examine each verb and imagine what the word indicates. Do you see something happening? Or are you reading a word that describes a condition or opinion rather than an action? For example, *gallop* is a verb that shows action. *Expedite* describes a condition but doesn't show action. We use all kinds of verbs in writing, but the very best writing relies on verbs that show action and create specific images in a reader's mind rather than a collection of instructions or conditions.

Are many of the verbs on your list these words: *go, do, be, get, make, can, have*, or *want*? You can do better. Flip open a thesaurus or dictionary (I avoid using software resource tools that slight the language), finger down the columns and nail the words that build a superb article and hold the reader's attention.

One way to consider the outline of a travel article is to compare it to directions for a film script. Using video terminology, we might describe the construction of the travel article like this: Open with a sensation-filled lead with a strong hook to grab the reader's attention. Using close-ups or by shadowing a specific character, ground the reader in the specific location. Use special effects to parachute the writer's voice into the narrative to establish a point of view and develop curiosity about the story. Long shots fill in the historical, geographical, and factual background. Mix with wide-panning description to show the landscape and daily life. More close-ups show characters and interactions, and orient the reader in specific locations. Story details activate the reader's visual imagination and senses. The ending wraps up the story by referring to anecdotes, scenes, or situations described earlier in the story.

STRUCTURAL ELEMENTS

Now, let's look at the structural elements in two published travel articles. I wrote "Along the Pyrenees Trail" for *Potomac Review* (Fall–Winter 2002) and Peter Mikelbank, who freelances from Paris, wrote about Orkney, Scotland, and the world's shortest regularly scheduled air flight, published in the *St. Petersburg Times* on December 7, 2003 and in other papers, to tie in with the one-hundredth anniversary of the Wright brothers' flight. For reference, these two articles appear on my Web site, www.adventuretravelwriter.com.

THE LEAD OR OPENING

Learning to write a lead that snaps a reader to attention is a specific skill that has much to do with storytelling, conversation, humor, and timing. A lead should almost always be short and captivating. When the lead is lengthy, the reader is presented with too much information to absorb too early in the article. People read travel articles for pleasure, so the writer might consider using a lead that eases the reader into the mood.

Although the lead is the opening to the travel article, it is not a "topic sentence" as you might have learned to write in high school or college composition class. In the lead of a feature travel article, it's important to intrigue readers and bring them into the substance of the article that follows. A bright lead might set up a situation or conundrum that will be explained in the body of the article, such as "The search for the gold market ended at the bank." The lead might unequivocally establish the writer's perspective that will be developed through the piece, such as "I hate beaches." Perhaps the lead highlights a representative aspect of the place being described: "Wind owns the Outer Banks of North Carolina." Sometimes the lead is a question or a quote, which invites the reader to continue by provoking curiosity: "Do you know how to sleep in a tomb?"

The walk through the Pyrenees opens with a lyrical orientation to time and place designed to place the reader fully inside the narrative. It's fall and chestnuts are falling. We see women gathering the chestnuts, a reference to times past, and a close-up look at the chestnuts on the road and in the pickers' hands.

The hook designed to attract reader interest is the homey allure of ripening chestnuts and the local women who gather the nuts. Readers have to think about why the nuts are so valued, why there are special baskets, and the care the gleaners take to protect their hands. For a reader who has never handled a chestnut still in its rough casing, this might provoke mild curiosity.

The story about the world's shortest scheduled air flight, a curiosity in itself, opens with an environmental lead, placing the reader inside the experience. The lead sets the tone for this sense-driven narrative. We hear sounds—wind, propellers—see the panorama below and hear the pilot's instructions. Immediately, the reader is in the tiny airplane. The power lies in using sense-driven verbs.

The lead in a travel article presents writers with an opportunity to play with words and images, to experiment with voice and tone. Boldness and overstatement in the lead tend to inspire reader interest. Consider approaching the lead sentence with a plan to write one that has never been written before. Remember, brevity is a significant quality.

If a reader thinks "So what?" after reading the lead, the opening has failed its mission. The lead is supposed to seduce readers; weak leads rely on comparisons to other places or experiences that might not have meaning to the reader. For example: "We had the time of our lives at Disneyland; the kids loved it, too!" That's a phrase for a postcard, not a travel article. Long, rambling, fact-filled leads that describe the destination are particularly annoying.

Don't ever do this: "Nova Scotia, which means New Scotland and was settled, by, well, the Scots, is an oblong island north of Maine tucked along the rocky Canadian coast." Similarly boring is the writer who uses the crucial first sentence to open chronology or discuss why the trip occurred: "I traveled to France in March, the off-season, in order to avoid the crowds, rather than experience Paris in April, as the song says." This is a boring non-lead; the editor will not read further. And the syntax is atrocious. Description unfolds in the body of the article, while the lead should tantalize and invite. Bland statements and sentences that report the obvious or merely rework familiar concepts falter as leads.

Where does the lead sentence come from? There are writers who can't or won't proceed with a story until the most wonderful lead in the world sings: Write me! Other writers are confident that the best lead sentence will emerge as the story progresses. It's a matter of personal taste, talent, and tenacity. People who are willing to sit and scribble drafts until the right lead tangos in stage right should do so if it works for them. Other authors more comfortable going ahead with the writing and dealing with the lead later will also meet success. There is no set rule for finding a lead. Just remember to write it before you send your story to an editor.

If an editor doesn't see the point of the story in a glance, close to the top of the article, the editor probably won't accept the story for publication. Your ten seconds start when the editor casts an eye on the first sentence. If that flies, the editor may push on to the bottom of page one, read another page, flip to the middle and end of the story, and make a decision to hold or reject. Sometime later, editors read the stories saved for another look and if your piece makes that cut, you just may be headed for publication.

The lead may arise naturally as you begin writing, but I think you're better off typing "The Lead Goes Here" at the top of your story and then plunging into the narrative. Why do you put that reminder on page one? Because nearly every novice writer forgets to write a real lead. Here's another argument for waiting until you've finished the story before crafting the lead: How can you write an alluring entry point to the story if you haven't written the story yet? Try waiting until the story is finished and find the lead as you reread the article.

Leading with a personal reference might work if the reader can easily identify with the writer, but all too often writers start off with a lackluster, commonplace statement about personal travel motivation or the chronological start of the trip. There's nothing more distasteful to an editor because it signals a banal travelogue. The "all about me" lead usually tops leaden day-by-day narration of where the author went and what he ate and saw, plodding predictably to the flight back home. It could be a great account of your activities to remind you in your dotage, but that's not a travel article. The real travel story isn't about you or your trip; it's about a place and the people in that place. Sculpt a lead that signals a theme about the locale, the history of the place, or the people you encountered.

The lead establishes story personality. If it reads smartly, the rest of the story will snap into place. Once you find the lead and paste it on top of your story, go back over the whole story and see how you can trim or insert references that link back to the lead, thereby improving internal structure. Maybe there will be a sentence or two that needs to be added deep in the text or close to the end that will reflect the lead and enhance its power. Tweak the language or punctuation in the lead itself. Break the lead into two sentences. Make it short and punchy. Try out various ways of presenting the words and images.

One way to identify a missing lead is to read the text aloud or have someone read it to you. If there is an obvious lead buried somewhere, it should emerge if you are paying attention with an open mind. More than likely, it will be a sentence or two that stands out as the essence of your travel experience or condenses many impressions into a provocative question or statement. It may be a nugget of local wisdom, a description of a singular person, a moment in time, or a commonly held adage about the location.

Whatever emerges and works as the lead will also influence the ending, so don't lock placement for that sentence just yet. If you lack the lead, but you've already written an ending, examine it for cues to constructing the lead. The opening and ending work well when there is a relationship. Not exactly like twins or a mirror image, because over-attentive matching of lead to ending can get a bit too precious. There should be a strong supportive resemblance of mood, diction, and subject.

GROUNDING THE READER

Following the lead, or even in the lead, the next structural step is to ground the reader. High up in the travel narrative, engage readers by placing them firmly in the place you are describing. In the first two or three paragraphs after the lead frame, the goal is to get the reader to see and experience the same place you, the traveler and writer, have been. Occasionally this can be achieved in the lead sentence, but usually in the dozen or so sentences after the first sentence the writer familiarizes the reader with specifics about the location. The grounding paragraphs tell where the story is taking place, show a panorama of the landscape complete with geographic characteristics or other surroundings, and discuss the season or climate and any other details that help the reader understand the story environment.

Consider this lead and grounding paragraph:

> One way to experience the real Florida is to dig it. At the Calusa
> Indian Mount site on Pine Island, Florida, just west of Fort Myers,
> visitors and volunteers sift through the soil and shells at the Ran-
> dell Research Center, an archaeology dig sponsored by the Flori-
> da Museum of Natural History.
>
> —L. Peat O'Neil, *The Washington Post*, December 31, 2000

The story sends geography cues right away—what we're doing and why people go there. With the phrase "visitors and volunteers sift through the soil and shells" we have a hint of action to come.

Look at the grounding (even though this passage takes place in the air, the sentences signal location to the reader) paragraph from the Orkney story:

The World's Shortest Regularly Scheduled Air Flight churns its twin Lycoming 260-horsepower motors against a screeching wind of equal force.

Before an onrushing skirl of sea and sky—one final molar-rattling shudder, wheels licking fresh sea foam, she rises violently into the air. Angled between earth and sky, hands straining the stick, the veteran RAF pilot forces the boxy aircraft upward. Above the furor, he calls, "Right then, EVERYONE tucked in?"

The writer steers the reader into the story. The location, a time frame, and mood are conveyed at the top of the story. We know we're in an airplane, it's noisy and a bit perilous, and there's sea below. But we're not too frightened because of the obviously competent pilot's voice and the earlier comparison of the airplane to a "Walter Mitty of airplanes" suggesting an imaginary, fantasy flight based on the James Thurber character.

ENTER THE WRITER

In the Pyrenees story, the writer's presence as character enters the narrative in the second paragraph and suggests why the writer is walking these mountains.

… the crisp feel of autumn met my steps as I set off to walk across France on the Pyrenees Mountain trail that runs from the Atlantic Ocean to the Mediterranean Sea. In France, on the Grande Randonnee (GR) path system, you're never far from a village, so detours for lodging at an inn don't represent a day or more off the trail.

I had other reasons for hiking in France. The food is immeasurably better than in North America and for a woman alone, it's safe.

Although not specifically stated, the reader may pick up clues that the writer is alone, likes to eat well and stay in comfortable lodgings. We also know where we are, the season, and something about the mood of the locale. Apart from the overall sketch of the plan, the route and logistics for the upcoming walk are not spelled out. That's content for the story. Leaving a slight ellipse in the information chain permits the reader to think and draw conclusions, an essential ingredient in clever storytelling.

Would the same effect be achieved if the sentences went like this: "I planned to go off the trail each night, eat a fine meal, and find a comfortable hotel. Though I wasn't afraid of walking alone, it was autumn and camping in the mountains would be cold. I knew I could find safe lodging easily from pre-trip research."? In the published example, the focus is on the place. In the example immediately above, the focus is on the person. Travel writing succeeds when it centers on the place.

The Orkney flight story introduces the writer, first in the "molar-rattling shudder" of the plane, through the other sense-focused description and then, in the third paragraph: "Moments like these, heart slowly resuming the task of beating blood back into your brain, you ask yourself: 'Is a career in travel writing everything I imagined?'"

Do you hear the writer's voice and catch a glimmer of his personality? Take a moment to look at the complete story. Are there places where you might add more of the writer's presence? Or is it engaging just the way it is written, without obvious author presence in a continuing flow of I, me, we, our, etc.? Trim use of first-person pronouns, as this author did, because it distances and excludes the reader.

CLOSE-UPS

Building on the lead's grab, these tightly constructed paragraphs convey mood, tempo, smell, sounds, and physical description. They also plant clues about the rest of the story. After orienting the reader in a specific place, it's time to narrow content and visual description. Select visuals that sketch out experiences and perhaps mix in a few facts. The close-ups should be related to the ensuing story, so choose well.

Here's a close-up—a post office scene—from the Pyrenees story:

> I joked with the clerk about taking too many things, but he kept silent, wrapping the bursting box with string and stamping the bright yellow cardboard all over with purple cancellation marks.

And an Orkney story close-up:

> Hands spiraling controls feverishly, adjusting speed, fuel mix, ailerons, he loops, leveling out near sixty feet. Through a steamy windscreen, one island becomes retreating memory; the other, devoutly wished for across a mile of churning chop.

WIDE VIEW OF LOCATION

To show the landscape and way of life, a travel article uses description to fill in the background for readers. The pace flows from long view to close-up, broad view to detail, but vary the placement. Sentences displaying scenes should vary in focus, but not so often that the story rocks wildly from scene to scene, time frame to time frame. The end of one paragraph should flow easily into the beginning of the next. A reader feels guided and cared for, not shunted abruptly here and there for a rapid series of many quick scenes. Try to linger on a few key highlights, rather than striving to report every incident you recall or find in your notes.

OVERVIEW

Pull back from the close-ups for a few paragraphs and word paint the history, geography, or other background material necessary to the story. A broad-brush paragraph from the middle of the Pyrenees story conveys history and geography:

> Though the border between France and Spain, set by the Treaty of the Pyrenees in 1659, roughly follows the Pyrenees, there are pockets where one nation or the other spills over. Basque country—Euskal Herria, or "land of Euskera speakers"—on the Atlantic is really a separate nation, culturally and politically, though the three provinces in France and four in Spain must still answer to their respective governments, on the Spanish side betimes violently.

Now, take a background look at Orkney and the short flight:

> At apogee, a point where the Atlantic Ocean slam dances the North Sea into roiling forty-foot-high breakers, the daily flight links two remote outcrops: Westray (pop. six hundred) and Papay (pop. seventy) across a roiling straight known as Papa Sound. Its 1.5-

mile long hop won *Guinness Book of World Records* recognition and notoriety as the world's shortest flight over a decade ago. And while officially it's a scheduled two-minute flight time, informal competition among pilots long ago lowered that mark to less than one upsa-daisy!-white-knuckling minute.

ENDINGS

Now we're at the end. It's time to wrap up the story and leave readers satisfied and pleased that they went along on the excursion. Look back to the lead and the body of the story—what themes could you use as ending material?

Think of the travel article as a piece of weaving. Through the piece, certain images or themes continue. That's the story line. In the Pyrenees piece, continuing threads include writings by mountain hikers from times past, vestiges of World War II resistance to Nazi occupation, and encounters with local residents. In the Orkney story, themes include the fragility of the airplane, elements of nature, the whimsical notion that this short hop is still a regularly scheduled flight, and the author's desire to regain terra firma.

The ending for the Pyrenees story doesn't work with the elements contained in the story. Instead, this ending is a chronological event, an accident that terminates the walk and the story. It provides a literal, chronological ending to the narrative. At the end of the Orkney piece, the writer uses a quotation from the pilot that signals the end of the flight and the narrative, reemphasizing the brevity of the flight.

Story endings may employ elements from the lead or resolve a question raised during the narrative, or the ending can stray from the specifics of the story. When the ending paragraph evokes ambience, provides emotional or visual closure, it accomplishes the goal of wrapping up the story.

CREATING A STRUCTURE

Now that you've gone over a couple of travel articles and seen how certain paragraphs accomplish visual narrative similar to cinematic storytelling, we'll look at other aspects of structure in travel writing, expanding on the points discussed above. Structure also is created through the story line, the thread or threads of visual image or topic that run through the whole piece.

Knowing the basic structure of a travel article is important. After you know what is expected, you can bend the rules. When I started working on travel articles, I analyzed published pieces, paragraph by paragraph, to determine how the story was told. Scrutinizing a travel article in *The New York Times*, I jotted down what happened in each graph. Present time, geographic location and facts about the place, present time, flashback of the author's voice telling why the author is there, present time, historical information, anecdote in present time, historical facts, and so forth.

Once you are confident that you understand the structure for a travel article, you can bend the rules, expanding or contracting length for anecdotes, digressing with a personal association, or experimenting with style. Though the structural outline noted below is a useful general guideline, remember that how a writer organizes the anecdotes, encounters, factual background, close-ups, long shots, historical detail, flashbacks, etc. depends on personal choice and writing style. Much depends on the expectations of the editor and the publication. A skilled writer weaves in crucial points early in the story: where, when, who, why, how, and what. Remember that a travel article, though classified as a feature, still uses many of the traditional elements of a news story. Readers need to know where the story is based, who it concerns, how action unfolded, and so on. In a feature article, which includes travel and food articles, there's some latitude for where answers to those essential questions are placed in the story, but the gist of the story still covers the news fundamentals: where, when, who, what, why, and how.

Of course, the precise order of those orientation paragraphs is a matter of individual style. You may want to introduce readers to a particular character you met during story research before you explain the focus of the travel. Travel writing hews to a structural formula, but the writing shouldn't be predictable.

A travel writer starting out in the trade may use this checklist as a useful reminder of the elements to be covered in an article. Let's remember that not every element needs to appear in the same order as this list, and some may be skipped (when, who, why), depending on story content or the editor's inclination.

- Lead—snappy opening to attract reader interest
- Where—the place, grounding the reader in geography
- When—the season, grounding the reader in time, climate
- Who—introduce the writer, to identify with the reader
- Why—reason for the trip, the motive, draws the reader into the story
- How—the process of travel unfolding, framework and story line
- What—the story details, quotes from people in the place, anecdotes and facts
- End—wraps up the article, perhaps linking ending to lead

Once conversant with the structure and the cinematic aspects of how to show a travel story, as discussed in the two articles above, you should begin working on specific articles. Remember that the chronological format is not the best way to tell a travel story. The temptation might be to "tell my story" as it happened. Yet stringing events as they happened in real time doesn't craft a story. Resist the impulse to report every element of your journey, or every anecdote from your journal or collection of e-mails, in the travel article.

By creating a strong organized structure—a conventional feature article structure—you signal to editors that you are fluent in the technical basics of the trade. An article that rambles on about personal forays and ignores the need to inform readers early on about location and purpose may create doubt in an editor's mind. Can this person write travel articles at all?, wonders the editor. Why is this writer ignoring basic principles of news and feature writing?

This isn't a travel article; it reads like a personal reminiscence, thinks the editor.

I know you don't want editors following that thought path when they read your work. Be attentive to structure and edit superfluous personal commentary and commonplace experiences. Self-indulgence in the name of art could be just poor writing.

THE WRITER AS CHARACTER

In the classroom, writing students ask me how they can manage to tell the story from their point of view without using "I" or "we" in every sentence. Others wonder why newspaper editors reject first-person travelogues but publish travel articles with a strong writer's voice.

This is how I explain it: There is a difference between a first-person travelogue and a travel story with a vigorous authorial voice. The first-person account of a travel adventure written by the earnest novice relies on the chronological order of events or simply compiles random events from one trip. Perhaps this writer thinks that because the anecdotes occur in one location, the place itself offers structure. Usually, the first-person travelogue (the chronological report of what the traveler did) isn't skillfully written. It lacks a compelling voice that can compensate for absence of structure. The piece has a hollow feel, no voice, just the plaintive "I" moving around in a new place seeing and doing things. To review, the writer's voice is not to be confused with sentences that are written in first person (I, we, my, our).

The travel story with real structure and authorial presence doesn't need the "I" expressing action or impressions delivered from the writer's perspective. So many cinematic elements need to be communicated—the grounding of the reader, the close-ups, encounters with other people, the history and geography—that the author's voice is conveyed through diction, slant, vocabulary, and sentence pacing. The writer's "I" has one specific place to appear, after the reader is grounded. The author explains "why I went" or "what I was looking for" or some other statement that establishes purpose. Then the writer steps into the background, allowing the place and its people to occupy center stage.

So, the reader knows where the story is happening. How did you get there? This isn't the time to explain which airline flies to the destination discussed in the travel article, which road to drive, or advice on where to gas up the car and check the oil. Helpful details like those belong in an information sidebar or box that accompanies the article. Such specifics can be woven into the text but tend to be distracting in a gripping story.

Explaining why the writer (or anyone) would visit the place may give readers an understanding of why to travel to the same place and stimulates interest to continue reading. Share your travel motivation to heighten identification and gain reader sympathy. You want readers to feel a connection with you or at least form an opinion about you. Even if your story spells out a harrowing adventure, something of your personality and intellect comes across to readers. They'd like to think that they, too, could be in Tanzania or Tuva, feeling the same thrills, discomforts, curiosity, or disorientation as you are now communicating.

Many travel articles present information in a straightforward way, with the writer never making a cameo appearance. Some publications prefer third person or second person. How do you find out? Read the publication or ask the editor. However, some of the best contemporary travel writing introduces the writer early in the story. The writer continues as a player in the action, where appropriate. For the duration of the story, the writer becomes the reader's guide and pal. The reader learns why the writer went to this place, how the writer felt and interacted. Although the writer's presence is not the focus of the story, judiciously worded explanations of the writer's point of view help tether the story flow. Telling the story with the writer as player helps strengthen structure.

Think about how you talk to a close friend about your trips. You the traveler have a role. Things happen to you, you participate in daily life. When you describe the trip to a friend, the narrative dominates for a while, then you probably launch into an anecdote or describe a curiosity about the place. In the written version, a tension exists between the personal events selected to reveal the writer's personal story and the background knowledge and panorama of the place, the narrative backdrop. How the personal anecdotal stories are presented determines the difference between it-happened-to-me monologue and engaging, or even thrilling, travel writing.

UNFOLDING THE STORY

It's all in the details, as interior designers say. After geographic orientation and a broad brush of necessary background, the highlights of the story unfold. Only you can choose what details go into your story. You want to paint a portrait of the place and might include anecdotes or encounters noted in your journal or saved e-mails or postcards. Go ahead and display your observations, mixed with facts. The details will show the reader what the place looks like, how the people live, what they say, how they gesture, and what you observed about real people. Your story is not about buildings and empty landscapes but about people in a place. The elements you select will depend on the type of travel article you are writing—the size, geography, population, founding history, tribal beliefs, cuisine, religious traditions, agricultural products, trades and arts, climate, color of the dirt, system of government, and on and on. You must realize by now that there will always be too much material available. Part of the travel writer's skill is omitting information that is already widely known yet selecting nuggets of interesting data that explain life in a given place.

Let's look into a travel story about Iceland discussed briefly in a previous chapter. No need, really, to replay the founding history or comment on the size or homogeneity of the population. Don't waste precious space on information that doesn't add drama to the story. On the other hand, if the travel story is going to focus on the small population and many geysers and hot springs in the island hinterland, the story could lead with numbers. "Iceland's population is 293,966 and nearly all of them are soaking here in the Blue Lagoon hot springs." The population detail works in this story; in another it would be dead wood.

Continuing to write this hypothetical Iceland story, you'd cull details from notes and reliable reference sources that supported the story line of the sparse population in the harsh environment, finding examples from notes and memory. Maybe the story moves through several springs and ultimately lands in a vacant spring. Reread travel notes and e-mails to friends and family to discover atmospheric details that support the story themes. Perhaps there are two or three secondary themes, such as how the geothermal resources have been developed or how the geyser fields attracted geologist-explorers in the nineteenth century and earlier. The lead might be written first or crafted after a careful look at the incidents that are available for the story.

How do you figure out which details go in and which are omitted or saved for another story? Select anecdotes or encounters with people, include details about the landscape and daily life, describe street scenes, and work in the factual and historical leavening. Add your own two cents when it advances the narrative line.

PLACING THE FACTS

Facts are not seasoning to be sprinkled randomly through the text. They should relate and support your story and be necessary to the story. Sometimes facts can be the nucleus or turning point of a story. A Web site or encyclopedia may describe certain customs or weather conditions that your first-hand experience belies. In the place-specific or destination story, though, idle fact-dropping is no more interesting than name-dropping at a cocktail party. It's tedious. Usually it takes a skilled stylist to use bald facts to steer a story; humorists like Dave Barry or P.J. O'Rourke come to mind. Look ahead to chapter six for a discussion of fact-finding resources.

MOVING A DRAFT TO COMPLETION

Let's look at the published and draft versions of elements from a story about taking tea at the Ritz Hotel and with a rickshaw driver in Agra, India. The published lead:

> "Tea! Thou soft, thou sober, sage, and venerable liquid ... to whose glorious insipidity I owe the happiest moments of my life, let me fall prostrate." (Colley Cibber, *The Lady's Last Stake*, 1708)
>
> This particular lady isn't quite at her last stake, but she can sing the praises of tea. I am thinking of two very different teas, one served in India, the other in London about a year later. Both were rich in ceremony and human connection, though vastly different in circumstance and location.
>
> —L. Peat O'Neil, *The Washington Post*, January 20, 1991

And the draft:

> Taking tea is accepted the world over as a social pleasure that refreshes the spirit as much as the palate. More people drink tea than coffee, beer, or designer water. The shared ritual transcends social status and income. Tea erases economic borders and binds wealthy London socialites to New Delhi beggars. A properly brewed pot of tea is rich with ceremony— the preheated pot, the measured leaves, the boiling water poured just so—whether the cuppa' tea is prepared in Soho or Kenya, Sydney or Kuala Lumpur.

The published version immediately involves the reader with the writer. Readers know they will be reading about (and traveling with) a woman who likes to drink tea. Yes, it's written with the first-person pronoun, but this may well be the only place in the article where "I" is used. Specific references are made to the places featured in the story, grounding the reader early. The paragraph goes on to provoke questions: What were the "vast differences" of the teas in London and India? What kinds of "rich ceremonies" were experienced? Who else participated in the "human connection"?

In the draft version, factual information dominates: "more people drink tea" than certain other beverages; "the preheated pot" and other details of making tea; "taking tea is accepted the world over ..." But the writer and human connection are missing. The notion that tea is universally enjoyed and thus levels economic and social borders is impersonal. Maybe too much information is conveyed, leaving the reader with no questions that the story promises to answer. References to exotic places where tea is drunk create a teaser for the reader, but a false one, because only Agra and London are actually discussed. Rather than grounding the reader and letting the reader know the location of this story, the recitation of faraway tea places confuses the story's focus and ultimately weakens its structure.

TELLING WHAT HAPPENED

Next, show what happened, but not so simply as ... and then I did this ... and then I saw that. You've gained the reader's trust and attention by briefly introducing yourself and your reason for traveling. Now you have to back yourself, the overreaching "I" or "we," to a minor role in the text. The story isn't really about you but the place and what happens there. Rewrite sentences that start with "I" so the scene is conveyed more precisely. For example, instead of "I planned to visit the Museo Archeologico, which is a marvel of modern architecture and the world's most important museum of Meso-American cultures," consider "Hidden behind eucalyptus trees, the stone walls and suspended stone roof of the Museo Archeologico building replicates the Meso-American stone architecture displayed inside." One sentence focuses on the author's intentions; the other sentence shows the place.

Readers want personal observation from an acute eye and ear, written with flair and contemporary voice. Stilted sentences, each one grammatically matched to its predecessor, make for tepid, if technically correct, writing. Strive for voice, a narrative that includes yourself and your observations without relying on the pronouns "I, my, we," which can distance the reader.

Returning to "A Tale of Two Teas," close-ups allow a reader to step into the writer's shoes and experience the immediate surroundings. The writer is still present, but the reader sees through the writer's eyes.

> Tea at the Ritz Hotel does have class. Under the high ceilings that simulate celestial heavens, the Palm Court conveys the illusion of spaciousness and wealth. The ballet of the tea service begins with waiters adjusting their cuffs and jackets and polishing the silver-plate trays while guests settle themselves and eye one another with airs of expectation. To stately Britishers and tourists alike, this is life as it should be.

Later in the story, the writer has tea in Agra with a rickshaw driver. The writer is present, but from the perspective of the local children:

> At the tea shop, other customers slid away from the only bench to make space for us. A man who looked like a young Marlon Brando chatted with the proprietor, then left in a hurry. Children smiled and chirped, "Hello, lady."

STRUCTURAL GIMMICKS

There are so many ways to tell a travel story. Finding the right story line for you, one that is also strong and unusual, is important. The story line is the spine on which the anecdotes or details of travel will hang. It may be useful to compare the story to a piece of weaving. The story line or several lines run through the whole piece and give readers, literally, something to hang on to. A vague or weak story line fades out or disappears when the writer rambles, strays off the topic, introduces too many variables, and gabs about extraneous information. Think of a person who interrupts to discourse on a tangent, then returns to the main topic, strays to an unrelated anecdote, introduces another topic, and strays from that one. Distracting, isn't it? In your travel writing, you will eventually learn to play with several themes or story lines in one article, but as you are learning, try to confine your details to a designated path.

With so many options available for mapping out a story, a writer may use the basic movie camera directions explained at the opening of this chapter, but utilizing different themes. The story could have a geography focus and use the ecology or geologic evolution of a place to structure the travel experienced in the present. Or use an historical focus with flashback quotes and description as in "Along the Pyrenees Trail." Follow the footsteps of an historical figure. Use the built-in pattern of a mini-journey as the foundation for the story, as the Orkney piece does. Tell the travel experience as a slice of local life or focus on food preparation, a process that allows for conversational digressions to tell the needed background details.

USING CLICHÉS

What, use clichés? Elsewhere in this book, you will read that clichés should be avoided like the plague. And that, savvy readers will recognize, is itself a bounder of a cliché. Perhaps a place is so thoroughly identified with a fact that it becomes cliché: the rain in Spain falls mainly on the plain; Mombai teems with crowds; the jungle is steamy. Brave the snickers and editorial rebukes; write a travel story revolving around a cliché. You risk overdone images and well-worn anecdotes, but by sticking to your own experiences, you could emerge with a vigorous piece of writing.

Use contrast to advantage. When I proposed a story about Christmas in a Muslim land, the travel editor at the *St. Petersburg Times* said, "Send it immediately, I want to run it before December twenty-fifth." Fortunately, I had most of the story ready to go and photos at hand. The idea isn't that extraordinary because cultural contrasts form strong stories. Still, many authors try to cover too much, stray from the main theme, and criticize. However, my angle was to compare the Christmas season in the world's most populous Muslim country, a country that enshrines freedom of religion in its constitution and has a long-established Christian minority, along with many other religions. The story turns the cliché on its head (another cliché, if you're paying attention) by showing that the Christmas season is not the sole purview of "Christian" countries.

WORDS INTO PRINT OR WEB SITES

You've proceeded with that long draft, and perhaps you've already started writing based on what you've learned in this and earlier chapters. I'll bet you have several two- or three-page drafts, forays into the world of travel writing. Or maybe you even have a long piece that you consider finished. Just for the sake of exercising your emerging skills, take the time to really run the distance and write a long draft, using the structural guidelines in this chapter.

Block out at least an hour or two. It may take several sessions to recall enough material for a full draft. Get comfortable. Close your eyes and think deeply about the journey you want to describe. Once images float in your mind's eye, or as you recall people you talked to, start writing those memory flashes, thoughts, and concepts. Don't worry about grammar or sentence structure at this point; just write.

Describe everything you remember about a single situation. Sit yourself down in that café again and explain it to a child, spelling out the confusing and strange and bizarre, noticing the simple and ordinary. The too-tight fit of a waiter's jacket, the stain of coffee across the lapel, the frayed cuff on the elderly lady's suit, the heat of sunlight outside the shade of the parasol, the sweat on the beer glass, the spilled espresso absorbed by the paper on the wrapped sugar cubes, the marks of the chair slats on the bare legs of the tourist as she leaves, the rattle of newspapers, the feel of thick old china cups that have touched millions of lips.

This is an exercise in training visual memory and selecting detail that shows a story so you don't have to say it. Will you use all this draft material? Probably not in one story, but somewhere you will. For a writer, experiences stored in memory are potential; experiences on paper or computer disk are reality.

Don't fret if you've found the draft-writing process difficult. Of course you have travel journal entries and perhaps a collection of e-mails saved from the road. Perhaps you transcribed journal selections after the discussion of travel journal writing in chapter three. Whether you write a long draft from memory, collect e-mails you've sent from the road, or transcribe the journal entries that struck you as important at the time you wrote them, you will be jump-starting your travel article.

Consider these reasons for writing a long draft. You'll have lots of material to select from as you cull details to tell the story. You'll feel a sense of accomplishment. You may have enough material to construct two articles. Twelve pages of draft material churned out in a couple of days or a week of steady, focused writing are more useful to a novice writer than two pages of highly polished writing. Why? Because an inexperienced writer's idea of polished writing might not be what an editor considers polished writing. Better to spend your time practicing the act of writing than sanding away at paragraphs that weren't outstanding to begin with. For now, aim for quantity; the quality will develop as you pound those words out. Self-editing is a skill developed through process.

Draft after draft, there are travel stories that take time to emerge fully. Be patient and stick with your goals. If the draft you are working on seems to be stagnant, put it aside for a few weeks and crank out a long draft about another travel experience. Jumping from story to story may seem unfocused at first, but actually the change heightens your attention, and working on another project may improve your writing style. Even though the writer is the same—you—the subject matter will be different, and this should inspire your writer's pride to find new ways to tell the story. Each piece we write teaches us and influences our writing facility.

exercises

EXERCISE 1: Use words that convey extra meaning. Write descriptive phrases, using adjectives and nouns that do double duty. For example, to communicate the sensation of skiing in a driving snowstorm, consider these descriptive packages: white fluffy snow, cottony snow, puffy snow, knife-cold snow, bitter icy snow, deceitful snow. All snow is white, most is fluffy, cottony, and puffy, but the last three sets of words *communicate* more than *describe*. They convey physical feeling. The words work harder, putting the reader inside the writer's ski boots.

EXERCISE 2: Alone in a metro or train compartment late at night, you doze off, then realize the train has halted and the lights are flickering. Construct half a dozen phrases that communicate your startled state and the stopped train. Search for words that suggest fear and concern. Here is an example:

> The train hurtled into the threatening night; I dozed, unaware. My sleep and the train died at the same time. The train wheels ceased their lulling rhythm and my sleepy brain jerked alert at the soundless alarm.

EXERCISE 3: Construct an outline of scenes. Using the movie camera directions described at the beginning of this chapter as your guideline, work with your long draft or transcription of your travel journal. The typescript or printout should have wide margins to accommodate written notes or use stick-on notes. Read through the draft and label scenes. Which are close-ups, which are the long shots, which are wide-panning scene shots? Mark where the reader is grounded. Mark where the author's voice enters. At the beginning, you may find you've only written close-up descriptions of specific buildings, scenes, or people or things you saw and wide-angle general observations that sweep across the landscape.

If you have other typescripts of travel articles you've written, go over them and label them with the camera position they represent. Do you have more of one kind than another?

EXERCISE 4: Select appropriate detail and relevant, intriguing facts. Using the same typescript and a different color pen, or make a fresh copy if you prefer, read over the story and analyze what kind of story details you have to work with. If there are so many paragraphs or subjects that you can't find a focus, make a grid to analyze the material. On a separate piece of paper list general headings, like animals, buildings, local people, plants, food, street life, and so on. Obviously, you'll tailor the headings to the subject matter in your draft article. So, if the story is about a group horseback riding tour on Cape Cod beach, the headings will reflect that—horses, tack, stables and outbuildings, people in the group, the guide, plants, ocean, etc. Then write down these headings next to each anecdote or paragraph or however you have divided the elements. When you've finished labeling, go back and read the headings.

To continue the example of the horseback riding tour, are there more headings about the people in the group than the horses? Do you have more anecdotes that feature the guide's salty personality than the scenery and the ocean? Use this analysis to figure out the story line. If most of the draft notes focus on the horses, the story line will revolve around them, although you'll use selections from the other details to keep the story interesting. By breaking down the draft material into labeled paragraphs and anecdotal units of specific detail, you now know what building blocks are available to work with.

EXERCISE 5: Write sentences that explain travel situations you experienced relating to buying tickets in foreign places—long distance transport, theater, bus, metro—any kind of tickets. Start the sentences without using personal pronouns, including I or we, but make sure the reader knows why you are there. Here's an example:

The hawker spoke in a low voice, asking people on the crowded London sidewalk if they wanted to buy an extra ticket to today's matinee. Another hawker muscled up, "Wot have ye got here, miss?," determined to stake claim to his piece of the public walkway. "One ticket, face value," I answered. Just then a bearded stranger shoved a twenty-pound note in my face and bought the ticket. He must have been a hawker, too, because the person who actually showed up in the adjacent seat was a bulky Dane with a cold.

EXERCISE 6: Write sentences that quicken the pulse of a story. Use action verbs. Do not use any tense or form of the verb "to be" (*I am, you are, he is, I was, you were,* etc.) These sentences should describe people in a public place—a market, city hall, the beach, etc.

Ripping aged leaves from the heads of cabbage, the balding market vendor whistles an aria from Verdi. Shoppers pause and pretend to consider the vegetables, but their hearts thirst for the opera.

San Francisco's North Beach lacks sand and surf, but the local bohemians parade a fair amount of skin. Fashion reigns in two colors here, black and leather.

EXERCISE 7: Write with a descriptive voice without starting sentences with the pronoun "I." Remember that you can communicate voice without using "I." Strive to write simple declarative sentences.

Outside the train window, sagebrush chased dust across the red dirt desert floor. Sure was windy, but the passengers inside the snug dining car couldn't feel it.

STYLE AND TONE

A writer's style is as personal as a signature, memorable as a face, subjective as a name. The writer's attitude to the subject matter and the act of writing contributes to the development of style.

A travel writer demonstrates style in the lead that grips, artful description that makes readers feel like they are accompanying the writer, and the inspiring or funny ending that ties the story together. Along the way, clever turns of phrase, allusions, metaphors, contrast, vocabulary, juxtaposition, and other tricks of the trade will keep the story moving stylishly.

What is style in writing? Like a person's taste in art, affinity for a certain writing style is deeply individual. To paraphrase a comedian on the subject of art: I can't define it but I know it when I see it. To have style in writing, the words must be written in a way that distinguishes them from ordinary composition. However, before writing can be appreciated as having style, it has to at least meet those standards of composition in English. In other words, knowing and using the elements of style—the rules of usage, grammar, diction, sentence structure, styntax, and the principles of composition—must come first in a writer's effort to create stylish prose. Then, having mastered the mechanics, a writer may explore individual ways of expression.

It might help to examine your own writing style. How are you nurturing your diction and vocabulary? What books—not necessarily travel books, any literature—are you reading? Who are the literary authors you enjoy? Do you recognize a writer's style? Can you hear a writer's voice?

In order to learn and create, sometimes we must discard habits. All of us have stylistic tics that need revision. Reread your writing from a few years or a decade earlier. Do you still sound the same? Has your sentence flow or vocabulary improved? What aspect of your writing do you think needs attention?

Before the writing can be assessed as having style, it has to be clear and competent. And the person making the assessment, in this case the writer herself, really has to have some standards of taste, a knowledge of what constitutes style. So, crack open a college-level grammar review textbook or reread William Zinsser's *On Writing Well* or Strunk and White's *The Elements of Style*. Do the exercises in the grammar text and take a red pencil to your own travel articles. Trade articles with a writing friend and ruthlessly correct grammar and sentence structure. Identify elements in your writing that address style—metaphors, similes, diction, vocabulary.

Reading what other writers have said about style can be useful in identifying or cultivating your own. Discover a model of elegant writing by choosing from what accomplished writers offer. Take a look for yourself in *Bartlett's Familiar Quotations* or H.L. Mencken's *A Dictionary of Quotations* to get a feel for the variety of opinions on style from the giants of history and literature. Select essays, memoirs, and diaries of respected writers whose words have survived the test of time. The works needn't be travel essays to be worthwhile in your self-tutelage. While you are at the reference shelf, look up "style" in Webster's or an equivalent online dictionary. You'll see some variation of this definition from Webster's: " ... a manner or mode of expression in language ... distinction, excellence, originality, and character in any form of artistic or literary expression."

Style can be breezy, ponderous, sympathetic, humorous, poetic, satiric, academic, cozy, and so on. Although writing style seems an amorphous quality, it is composed of measured elements. Selectivity of content is a basic ingredient of a writer's style. Originality of voice and expression—the point of view— conveys style. And of course, the quality of writing technique is crucial to style. In a way, style can't be taught because it is so individual. But a writer can practice experiments with phrasing, improve vocabulary, and absorb techniques used by other writers. A writer can learn what isn't stylish, steering around elegant variation, studied irony, and purple prose. More about those traps later. In this chapter, we'll look at the elements of style that show the writer's imprint on the piece and examine ways to nurture stylish writing.

CRAFTING STORIES WITH STYLE

The best travel writing evokes a clear and vivid sense of place. Accurate descriptions of a place contain illustrative details, anecdotes about the people and experiences felt by the writer all laced together with a nod to history and geography. The travel writer's first editorial task is to select travel incidents that show the character of a place in a story. Developing style in nonfiction writing is a lot like developing a point of view for a fictional character. The details you select to tell the travel story should demonstrate something of the character who took the trip—you. When we first start traveling and looking at the world with a writer's eye, there may be a tendency to see everything, write down too much. Since you enjoyed your experiences, you feel an urge to pack all the details into a travel story so the reader can have the same experience. This approach doesn't work. The interesting travel story is carefully composed of selected details that reveal the writer's sensibility through details that affected the writer's senses. By strengthening your ability to pull the illustrative details from your journal and memory, and tell them with a consistent and distinctive perspective, you develop your writing style.

Consult the richly colorful entries from your travel journal. Or cultivate your memory by running through your files of digital images or photo albums. Write sketches of places and incidents that these images trigger. You are now ready to select entries that will form the basis of the article and express your style. Difficult as it may seem at first, not every observation you record in your travel journal will support the story flow nor be interesting or useful to readers. It's agreed, then: Style is a matter of selectivity, individuality, and quality. Review the anecdotes and scenes from your personal journal of travel experiences. If you've already written a draft of your travel article, read it and pretend you haven't been there. Do you know enough after reading the piece? Are you curious to learn more? Do you have the information to start planning a trip to the place?

Put yourself in the reader's place: What would you want to know if you were going to take this trip? Read what other writers have reported on the place. You also have the travel journal to work with. Remember the reader who is interested in a vicarious travel experience and use buoyant language, inventive metaphors and similes.

With this material in the background, focus on story content. Here you come, fueled with a love of travel and appreciation for varied cultures, and it's natural to want to share everything you've observed and experienced, but selecting the right illustrative events goes to the heart of style. You can even deliberately leave out information to stimulate curiosity. But don't trick readers; if you omit a detail that figures in the story line, with the idea of spurring readers to the end, you are obliged to return to that detail and explain. For me, learning how to streamline travel articles was the most difficult lesson. I hated to omit information I enjoyed and considered important, but I came to understand that some material bloated the story, distracted readers, or slowed the narrative line. I was sacrificing style for facts and explanations. With the help of skilled and generous editors who hounded me with questions ("How does this move the story along?" "Does this show your relationship to the place?" "What does this add to the story line?" "Do readers need to know this information?"), I learned that less is often best.

Pay particular attention to editing phrases, asides, and references that are not timeless. We strive to put ourselves in the narrative, but don't weigh down the story line by insisting on reporting your every movement, thought, and conundrum. Let the place and its people dictate what's important rather than your need to place yourself in the narrative.

Improve clarity by cutting asides, personal commentary, and parenthetical remarks that indulge the author and other off-the-cuff material that the author inserts for personal flavor, and indeed, do add voice, but when used excessively—more than one or two per story—it weighs down the story line. Like that sentence, perhaps? See how convoluted it reads?

Does this mean you can't put any asides in the travel story? No, just evaluate carefully what the comments add to the mix. If the material is in there to satisfy your view of yourself or to enhance the presentation of yourself to the reader, consider that the story might be better off without the personal asides. Consider breaking the long sentence into shorter statements.

GRAMMATICAL VOICE AND WRITER'S VOICE

You remember the lessons about voice from school: first person (I, we) second person (you), third person (all-seeing). The grammatical voice you (or your editor) prefer depends on the story, the publication, and your skill. When we talk about point of view, we're discussing who is telling the story. Is the writer a character? Use the first person. If the editor prefers third-person narratives, you'll probably use a mix of second- and third-person voices. This book, for example, uses all three voices—first, second, and third. Generally, it's best to stick with one voice per paragraph or section.

Writing voice is the way an author expresses personal attitude—through word choice, asides, sentence flow, paragraph density, and other individual stylistic devices. This voice is a function of style and authority. Style breathes life in the authorial voice and point of view. Rather than assuming a false voice, constructed to suit the material, explore your own mind and linger there as you write about the character of a place. Be mindful of sticking with the story theme, but give your writer's voice latitude for expression. Develop a writer's voice by setting aside expectations. Practice writing without a goal or a particular publication in mind to explore true personal voice.

In most contemporary travel writing, the writer participates in the article. The story is told from the writer's point of view, in a natural writing voice. But writer participation might not occur in every paragraph. As discussed in the previous chapter, don't write "I" or "my" or the plural equivalents to communicate the author's point of view and voice. First-person pronouns should be used sparingly. Some publications prefer travel articles written in second or third person, when the writer does not appear in the story.

In deciding which experiences to include in a story, I listen to my individual storytelling flow, my instinctive inner voice that is the essence of personal writing style. Learning to narrow focus and accurately select incidents to build a visually suggestive travel piece is a matter of practice. It may be easy to say "trust the inner voice," but sometimes we have to nourish that storytelling sensibility and encourage self-confidence.

Uncertain about your storytelling ability? Reread a few children's books. Notice the narrative arc: Where does the action start? Who are the characters? What successes or obstacles occur? How many incidents do you remember after finishing the book?

The travel article is compact; only a few highlights can be included. Like a children's story, the narrative needs action, characters, and dramatic events (successes and failures). Stick to the story line by asking yourself with each sentence, "Is the reader still with me? Does this sentence follow on the footsteps of the last one or have I pushed the story into unknown territory?"

To develop your instinctive writing style, try to write the travel article as if you were narrating the story, speaking to an audience while pictures unfold. Select incidents and descriptive scenes that are consistent with your experience. What impressed you? Why?

Are you including an incident because you think readers will like it or because it is meaningful to you? Writers can't second-guess the reader. If the encounter or particular description flows with your story line and sticks in your mind, it belongs in the narrative. If the experience sticks with you and conveys a sense of the place you are writing about, express it with your style. Later, after the story is constructed, you'll again streamline the material. Like a sculptor, you'll chisel away excessive facts and sand off the surplus explanations and adjective-heavy prose. You'll add verbs that show your story.

I cut my beginner's teeth on a travel piece for *The Washington Post* about an overland trip across North Africa. I had written freelance travel articles for small papers and magazines, but this was my first major sale. Mysterious and exotic, Algeria and the surrounding region offered many story angles. Too many. Doing justice to the story of driving across North Africa, camping in the wild, shopping in markets, and meeting local people could fill a book. Sunday travel section readers don't relish wading through dense material and editors won't buy it anyway. So, I had to focus. First, I selected one portion of the journey. Algeria was certainly the least known country of the three, and by limiting the story to Algeria, I increased the article's market value at that time. Travel editors are curious about stories from places off the beaten track, but the timing has to fit. There was a window of opportunity for a travel article about Algeria only after political unrest abated. Since then, however, Algeria has again succumbed to internal strife; a travel article about the region might not sell today.

Let's look at a travel story that isn't so esoteric, about kayaking along coastal South Carolina. During the writing phase of the article, I selected anecdotes that would illustrate my story premise or thesis. One theme was the friendliness of Carolinians, that the state with a palmetto tree on its flag was populated with warm, sympathetic citizens. I also wanted to show how a couple of outsiders fared there. My personal writing style is rooted in developing and enhancing human connections, and I tend to be impressed by small, unexpected acts of kindness. Thus I strive to align my writing style with that orientation. I had no shortage of encounters with helpful strangers in the barrier islands of South Carolina, but a balanced story needs adversity, so I deliberately included material that showed the pitfalls of being a hapless newcomer to the region.

All of these incidents demonstrated how the locals connected to strangers and showed aspects of daily life in coastal Carolina. Many of the encounters served dual purposes. Extra information was used in the sidebar section of the story, the information box of travel facts that most travel editors require. My guideline for placing incidents inside the story or in the "Ways" section was this: If the item related directly to the story action, it would be fodder for the main story. General travel and kayak information was relegated to the sidebar.

Some of the material contained in the journal of this trip was completely omitted from the travel story. For example, I could see no useful purpose in a lengthy description of the unfortunate night at a bed and breakfast in Beaufort. One way to test the interest value of your experiences is to give friends and family a rundown of your travels and note which anecdotes hold their attention. Compare the events you selected for your story with those that elicited questions and deeper interest from your audience. Watch your audience and remember how they reacted.

Telling a story with flair to a live audience is challenging work. In print or online, the task is even more demanding. There is no opportunity for eye contact, gestures, or feedback from the audience. The onus is on the writer to keep the narrative moving at a consistent level. Story momentum is easier to maintain when the anecdotes are all uniquely interesting. Hit the high spots, incorporating the incidents or experiences that elicited the most interest from the audience when you talked about your travels. Mostly, you are selecting and defining what affected you and appealed to you. Personal writing style depends on confident, individual taste.

Before writing a travel narrative, spend some time thinking about story elements. Jot down the events that affected you—incidents that communicated the core nature of a place, the people you met. By avoiding, for the moment, a circumstantial, linear list of where you went and what you saw, the focus is on the experiential elements of travel that fascinate the reader. Not what you saw, but what happened in the place. Not where you went, but how the locals live and how you interacted with them.

Readers want to feel like they are at your side, taking the trip with you. A trip has periods of activity and stretches of sameness. You want to communicate the periods of activity and hint at the things you did that were routine. Using the tips outlined in chapter four, on building a structure like a movie, select events and experiences that fulfill the need for close-ups or long shots, incidents that show intense personal connection or broad general impressions. If your travel journal doesn't have the anecdotal material you need, strive to remember scenes that correspond to the structural elements described in the last chapter. Focus on human encounters at various places along the way. Impressions of the awesome landscape and the historical sites are communicated through the important "high spots" of human interaction. Interweave with general descriptions that show the passing scene.

ORIGINAL VOICE

Style is a matter of tone and voice. Will you create humor in the narrative by mocking yourself? Will the story touch a deep emotional nerve? Do you have cross-cultural bonds to develop? Is humor your strong suit: Can you tell the funny side of experiencing other cultures? An anecdote can amuse or offend, depending on how the story is told. What is your attitude toward the place you are describing? Your biases and opinions about your experiences there will influence the writing style that emerges as you compose the article. Were you changed? Disappointed? Surprised?

Establishing voice and tone early strengthens an article. Readers will want to stick with this voice because the tone is friendly or funny or smart. The words are cleverly chosen, juicing the reader's mind. Phrases that sound familiar resonate with the reader, making him feel included. There is no single correct writing style to achieve tone or voice. There is only the one right way for you to say what you know.

FALSE VOICE

Thankfully, we've thrown off, for the most part, the nineteenth- and early twentieth-century convention that required travel writers to modulate sarcasm, criticism, and strong opinions that might chafe the sensibilities of genteel armchair readers. Few travel writers today would presume the arrogance of the past that denigrated the ignorant natives, so different than me and thee. Travel writers then practiced the high art of invention, stretching description to fit the direction of self-image, painting themselves buccaneers and explorers when they were borrowing from other writers' already inflated descriptions for their own elaboration.

Today's writer forges truthful reports about travel and shows culture, customs, climate, and accommodation without shying from the strange.

Previously, and still in certain "advertorial"-type publications, artificial editorial standards concerning a writer's voice and experiences encourage the notion that travel is always fun, comfortable, and stimulating. We know that's not true, but travel articles are sometimes published to sell products. Certain customer magazines designed to enhance the image of the travel industry encourage the notion that travel narratives should be tweaked to suit artificial intentions, to promote business. Indeed, you may find yourself writing such artificial travel articles to develop a portfolio or for the income. For more on work-for-hire travel writing, read chapters eight and nine.

Today, we hope that truth guides the hand of the travel writer. We hope we can recognize what is fantastically unbelievable and mildly improbable. And we strive to be honest about what we see, avoiding comparisons that might sound smug or complacent, focusing on what the place and its people offer rather than finding fault because it isn't like home.

Examine voice in your own writing. Does the reader gain an understanding of the narrator? Do you take the time to show yourself, as author, so the reader will identify with you, the narrator? Exercise self-criticism: Is your writerly voice annoying? Do you rely on first-person pronouns to tell the story? Are you a fair observer? Do you explain to the reader when you stray from absolute truth?

EDGE AND ATTITUDE

Sometimes writers wonder how much voice is too much. Usually, unless the writer is noisily whining or using excessive sarcasm, the voice you naturally write with—an easy conversational tone—will please your readers. Some contemporary writers invoke a mean and edgy tone, which can be irritating in a long article. Some of today's travel writers inflate their experiences to evoke greater danger or characterize encounters as risky or threatening to enhance their imagined status as intrepid adventure writers.

Brisk, straightforward expository writing works best for travel feature articles. Personal asides, rhetorical comments, humor, and other comments are fun to interject, making the story move along faster in an informal manner.

DICTION AND CLARITY

Consider the tone of the article in relation to its subject. Expand your word choices. Sentence fragments—incomplete sentences—are permissible if your intention is to whip up the pace and create a loose ambiance. Jargon and slang are occasionally useful, but remember the reader's needs when you select similes and metaphors. Remember the reader: Not every reader is aware of television show characters or electronic game scenarios. And it could be equally annoying to read allusions to classical Greek myths or sports references. Consider the specific audience you are writing for.

RISK-TAKING IN LANGUAGE USE

What are your favorite metaphors? Do you rely on sports, military, or business words to construct images and convey secondary meaning? Consider whether these similes and metaphors do justice to your topic. Stretch your imagination and invent some new metaphors. Compare music to mathematics; food to cloth; construction projects to nature. Drive all over the open desert stretches of highway and cut through the clouds in the vast blue sky that is the art of writing. Just don't mix and overuse metaphors in the same sentence or paragraph, like that last sentence.

Try a few examples of figurative language like these:

> Woodpecker attacking a hollow tree sounded like a snare drum...

> Background choruses of gossiping tea drinkers like a forest of cicadas...

By taking risks I mean stepping out of the ... no, not the box, that's become a cliché, as has out of the closet, off the grid, off the map, off the page. What would be an effective fresh comparison to convey exploring turf beyond the well known? Venturing out of the hard drive? Off the deck? Maybe those phrases have become hackneyed as well. Write sensibly, but write with surprise. Sometimes the right metaphor or simile strikes like a wasp sting (never lightning!).

MOVING BEYOND CHRONOLOGY

Writing with style may involve shifts in time, perspective, and mood, although not so often that the reader can't follow the story line. Alert readers to highlights in the story by placing a clue in the opening paragraph, then fulfill the promise with an explanation later in the story.

Engaging writing establishes a mood. Establish right at the start of the story elements of the personality (the writer) who will tell the story. A reader commits to finish the piece when there's something personal about the storyteller close to the start. That familiarity takes the reader by the hand and says, "Come along, you'll have a good time if you read this."

Style might involve what is left out of the opening, or a comparison to establish an understanding of what exists. This writer uses what is missing to describe the setting:

> Five golfers, each of whom can strike the ball brilliantly, are standing on the first tee at Tour 18, staring at the face of a lighthouse straight down the fairway. The hole is supposed to look like the eighteenth at Harbour Town, the great course at Hilton Head, only there's no ocean along the left side of the fairway, just a swamp, because we're not in coastal South Carolina but rather suburban Houston, in what used to be an oilfield.
>
> —Joel Achenbach, *Smithsonian*, August 1993

When you cast about for an image to use in a comparison, strive for bold originality. Steer clear of preposterous similes that distract the reader and detract from the story. Jolt a reader's curiosity, but remember to be fair to the reader and answer any questions raised in the early part of the article.

> Bankruptcy is an awful thing. In 1990, it became an American brand of purgatory; many considered it a payback for an era of greed. For me, bankruptcy ushered in a time of personal grieving, searching and guilt. At least I hoped for another chance. And trail cooks spend a lot of time on their knees.
>
> —Patricia Lewis Sackrey, *The Boston Globe*, August 14, 1994

In this example, the question arises: What does bankruptcy have to do with a travel article? The reader is curious about how the road from bankruptcy led to being a trail cook. Note how humor lightens a potentially difficult subject. The writer calls bankruptcy "an American brand of purgatory" and summons the same metaphor with the phrase "trail cooks spend a lot of time on their knees." And she answers the questions by the end of the story.

BORING WRITING

How does a boring paragraph begin? Could this be one? Probably not, because you're already wondering, just what kind of sentence is boring? If the reader is thinking about the ideas presented, the text doesn't fulfill the first element of boredom: lack of engagement. Boring writing lacks surprise. The sentence rhythm is repetitious; the words are predictable and sound like other sentences and phrases we've heard before that lurk in the subconscious. The next word or turn of phrase is what is expected and reader interest ebbs. Boring writing lacks a natural voice. It is removed from the way people talk and think, is self-conscious with a poky dedication to traditional phrasing or an artificial high-minded diction. Boring writing is often in passive voice.

At the risk of losing your interest, here are a few of examples of weak style:

> Upon completing our repast, we surveyed the piazza and strode with purpose through a throng of gadabouts to the morning's artistic quest, St. Mark's Cathedral.

Perhaps this writer thinks he is a nineteenth-century tutor on the Grand Tour. Unfortunately, scores of novice travel writers affect a style like this. Words that time and custom have relegated to infrequent usage (repast, surveyed, strode with purpose, gadabouts, artistic quest) should be used sparingly in contemporary writing. Alliteration (through a throng) also has its usefulness, but dropped into this already ponderous sentence, it has the affect of choking the flow. A case could be made that the example above shows sarcastic edge; it would depend on the rest of the article and the overall voice.

> The rolling green hills of Prince Edward Island are all that a bucolic place should be.
>
> New Orleans is the capital of jazz, a good-time rhythm and blues town.

In both sentences, the end is a vague restatement of the first part, which deflates the image. Sentences that rely on commonplace generalities (all that a bucolic place should be, a good-time rhythm and blues town) lack style and information.

A key to engaging a reader in this age of competing information sources lies in the construction of the lead and the next few sentences, as well as every opening sentence for subsequent paragraphs. What grabs a reader's full attention? Ask yourself what happens when you read travel articles: Do you continue with this writer or are you tired of her already?

The top of the story (lead and opening paragraphs) sells your piece and alerts readers to the savvy narrative that follows. Use a gimmick, an anecdote, a story, a quote, and some phrase with universal appeal. Ask a question, state a fact, inflame curiosity, and be bold. The more original the lead, the greater the survival possibilities for the story. Before writing your own story opening, take a moment to review the section on leads in chapter four. Of course the goal is to write lively and entertaining prose. Readers who are involved in the material expect to be served juicy text. And you, as the involved writer, should want to produce your best.

So, how about that boring paragraph? The sentences are constructed alike and sound similar. The writing style is flat and ordinary. The pace and tone rarely change. The sentences are all the same length and style. The vocabulary is limited to words in common parlance. The diction is pedantic and repetitive or overwritten and overly dependent on adjectives and adverbs. The reader stops before the end. Like that paragraph you just read.

STYLEBOOKS

This might be a useful point to discuss stylebooks and publication "house style." Most newspapers, wire services, and publishers, as well as print and online magazines, follow a specific set of rules concerned with grammatical points, capitalization, punctuation, and so forth. These stylebooks or the "house style" are drawn up by staff editors, or the publication might use a widely accepted stylebook such as *The Chicago Manual of Style, Words Into Type, The United States Government Printing Office Style Manual, Wired Style: Principles of English Usage in the Digital Age*, or *The Associated Press Stylebook*. The *AP Stylebook*, for example, offers an alphabetical format to explain this venerable wire service's house style. Randomly looking up *whiskey, whiskeys* I read: "Use the spelling *whisky* only in conjunction with *Scotch.*"

So, next time I write a travel story about Scotland for the AP and Scotch whisky is mentioned, it would behoove me to use the AP accepted spelling.

SELF-EDITING FOR STYLISH WRITING

Let's consider elements for improving story structure, developing characters, expanding vocabulary and figurative language, the sound and pace of sentences, and knowing when to end a successful travel narrative.

While writers always strive to use the right word to convey mood and meaning, some phrases and images are especially useful in travel writing. As you probably know, travel writing is sense-based. That means you key the narrative to the reader's senses more than their powers of analysis. The travel writer communicates how a place smells, what sounds are heard, how the people move, what the local food and hooch tastes like. A successful travel writer includes a rundown on the weather, snatches of conversation, and an eyeful of the texture of daily life.

Fancy adjectives, frivolous subjunctives, and obscure personal witticisms are no remedy to flat writing. Humorous asides inserted whimsically with the idea that they create voice almost always fail. Elegant words are not necessarily the ones with the most syllables or snob appeal. Sometimes simple words, used with imagination, create a more unified story.

Now, fish out that story you've been working on or pull out a draft you've set aside to work on later. Perhaps you have a travel article that was rejected by an editor. Read the story aloud and listen to your voice or tape record yourself reading and listen to the playback for the true effect. With highlighter in hand, mark all the verbs. Make a list of them. How many are truly action words? Replace the verbs that don't demonstrate motion or activity. Rearrange sentences so they are in the active voice. Passive voice places the subject as the receiver of the action while active voice has the subject as the doer of the action. For example, the chauffer drove the car (active voice). The car was driven by the chauffer (passive voice). Next, highlight the adjectives. Do they pile up before nouns like a chain-reaction car crash? Knock off one adjective if there are two for a word. Are the adjectives specific or bland qualifiers? Does the adjective immediately summon a mental picture? Shift the descriptive work to the verb and the noun itself if the adjectives are overly familiar. English overflows with words exactly appropriate for every scenario. Adjectival props show a reaching writer. Qualifiers (e.g., rather, sort of, seems like, kind of, nearly) sap the strength of a sentence. Are you comfortable and confident that what you are hearing is muscular, verbal, evocative, resonant English? Does the article need to be rebuilt or will it run with just a tune-up?

Polishing tedious material is not an editor's job. It's our job. We writers have a responsibility to ourselves and our readers to craft prose that informs and enlightens, educates and inspires. Our writing is our self, our mind's expression. Let's resolve to shine our writing before attaching the file to an e-mail query or sliding it into an envelope.

Guaranteed, no editor will be spending time wrestling with listless words and a thesaurus. The manuscript that needs that kind of work is ignored or rejected. Editors sometimes will suggest rearranging paragraphs, insist on stronger transitions, and help with continuity, but that advice would only be offered if the article is worth publishing. If the story is accepted, editors have been known to make a few cuts, sometimes without even consulting the writer! But don't count on an editor to devote any time to improving an article that lacks potential.

Developing a style, writing with punch, and choosing straightforward language are hallmarks of a serious writer. After an editor expresses interest, listen carefully to suggested edits. Though the story may be crafted with original metaphors, appropriate images, and vivid vocabulary, you still may be asked to make changes. While staff writers may defend the piece if an editor recommends changes, the freelance writer may not have that luxury. It doesn't improve your position with editors to challenge every suggestion for revision.

GEE-WHIZ DESCRIPTION

Life is being celebrated every day in countless different ways. The traveler is the go-between, bringing news of wondrous events to eager ears back home. The travel writer goes one better, discovering, experiencing, and then sharing impressions with a broad audience. Your description in the article expresses your wonder and the truth of your experience, but search for language that reaches a broad audience.

In trying to avoid flat writing, some novices assume the wide-eyed tourist's voice. Sorry, no room for "gee-whiz" or expansive description of ordinary experience in travel writing that will be published. Examples of overblown gee-whiz description might be: You're traveling and see a fabulous sunset, an experience most humans on this planet have had, so you rave about the colors in the sky, but what's so unique about a pretty sunset? Nothing at all.

Perhaps you've never seen a certain activity—the changing of the guard at the presidential palace in Athens, a fire-walking dance in Bali, or a pig roast in rural Hawaii. Don't be naive. Though the perspective is personal, a keen eye for action and nuance and some knowledge of ritual archetypes and myths will bring balance to a story about cultural performances. Perhaps some of your readers know these rituals well.

You may be writing about a seaside location where the local men and women wear pants and a sarong for swimming, or conversely, the local women wear no upper body covering at all and parade the beach. Prune the "gosh" and "golly" observations and language that express astonishment at what is ordinary and commonplace experience. Be just as ruthless in weeding out phrases rooted in prejudice, cliché, and condescension. Artful understatement grabs more reader attention.

Sublime writing is not in all of us, all of the time. But everyone who diligently plies the pen—or keyboard—will surely someday turn a magnificent phrase. Meanwhile, there are legions of efficient, interesting sentences informing and pleasing readers.

Keep in mind that bad writing is published every day. Your job is to be part of the fine writing that's also published every day.

You make the choice as you construct a piece. Will each sentence carry its share of the story line? Or will you overlook a few bloated sentences, even though they sink the piece? Learning to self-edit is perhaps the most difficult part of writing, but improving that skill promotes development of a recognizable writing style. Each time you sacrifice a marginal, though beloved, sentence, your style tightens and improves. The work of rewriting, cutting, and moving sentences is the heart of the process of becoming a skilled, professional writer. Always pause to read aloud and listen for the continuity of the voice.

Settling for less than sublime writing does get the job done. After all, you want the piece finished and under the eyes of the editor who expressed interest. Recognize the point between half-baked, lazy writing and the best writing you've ever done—that midpoint is a realistic starting point for a last edit. As you refine your writing and editing skills, the whole process becomes more fluid.

Bang out muscular sentences that heft a story high. Editors don't call their jobs "moving the story along" for nothing. With writing practice, training the imagination, and reading selectively, the serious writer will create an often outstanding, occasionally arresting and usually salable piece.

Nourish your writing style with excellent reading. A unique personal writing style develops with its roots in literature.

THE RIGHT WORD AND THE LAUNDRY LIST

Precision in language is an art and a skill. Selecting words of determined meaning will toughen writing. For example, I've seen many travel articles rejected because they contain a sentence similar to these below. The writer obviously intends to communicate that the resort or destination has an array of activities. Because the presentation is flat and predictable—usually a list separated by commas—no meaning is carried in the sentences. No image comes to the reader's mind; the words and space are wasted, the print equivalent of broadcast dead air.

Take a look at these sample sentences. The goal in this hypothetical travel article is to inform readers about activities at a destination resort. Write a critique for each of these sentences.

1. Daily activities boards list things to do here, including swimming, golf, and croquet.

2. Daunted by the activities menu, I lazed by the pool all day.

3. What a fabulous array of things to do! I found activities for every taste.

4. There are many activities such as sports, dancing, tennis, board-sailing, surfing, and sunbathing.

5. Imagine a place where there's plenty to do for everyone.

6. You'll find sufficient diversion, such as snorkeling, diving, sailing, and sea kayaking.

7. There's no lack of entertainment, whether you're a doer or a watcher.

8. Things are happening here. Lots of things, as long as they are all sports.

9. Visitors can choose from activities such as horseback riding, tennis, golf, swimming, croquet, water sports, aerobics classes, and just sitting back and watching the world go by.

10. At breakneck speed, we worked our way through the activities menu. By the end of our three-day marathon, we'd sampled twenty athletic diversions, not one of them in the pool.

Herewith, my critiques:

1. Questionable diction—what are "daily activities boards"?

2. Stylish with use of humor.

3. Gushy, gee-whiz writing. Needs specific information.

4. Unrefined, flat laundry list of activities.

5. What's this, the land of volunteers? Everyone "doing" for everyone else?

6. Nothing but a laundry list.

7. Ambiguous, could be improved.

8. Vague. Attempt at humor falls flat.

9. Laundry list and clichés.

10. Visual language communicates activity and information.

Why do we need to use precise language? Because although description is intensely personal, the end product is intended for a varied audience. Striking, zippy language reaches a broader range of people. You want your writing to endure, don't you? Why settle for worn-out phrases when travel writing offers an opportunity to use personal imprimatur? Forget lists of things; show people doing the activities. Hack out those rusty clichés. A good test: If you've seen or read the same series of words recently, the phrase is lurching to the wrecking lot of dead metaphor. Don't drive clunkers; test-drive fresh words and innovative comparisons.

Elements of humor always win out over bland statements of fact. Audacity and boldness in point of view grabs attention. Don't forget exuberance and gaiety. Writing is a visual process. Words catch the eye before the brain. A string of long, heavy words are difficult to read and retain. Short, brisk words paced in sentences that roll off the tongue are preferable to cumbersome, otiose, convoluted conjugations. A few well-crafted sentences will attract reader notice far more than long-winded bombastic material that overwhelms the reader. Nouns are naming words and must be specific to show what is happening. Verbs are action words. But even action words can be inactive—passive voice verbs avoid responsibility for action by deflecting the source of the motion. Active verbs give momentum to a sentence. Readers can see the action by picturing a person, place, or thing doing something. If you want to create visceral prose with tensile description, rely on the verbs, not adjectives.

IDENTIFY WITH THE READER

Enable readers to visualize themselves in your story. Use words with which they can identify. Keep your audience in mind. Know whom you are writing for and use language appropriate to the subject matter. Remember that writers are competing with other information sources such as the Internet, television, radio, and information databases. We are writing for people with limited time and, according to surveys, a disinclination to read. Writing for nonreaders who are in a hurry means that the text has to appeal quickly so the reader will persevere. Because statistics tell us this average person doesn't read very often, she may not have a high level of attention or retention. I don't think this means you should "dumb down" your article, as the cliché goes, but rather smarten it up. Use words that are stimulating rather than soporific. Make readers work, but not too hard.

Help the reader along. Don't leave holes that raise distracting questions. Tweaking curiosity doesn't mean leaving nagging ellipses in the story line. As William Zinsser, author of the seminal writing book *On Writing Well*, said in a lecture a few years ago in Washington, D.C., where each sentence ends, the next should pick up the thought and the story line. Don't leave your reader hanging—take him along each phase of the story.

SIDEBARS

Sidebars and boxes help the reader receive factual information in a compressed package. With the "how to" facts in a sidebar, the travel story focuses on experiences and visual description. Most newspapers and magazines require sidebars with an article. The word count is usually included in the overall article. However, always ask an editor who is interested in your story idea the kind of sidebar information expected. Some publications require the basics of which airline flies to the destination and a couple of hotels. Others want information on hotels at various price pegs, data on nearby attractions, and several reference Web sites.

Placing factual data in the sidebar allows the writer to keep the story moving. Don't get bogged down in lengthy explanations that the reader can grasp by a quick look at the sidebar.

If you throw in facts that rank size or frequency or some other characteristic, such as longest river in the world or oldest restaurant in Paris, put in a reference or comparison that is accessible to your readers. For example: a river so long that if it were straight it would stretch the length of the Mediterranean Sea; if it's the second deepest lake in the world, note which one is the deepest. When a fact is important enough to include, define it fully so the meaning supports the text. Place historical dates in a context your readers will recognize: a restaurant in Paris that opened when George Washington was working in western Maryland as a surveyor. A border treaty signed the same year J.F. Kennedy was shot.

SELECTING WORDS ABOUT PLACE

Travel writers are painters trying to be both believable and creative at the same time. Travel writing has to appeal to people who have been to the place and to people who have never been there. Your idea about what makes the place unusual drives the story. The words you choose to express that experience elevate the quality of the story or doom it to the commonplace.

One way to capture the mood of a foreign place is to use words from that country in the text. Foods, native dishes, and special drinks mentioned in the story in the original language recreate an authentic mood. Some words like *cappuccino*, *espresso*, and *baguette* are in current use. Strive for words that create curiosity and ambience without being impenetrable. *Brioche* instead of round French roll; *risotto*, not rice in sauce; *dim sum*, not Chinese dumplings; *minestrone*, not vegetable soup.

Explain foreign words with pronunciations in brackets or quotation marks, but limit this format as it can defeat a reader. If there are many foreign phrases in your story, make a glossary for the sidebar.

Words that are rich with sound, the he-haw-he-haw of European ambulances, the ta-ka-ta-ka-ta of the airplane in the Orkney story we looked at in the previous chapter, the ka-thunk, ka-thunk of a train track, or the thuck-a thuck-a thuck-a of a flat tire on pavement add texture to the article. Try to jot down the sound that accompanies an experience so you'll remember the ting-a-ling of a pedicab's bicycle bell in Penang or the chucka-chucka of helicopter blades over Hawaiian volcanoes.

READER DISCOVERIES

Readers of mystery novels will recognize this technique. The first three chapters of a mystery reveal clues and information that may provide the key to the solution. The travel writer can "plant" clues in the early part of the story to entice readers to continue reading. This isn't trickery but rather a narrative device designed to heighten the sense of drama.

A travel story about Kamchatka, in the Russian Far East, shows this technique:

> We'd hiked most of the day when I found the spoon. I was walking behind Gosha's lumbering beige horse, my heavy backpack roped to its saddle. I happened to look down and found a tablespoon with a pretty scrolled handle embedded in the soil. The spoon bowl faced up. I pried the spoon from the weeds and dirt and stashed it in my pocket, then scrambled to catch up with the group. It would be a while before I learned the meaning of this find.
>
> —L. Peat O'Neil, "Itel'men Tribal Harvest Festival," *In Search of Adventure: A Wild Travel Anthology*, CCC Publishing, 1999

If you do plant clues in the opening, return to the information later in the story. When a question is raised in the reader's mind, it is only fair to supply an answer. To resolve the unfinished question about the spoon I found, I could write the answer within the story without specific reference to the opening. Or I could write quite baldly, "Remember the spoon I found?" and proceed to explain. How the answer is woven into the text is a matter of a writer's style.

STYLES TO AVOID

Learn what isn't stylish and steer around writing traps such as overwriting and overstating (purple prose), elegant variation (studiously searching for synonyms), irony (a distancing device pointing out incongruities between appearance and reality), and eccentricities in language (slang).

OVER-WRITING

Over-writing, the so-called purple prose, seduces newcomers. Do you write with the idea that the more words you pile on, the richer the writing becomes? Think of extra adjectives and adverbs as deadly fat that needs to be trimmed from sentences. Weigh your words. Do the sentences seem circuitous? Are your valid and succinct observations lost and obscured in the incoming tide of bubbling, steaming modifiers, written in convoluted, compound sentence structure with mixed metaphors and uncertain subordination so no one can understand the defined, objective point to begin with? Like that sentence you just read? Cut to the quick. Direct expression isn't wordy or vague. Avoid repetition; use simple expression rather than complex diction; select words and phrases appropriate to the material. Read your work aloud. Find a single word to replace two or more imprecise words. Break up convoluted sentences. Make word choice appropriate to the material.

Cut generalized catch-all words: nice, fine, wonderful, beautiful, elegant, one of the most, among the best. Be specific: prim, porcelain, electric, riveting, midnight blue, crumbling. Verbs show, nouns tell, adjectives focus or distract, adverbs qualify or confuse. Watch those adjectives and adverbs for true meaning. In fact, consider ejecting adverbs and adjectives and focus on improving all nouns and verbs.

Be wary of stilted diction, pretentious words, and artificial writing. A house is not an "edifice" or a "place of residence." Walks and performances start or begin, they don't "commence." Precipitation is rain, snow, or sleet, not "inclement weather conditions." People talk or shout; they don't "opinionate" or "discourse."

The quasi-English academic voice often affected by novice travel writers isn't a natural voice unless you are a British professor musing about your peregrinations during the last century. Check your travel article for words that are pompous and out of place. Could you read this article to a group of friends and would they recognize your narrative style? Give it a try; read a couple of travel articles including one of your own to friends and don't reveal who wrote them. Did they identify your work by listening to the narrative voice?

ELEGANT VARIATION

Do you find yourself searching for synonyms for every word because you don't want to repeat the same word over and over? I do, because mining the language for ever more clever words is part of the challenge of writing, and using synonyms is an accepted stylistic tool. But the search for a different synonym or descriptive phrase for every word in an essay or article can easily be overdone. This is called elegant variation. You've fallen into this stylistic trap when words trip over themselves in an effort to be different from an earlier appearance in the text. When the effort to find a different word becomes overworked, awkward, and obvious, the writer has gone beyond conscientious stylistic variation into the dreaded elegant variation that isn't elegant at all.

Here, I've rewritten the opening of a published article to show elegant variation, which is anything but elegant.

> Mount Rinjani, a dormant volcano, is swathed in Indonesia's daybreak. The gauzy mist of dawn arises from the volcanic crater. In the early morning light, I've worked hard to get to the top of Lombok's humped black lava-strewn incline, more than two miles up. But my aching legs and shoulders are small payment for the spectacular sunrise view at the peak. Down in the cavity, the waters of Segura Anak are ethereal in the hazy break of day, and I thank the mythical resident goddess for giving me the fortitude to complete the ascent at first light up the formerly volatile mountain.

It actually was written for publication like this:

> Mount Rinjani is swathed in the gauzy mist of Indonesia's dawn. I've worked hard, and yes, even suffered, to get to the top of

Lombok, more than two miles up, but my aching legs and shoulders are small payment for the spectacular view. Down in the crater, Segura Anak is ethereal in the hazy morning light, and I thank the mythical resident goddess for giving me the fortitude to complete the ascent.

Note, in the elegant variation version, how many different words are used for morning—daybreak, mist of dawn, early morning light, sunrise, hazy break of day, first light—each one different, most of them superfluous. Words used to describe the volcano are resolutely different with each reference: Mount Rinjani, dormant volcano, humped black lava-strewn incline, volcanic crater, peak, cavity, formerly volatile mountain. Yes, there are synonyms used in the paragraph that was published, but the words don't break the story flow, and when the "gauzy mist of Indonesia's dawn" is repeated as "ethereal in the hazy morning light" there is a change of perspective from standing on top of the volcano and looking outward to a view on top looking down into the heart of the crater. Use synonyms, but don't be obsessive about finding a different word for each usage.

IRONY

Irony distances the writer from the material. Ironic comparisons use words that create a discrepancy between their meaning and their use in the sentence. Irony is writing one description while clearly the truth is entirely different.

> In the shantytown, each family matriarch guarded their palace from a throne on the porch.

> I was welcomed to the village, although I don't know how the chief discovered I was an American. Was it my digital watch or the Palm Pilot?

Irony can sound like a joke that you had to be there to appreciate. Occasionally, an ironic sentence can enhance the material, for example, as a rhetorical question. But the ironic voice sometimes does not stand the test of time. The joke or key that makes the statement clever one year may have been rendered moot the next. Don't you want your articles to be read and understood in the future? Before using irony that is specific to a time or place, ask yourself whether a reader will understand it in five years. Ironic comments on yourself or a companion may not be fully understood by readers who don't know you. If you finish up the description or story with a lame "well, you had to be there," the story doesn't bear retelling.

ECCENTRIC LANGUAGE

Yesterday's *hepcat* is today's *dude* is tomorrow's what? Slang words limit your writing to a particular place and time. Slang also infects diction styles. How many articles have you read where the writer states the information and compares it to itself with a "well" surrounded by commas? As in: "The band played marches just like, well, a marching band—loud and brassy." Ten years ago, in the first edition of this book, I railed against this stale construction. I still read it occasionally, but the better writers have moved past. Don't burden the article with cliché descriptors such as "poster child," "drama queen," "media star," "show pony," etc.

Dialect and jargon, when used at all, should be integral to the story line. Avoid substandard English forms such as double negatives, profanity, or extreme slang. Sentences constructed in local accents with regional witticisms may fit in a story about that region, but the same diction or word choice could leave other readers baffled. When I wrote a piece about Maryland's Eastern Shore, I included the phrase "'Mer-lan' as the locals say …" to give readers an indication of the local accent for "Maryland." However, continuing the anecdote in the regional dialect could become tiresome—one or two words are sufficient to establish accents.

Don't make up words. Though it may sound cute to you, made-up words can be stumbling blocks for readers. Cruise the dictionary and thesaurus for words. Use American English and standard spelling. Review the finer points of diction in a grammar handbook.

exercises

EXERCISE 1: Practice writing with various points of view. Writers with a well-developed point of view acquire individual style. Improve your writing style by playing with different points of view, attitudes, vocabularies, and agendas.

Describe an episode from a recent excursion in your city or journeys farther afield. Rewrite the scene in several different tones and voices, using the basic information contained in your first version or adding more details or anecdotes as you recall them. Write the scene from the point of view of the building. Or what does that prominent statue, the motionless military general on the horse, see? Cast the scene in a historical light, writing with the vocabulary and style of that earlier period of time. Another version might describe the scene humorously. Try writing the travel episode as a war correspondent might—with staccato short sentences and no pronouns. Pretend you are reviewing the destination for a convention of sports coaches or foreign language translators.

After you've written the scene from various points of view, go over the text and highlight or underline sentences, phrases, or words that show the particular style or perspective you were striving to create. Read each version: Is the tone consistent? In the humorous piece, does the reader feel that a funny person is telling the story? Does the version written with a historical perspective lose its tone because of contemporary jargon?

EXERCISE 2: This exercise can be used as a warm-up for those times when writers just don't feel like showing up at the computer. The idea is to stimulate innate love of language, gain confidence, and expand visual vocabulary. If you don't feel like staring at a computer screen or sitting at a desk, use a notepad and pen for a change. Write outside or in a nearby café. Change your location as if you were on the road.

In a column on the left side of the page, make two lists—of verbs (action words) and adjectives (descriptive words). Don't think, just write. Let the associative powers of your subconscious mind direct the flow. After you've filled a page, go back and craft sentences using the words. Focus on the place you'll be writing about as you construct the sentences. Ideally, none of the sentences will begin with an article or pronoun.

EXERCISE 3: Using visualization techniques, find the high spots of your trip by going back to the selected site for a sense-memory trip, a visualized walk-through with attention to sight, smell, sound, taste, and touch. Writers recall travel memories and write with their inner eye. Remember your personal discoveries to convey a sense of wonder to the reader.

EXERCISE 4: Communicate information through omission or allusion, leaving something for the reader to discover. Write a page or two about a travel experience. Read the piece over and identify ways of telling elements in the story without explicitly setting forth every action or experience. Here's an example:

> The soundtrack during breakfast on the veranda explained why these islands are called the Canaries.

Are we ever told that birds were singing during breakfast? Not exactly, but you have the information.

EXERCISE 5: Build descriptive phrases for specific people and places. Focus your inner eye on a person you've observed many times, or go out with your notebook and find a person to watch without being annoying or threatening. Describe the person's gestures, appearance, facial expressions, ways the person communicates, etc. Write phrases or sentences, whatever is most comfortable for you. Do the same thing with a building to capture the overall appearance and specific features, as well as the relationship of the building to others on the block.

EXERCISE 6: Write a list of "double-duty" verbs—verbs that create the illusion of affecting the senses concretely (e.g., scrape, reek, drum, lumber, plough, careen, slaughter, drizzle).

EXERCISE 7: Write a free-voice paragraph. Look into your memory. Enter your mind and linger. Focus your attention, but don't create a goal for the writing. Maybe you write a scene from a recent trip; maybe not. Maybe you rant about something or express sadness. Are you afraid? Elated? Or decide where you are poised—on the edge of a tipping raft, buying a watch from a posh jewelry shop, standing in the rain on a mountain top, huddled in a cave with a fading flashlight—and write the perspective. These are just scenarios to provoke a start; the real work is allowing your voice expression.

FACT CHECKING AND RESEARCH RESOURCES

Fact comes from the Latin root, *factum*. A fact is that which is done, according to *Webster's New World Dictionary*. Some event that has actually happened or is really true, the state of things as they are, reality. Travel writers deal in facts, things that have happened, and truth, the state of things as they are.

Travel journalism is nonfiction. Not "creative nonfiction," not "mostly facts and some made-up events," not a "creative product of the imagination," not "mostly what happened with some embellishment to make a better story" or whatever other excuse the writer might cook up. While a few travel writers may stretch language to create mood or heighten drama in the story, the genre deals in fact. The events, encounters, and experiences recounted in a travel article actually took place. Otherwise, the piece is wholly or partially fiction and must be labeled as such.

In this chapter, we delve into facts—where to find them, how to store them, how to check them, and how to weave them into your article. We'll look at collecting data before you travel, while you're on the road, and what to do with all the information you gather when you start writing.

GET ORGANIZED!

Do you have stacks of media discs and CDs without labels? Is your hard drive a compost heap of documents that takes you ages to scroll through? Confused about which version of an article you have opened? Not sure whether you recognize the text on your monitor? Disk cleanup is a chore that few of us enjoy, but whatever operating system you use—Mac, Windows, Linux, or something not yet invented—your productivity will increase if you keep text and image files in clearly labeled folders. If you don't know your computer tools well enough to create, move, copy, send, and delete files and folders, seek help. Take a course or employ someone who can clean up your hard drive and create a backup system.

Storing printed reference material in an easily retrievable system is a time-saver for a working travel writer. To build a travel resource library, save travel articles, brochures, excerpts from books, and other material for writing. Keep only the most recent material. Some writers scan research material and save it electronically. Discipline your hoarding tendencies by asking: Can I retrieve this information from another source? If the article is ten or fifteen years old, can I rely on the data?

When you are using research sources from the Internet, bookmark useful Web sites and maps for the regions you're writing about. Remember to organize your favorite Web sites into file folders, too.

Develop an instinct and a set of standards for evaluating Web sites. Note the last content update, who owns the site, and whether there are typos or errors. If you plan to reprint or quote material from a Web site or print source, review the fair use section of the copyright laws. Include a reference citation for any material you quote from Internet or print sources.

Many writers are print-focused researchers who collect swaths of paper for every story they write. I've been guilty of that pack-rat instinct, but I regularly weed my files of outdated material. And I review Web sites for current status before including the URL in an article. Remember, conditions change—the region that fascinated you last year may be a war zone now. The Web site you used to plan your trip might have vanished or changed focus.

By far the most common organizational problem for anyone in the information age is saving too much material, creating too many files, copying too much Web-based material and never having time to go through everything. Collect the data you need, but don't over-do it. At a certain point, you just have to stop reporting and hunker down and write. After the story runs, discard print and computer files that are no longer relevant.

Smart travel writers know that information Web sites and printed brochures are updated regularly. It's a good idea to retain source materials (printouts from Web references, URL addresses of your source information, photocopies of facts culled from books, a bibliography, handwritten or typed text notes from interviews). Having this material on hand could protect you in the rare case of errors creeping into the published version. If an editor or reader has a question, you'll be able to provide solid evidence as to provenance of the facts in the article. Once you've finished writing and your editor is satisfied with the work and fact checking, keep source material for a year or even longer, especially if you plan to develop several stories from the same research and travel. If you intend to restructure the story and sell it elsewhere, you will also need to consult source material for updates. When several years have snuck by, you probably aren't going to take the time to rewrite the story and the material is starting to lose its value. That's when it becomes clutter.

Writers who are reluctant to let go of source material should think about whether keeping the old stuff is holding you back from writing about fresh subjects. Before you toss everything, ask yourself if you could get the brochure, article, or guidebook again easily. Ask yourself if the material is still up-to-date and useful. If it isn't, pitch it or recycle the paper.

The Internet is a huge file cabinet available to anyone with access to a browser, but you can waste hours combing through irrelevant Web sites that appear after a data search. Since the mid-1990s, many publications have archived their print versions on the Internet, but you may have to pay a fee to retrieve a particular story. Articles that aren't archived by a publication might be stored on subject specific electronic databases, and again, access fees may be charged. Newspapers and magazines published in previous decades are usually stored on microfiche, if the bound originals are not available in a library. Consult a librarian for assistance in using periodicals indexes, electronic database tools and inter-library loans to locate research material.

BUILDING REFERENCE SOURCES

Every productive e-mail or phone call to a person working in the travel industry is a potential contact for fact checking. I save business cards, enter them in a computer contacts database or staple them on large Rolodex cards. A filing system using 3x5 cards would be just as handy. How you store information depends on what method you will actually use. If you can't find the information after you've "filed" it—on PDA, computer, in a file box, or a pile on your desk—then it's not much use to you, is it?

Some writers store contact addresses with mailing list management software that can print address labels. For e-mail business communication, maintain your professional contact list in an e-mail address book stored in your PDA, hard drive, or on server space provided by the ISP you use. The contacts database manager you choose depends on your computer and operating system, and on personal preference.

Really organized writers create a reference file for each story. Whatever information storage system you use, keep it up-to-date. Sorting through lists of Web links, stacks of cards or stick-on notes with names and numbers on them will slow you down. When it's time to check a fact, are you going to keep the editor on hold while you scurry through a computer hard drive looking for the right text document?

When you contact tourism industry officials for information about a specific region or landmark, take note of names so you can call or e-mail with follow-up questions. Establish connections with staff in the press relations departments of tourism offices, hotels, and local attractions. Later, you may need to request photographs to illustrate a story. In the beginning of your freelance career, you'll ask lots of questions to find the right person to handle your research questions. Once you find a helpful knowledgeable travel professional, treat her politely. Your telephone or e-mail manners will enlist the help of strangers or alienate them, so work on a pleasant, concise style in all business communication.

Barbara Patcher, a New Jersey-based business coach and author of many business communications books, advises, "Travel writers need to get to the point quickly in the e-mail, use short paragraphs and keep the message concise. People can be too quick to send an e-mail without really thinking what the content is saying." She suggests inserting the address in the e-mail only after the message is edited and proofread.

If you are calling to gather information or check facts, choose the time of day—morning or just after lunch—and the day of the week—Tuesday through Thursday—when office workers are usually less harried. There's more about how to build your network of travel writing contacts in chapter nine.

PRE-TRIP RESEARCH

Pre-trip research helps focus story idea development. While the Internet is my favorite research arena, I also recommend library research, simply because the bulk of human knowledge was compiled prior to the electronic age and not every book or research source has been transferred to Web-based sources. In fact, it is sometimes much faster to accomplish research tasks by consulting books than sifting through thousands of Web sites. While a browser's response to a carefully constructed search parameter can be stunningly fast, if you seek inspiration, ideas, and connections, you'll profit from print and archival research in a library. It's wise to use online library catalogs to seek specific titles, and many historical sources for travel writers have been transcribed into electronic libraries, usually available through university online libraries and archives. Eventually, though, if you plan to delve beneath the surface of the places and people you write about, set aside time to browse relevant books, manuscripts, and periodicals in a reliable reference library.

Depending on where you live, you may need to request inter-library loan assistance or use limited or paid access Web based research collections on the library's subscription. Select books on the history and geography of the place you are writing about, guidebooks, and photo essays for visual inspiration. Familiarize yourself with the literary and artistic notables of the state, region, or country you'll be touring. Consult online or CD-ROM databases of newspaper travel articles. You are reading to develop understanding of the destination and its people, to absorb what has been written about the place already. Of course, you can read too much, saturating your curiosity, drowning your natural alertness in predigested facts and other people's opinions.

This pre-trip reading should be a preview, an introduction. Try to read something written about the place at another point in time, an explorer's diary, a visiting eighteenth- or nineteenth-century writer's essay, or even a guidebook from decades ago. Seek information sources that can help you appreciate how places change. Look for commentary about the history and culture so when you are on-site, you'll notice connections. When you dine, you'll remember what you read about regional cuisine, farming, or fishing. If you attend a dance performance or religious ceremony, the background reading will have prepared you and perhaps help you begin to understand the culture. When a conversation starts with a local resident, you'll be a more informed participant. Fiction set in a certain locale can also enhance your understanding.

Prior to departure, visit the appropriate Web sites or contact the relevant travel promotion offices and ask for maps, guidebooks, and information about hotels, restaurants and cultural centers. Many states and countries support tourist promotion offices and maintain excellent information Web sites. Bear in mind that many places in the world are still developing a Web presence for tourism and accuracy can be problematic. Take careful note of when information on the Web site was last updated. During research, consider these caveats: Don't believe everything you read, and consider the source.

Generally, foreign governments, through the national tourism secretariat or commercial promotion entities, engage public relations firms to promote the country, city or region. In the United States and Canada, each state or province supports a travel promotion office, Web site, and toll-free phone line and may also engage public relations representatives to promote the location in the press. As a travel writer, you should be aware of the tourism industry promotional structure to gather information and photographs and, perhaps, to stimulate future business for yourself. Tourism promotion offices sometimes commission freelance writers to write about the country, state, or city.

A travel writer gains an advantage by scanning maps in advance. Prior to a long drive from Washington, D.C. to Mexico City, I studied the city street map carefully. I knew that driving in Mexico would be challenging and I wouldn't be able to nose through the road atlas while driving. My pre-trip map briefing was especially useful when I was caught in rush-hour traffic in the second largest city in the world and my companion couldn't find our precise location on the confusing map. Eventually, I recognized a street sign because I'd memorized many of the primary downtown arteries and we reached our destination handily.

Before I embarked on my first extended solo journey, I poured over maps of Europe, learning place names and figuring distances. My father, an architect, taught me to memorize city sectors by studying maps so I could wander without burying my head in a map on a street corner, labeling myself a tourist. With the map planted in my mind's eye, I roam around confidently. Warning: Don't try this without a map to consult in a pinch. Studying maps in advance can lead you to historic and cultural sites, parks, or markets that you didn't know about and could have missed.

If you are going to a destination in recent turmoil, consult the travel advisory Web page at the State Department for a safety update. An aspect of pre-trip research is talking or e-mailing people who have traveled or lived where you are going. They know the special places that aren't always obvious to short-term visitors and can recommend accommodations and restaurants. Such contacts may provide the names of friends where you are going, as discussed in chapter three.

DURING THE TRIP

While you are traveling, gather facts wherever you are. You also might find yourself in a library or Internet café searching for information. Even with the Internet at your disposal, it can be extraordinarily difficult to recover specific information after you return home. Collect materials to consult during the writing phase—pamphlets, local newspapers, business cards, and flyers. Realize that some of the printed material or brochures may contain outdated or inaccurate information, so gather names and e-mail addresses or phone numbers of people who can assist with data verification if an editor asks.

Another hurdle may be that printed materials may not be in English or a language you understand. When you enter a museum, public landmark, restaurant, or other sightseeing venue, take note of the street address, posted hours, and ask an attendant for a contact telephone number. If you are in doubt, verify information with the local or regional tourist office before you leave the locale.

Write down the names and titles of your sources in your notebook, journal, or PDA. I remember being stymied after a long research trip in the Mediterranean. I intended to write about visiting prehistoric caverns during a month's residence in Malta. Later, when I knuckled down to transcribe my journal, I found pages of interesting comments about what the caverns and carved rock rooms might have been used for. I vaguely remembered conversations with the bus driver on the way to one cave site, comments shared with other visitors, and speculations of an archeologist who happened to be at the ruin while I was there. The notes, however, were all jumbled together without attribution, my own ideas running in between comments from other people. Ultimately, all I could do was describe the comments in my story: "During several conversations that included a visiting archeologist, a local bus driver and other visitors ..." The Italian archeologist may have done important relevant research, but I neglected to get her name or affiliation. The only fact I could state without hesitation was that none of the information came from signs, brochures, or pamphlets on-site. There weren't any.

Even if you don't think you are going to write about a place or event, gather information while you are there. A helpful organizational tool is to carry large lightweight mailing envelopes, address them to yourself, and send brochures and papers back by printed matter airmail. I've sent packages to myself from many countries and never lost one. Send by registered mail if you like, so there is a written record that follows the packet. Obviously, don't mail valuables, but extra clothes and papers can safely be sent home to lighten your burden. If you are writing on deadline or must submit your piece immediately after return, it's best to keep important reference material with you.

WHY CHECK FACTS?

An unfortunate criticism of travel writers is that we don't use or check facts, relying on impressions or feelings to describe a place. We've all read articles that seem familiar because the facts used to support the story are the same ones someone else used in another travel story. Sometimes factual information has been lifted from other published material, often without considering context. For writers in a hurry, it's tempting to use the same bits of data presented in tourist pamphlets or on the first Web site that turns up during a browser search. You would think it's a safe bet. But think about how embarrassed you'll be if it turns out those facts aren't accurate. Bear in mind that foreign tourist bureaus may produce brochures in their own languages and then have them translated, increasing the margin for error. Even when there isn't a translation step involved, why subject your work to the mistakes of others? Consider this: Some Web sites that bill themselves as subject authorities are written by amateurs who may or may not know what they're talking about. Hone your sensibilities for sniffing out bogus Web sites, blogs, or discussion areas that waste your time.

This is not to say that Web sites compiled by interested amateurs aren't reliable. Wikipedia, for example (www.wikipedia.org), is a useful online encyclopedia compiled by anyone who wants to contribute. While the contributions are written carefully, a cadre of established experts doesn't review the data. Wikipedia, Suite 101, About.com, and other information Web sites may indeed offer excellent, reliable data, but always consider the source.

Does that mean that the *Encyclopedia Britannica* Web site or the *World Book* CD-ROM or other information databases are always reliable and correct? No, but there's a better chance with long-established information sources that a knowledgeable editor commissioned the work and someone verified the facts. Still, the self-policed shared information Web site might be more up-to-date than the material offered by a more bureaucratic, but enduring, publishing group.

So what sources can be trusted? Use up-to-date standard reference books, Web sites maintained by established information brokers, and CD-ROMs from reliable publishers as source material. Be aware that even the most reliable sources can change. Copy-editors at many news organizations use the rule I work with: Verify facts with two reliable sources.

Facts are rooted in a provable universe. When facts can't be verified, they probably aren't facts but speculation, gossip, myth, or innuendo. Fortunately the English language is full of qualifying words that allow us to communicate information without wagering our integrity. These phrases should be used sparingly, of course, and only in situations where information can't be verified but belongs in your story. Qualifying words and generalizing phrases that blur the edges of absolute statements include: said to be, believed to be, according to local legend, at the time I visited, according to received wisdom, the local buzz, legend has it, according to the rumor mill, etc. Using these phrases, though many sound cliché, saves you from the embarrassment of presenting incorrect information as fact.

PLAGIARISM

The current excuses for plagiarism include: "I didn't notice what I copied from my research notes." "I downloaded so much online material that I lost track of who wrote what." "It's just an accident that my words are the same as that other writer's."

Whether there's intention or not, plagiarism is "borrowing" or "copying" information written by another writer. If you use another writer's words in your article, you have to acknowledge with an attribution. Using the same fact, date, or historical anecdote that is widely circulated and cited in standard reference sources isn't plagiarism, but using another writer's wording is plagiarism. In academic publications, the acknowledgment of another writer's words or concepts would be contained in a footnote or citation of the previously published work. Travel writers simply put the excerpted material in quotes and include the author's name. Consider using a variation of this: *As (Name of Writer) wrote in (Title of Book), published in 1934, "Ethiopia is ...".* Before using quotes from another writer, consider whether you could make the point in your own words. Opening or closing a travel story with an attributed quote from some notable person is a useful technique to focus reader attention, but the body of the story should be entirely your own work. And references or quotations should always be attributed to the actual author.

Of course, if you use the comments of someone you meet or interview to develop the story line, place their words in quote marks and give a tag line or attribution. For example: Sibley Cross, owner and executive chef of the Criss Cross Inn, said, "We never take shortcuts with the quality of ingredients; you can taste the difference."

USING FACTS

Because facts are such an integral part of travel articles, we should be creative in choosing fresh facts or at least present them in original ways. When we've worked so hard to craft the travel narrative from personal journal entries, it would be a shame to haul out the same tired old facts used by every other travel writer.

Story narrative and structure still guide the choice of information; style will shape presentation of the information.

After telling the general facts that ground the reader in the location, focus on one or two factual aspects of the place that enhance your experiences. Keep any additional facts related to the story line. During the editing process, when you are rereading the piece, take a hard look at the facts. Perhaps you could you improve the flow of the story by organizing helpful facts in a sidebar. Are there any facts just thrust into the story—facts for facts' sake? Consider cutting them out. Facts should support your story narrative.

One way to convey factual information and sustain the story line is to describe how you learned a particular fact. For example, in a piece about Christmas in Santa Fe, you can effortlessly communicate a bundle of facts about the city's founding days by telling the origin of the holiday candle illumination in the civic buildings and cathedral.

AVOIDING ERRORS

Large-circulation publications have teams of proofreaders, copyeditors, and researchers that scrutinize an article as it makes its way into print or on the Internet. Factual errors are usually caught during this editing process. But you must do your own fact checking, proofreading, and grammar checks after you've finished writing the story, and always before you send it to a publication. Even though magazines and newspapers have systems to catch errors, it doesn't improve a writer's credibility when they find mistakes. Editors expect the writer to handle fact checking. At a smaller press, one person may handle several editorial tasks and not have time to verify facts.

TIMELINESS OF FACTS

Rapidly changing information and long publication lead times mean that writers have to be particularly sensitive to the timeliness of facts used in a travel article. Historical evergreen facts—those that endure despite political, social, and physical changes—are obviously more useful for extending the lifespan of your story. But their utility and accessibility means they probably have appeared in many articles. Those desiccated chestnuts may not add anything to the story line.

Even though the facts you select come from reliable reference sources, you'll have to be alert to political, social, and physical change. When the geographic and ethnic sectors of Yugoslavia separated and during the conflict that followed, the profile of the region completely changed. When the Berlin Wall fell and the Eastern European countries emerged independent, imagine the flurry of fact checking and word changing that had to take place to make upcoming travel articles conform to reality! Earthquakes and other natural events may alter the landscape. Competing religious or political groups may restructure governmental or cultural hierarchies. When you are writing about a country in the throes of transition, pay close attention to the facts selected to support the travel story. Strive to explain when information may change between the time you write it and the time it is printed or appears online. Temper your experiences and the facts you've selected with reality. For example, you visit a museum that is under renovation and certain exhibits are closed, but perhaps they will be open again by the time the article is published. Consider other ways to cover the situation by communicating the experience of the moment and what readers will encounter in the immediate future. Tell what it was like to see hidden glimpses of art masterpieces through the scaffolding of a construction site and how eagerly visitors await the unveiling of the new exhibits.

The stability of facts can be fragile, although we usually think of history as being inflexible. Earlier in this chapter, you were advised to find and check facts in well-edited and updated Web sites and standard reference books. And indeed, most current reference sources are reliable. Facts culled from an encyclopedia, almanac, or history book—such as the date a city was founded, by whom, or the architect of a particular building or the number of acres in a national park—would seem to be unchanging. But consider that there may be competing legends and two or three dates related to the founding of a city. Acreage in national parks may be augmented or subtracted or the purpose changed. The architect of a particular building may be revealed in time to be one of several people responsible for the project.

What's a conscientious writer to do? If all information is viewed in constant flux, there are no real facts. When information endures as fact for long periods of time and is recorded in well-established online and print reference sources, it has generally been accepted as fact. When controversy surrounds a subject or a date or border is in dispute, the reference source should include a statement to that effect. As the primary researcher, the writer then has a duty to pursue the information further, seeking other, more current sources. For help with current, reliable electronic and print research sources, seek the advice of a reference librarian at your local library.

All this fact checking probably sounds like a tremendous amount of work, but don't be intimidated. Your travel story will improve with a few facts worked into the story line. If you gathered information carefully while you were traveling, the fact selection process is fairly streamlined.

Bob Jenkins, travel editor of the *St. Petersburg Times*, has worked in writing and editing roles at several newspapers. Jenkins recalls one error-plagued story: "I received a query from a writer I'd worked with before to reprint a story that had run in a national magazine." The story was a service piece about national discounts for senior citizens. In St. Petersburg, where so many older adults live, the story would be useful. The writer accepted Jenkins' fee and the story ran with a chart provided by the writer detailing the prices for the discount airline coupons. "I personally had to answer sixteen phone calls from local people who were upset because the charts were wrong," says Jenkins. "The numbers had changed after his story ran the first time and he hadn't bothered to update."

Jenkins also tells of an experienced writer who reported, in a story about Rome, that the Colosseum was closed for repairs.

"We printed the story and two days later I got a call from someone who had been there ten days ago who had been inside the Colosseum. I called the Italian Government Tourist Office and they said the Colosseum was closed intermittently. The writer had wandered up, seen the doors closed and the scaffolding and assumed it was closed all the time and it wasn't." The message here is: Don't make assumptions.

"Even professional freelancers can make mistakes in judgment and timing," Jenkins says. "I believe the travel section has to be like any other section, accurate and have the pros and cons of situations. If a place is dangerous, alert people. If you can't drink the water in St. Petersburg, Russia, tell people. If there are muggers and beggars on the streets of Dublin, say so." Jenkins believes fact checking is a duty of the writer, not the editor. "I have not got time to fact check. I really think that people who pretend to be writers have to basically do their own fact checking." Indeed, time constraints are a perennial problem at almost all publications. Fact checking is labor intensive, time consuming, and tedious. In an effort to streamline the fact checking process, some publications ask writers to include photocopies or original source material when the manuscript is submitted.

Remember to check graphs, tables, photo captions, and the sidebar for typographical errors and errors of fact. After you've finished the article, do at least three editing reads, at least one of them on paper because it's much easier to catch errors in print than on a computer screen. While useful, the spell and grammar tools that come with word processing and office management software programs are unable to distinguish certain errors and tend to foster the creation of errors if the writer mindlessly clicks the "change" button during the check. Don't rely on software tools exclusively; read the entire story carefully several times.

Despite everybody's best efforts through the writing and editing process, there may be occasions when articles are printed with errors. When that happens, there are remedies. If the error entered the text after the manuscript left the writer, and it is substantial, the publication may run a correction. If the writer sent incorrect information, the editor may think twice before accepting future submissions. Letters to the editor sometimes illuminate errors. The writer or editor may respond in the letters column explaining or apologizing for the error. The best way to deal with errors is to prevent them.

The writer's responsibility is to include only information that is personally experienced or verified, preferably with a second source. Whether you write without pay for a small literary rag or online journal (e-zine) or contribute travel articles under contract to a multinational publishing giant, you the writer are responsible for the truth in your writing. If in doubt, leave it out.

HONESTY AND FACTS—RECORDING FACTS IN YOUR JOURNAL

The process of constructing travel articles from personal journal entries has a distinct advantage over writing from memory. Like a reporter's notebook, the travel writer's journal is full of description, dialogue, and personal observation. Because it is a journal and a diary, you may have written reflections, musings, fantasies, and digressions. As you record events in your travel journal, be scrupulous about writing what actually happened. When thoughts and words enter the world of fantasy or speculation, make a note about the transition: "I'm wondering," "I dream," or "My musings are." Later during transcription, you may not recall when the writing shifted from reality to projection or outright fiction. As a conscientious observer, there's an obligation to serve up a truthful version of events as you experienced them to readers who did not. Your experience shapes the description. An element of strong travel writing is the personal point of view. Just make sure you report what you saw, not what you think or assume you saw. If you aren't certain about the details, ask questions, check facts, and verify.

Countless times, I've neglected to ask questions about things I've observed. Those incidents are shrouded in mystery and supposed explanations. Sometimes the unexplained can be included in a story without unduly affecting balance. But when the scales are tipped in one direction or another, the travel writer has a particular duty to seek truth and balance.

Don't assume your view of a situation is the correct or sole interpretation. As visitors, we travelers can't honestly surmise that our first impressions represent the truth of the matter. Therefore we can't include incidents in stories without showing the range of possible explanations. Of course, we could write about an encounter without speculation, letting readers draw their own conclusions. Select incidents in order to describe locations fairly. Once a writer decides to write about what happens from a personal perspective complete with speculations and musing, the duty of honesty and balance should push the writer to investigate further, to determine the truth of the incident, or convey a range of explanations. We shouldn't allow hasty or false interpretations to color a reader's impression.

GENERALIZATIONS AND FACTS

Know the difference between your impressions, your prejudices, and "true" facts. Watch for outdated and biased notions. There is no need to perpetuate impressions and images that no longer exist. Spain and Italy were once routinely characterized in guidebooks as inefficient countries where the water was tainted, the food greasy, and the service slow. Guess where the greasy food capital of the world is now? Slow waiters and indifferent cleaning staff can turn up anywhere in the world—these aren't national or ethnic characteristics. Religion and other cultural hallmarks are always evolving. Be aware of your own biases and attitudes. Examine personal arrogance and expectations. If you aren't comfortable in different cultures or lack the ability to sustain a neutral mind-set when you're away from familiar settings, you might not have what it takes to be a travel writer.

We all have opinions, but it is important not to convey personal bias as fact. Strive to show both sides of a situation. Steer clear of stereotypes unless your experiences truly justify perpetuating an overworked image. For example, almost every travel article I read about North Africa trots out the tired image of visitors being hounded by freewheeling guides, touts, and salesmen. How many times does the reading audience need to hear about pestering salesmen rampant in Moroccan markets? Is that really the strongest impression that the travel writer carries forth? My experience was that a couple of engaging teenagers offered to show me their uncle's rug shop. I never experienced the cliché image of dozens of market flacks dogging my heels whenever I stepped out. What was your experience? It's easy to unconsciously rehash what other writers have set down, to blow our real experiences up to fit stereotypes. I sometimes wonder if strenuous pre-trip reading might unduly influence what scenes we focus on. Striving to record events accurately and in a balanced context enhances the reliability of the travel diary and keeps it rooted in reality. If we write down what actually happens in a timely fashion, the nuance of the moment won't be lost or skewed in ambitious storytelling. My journal reminded me that herds of street vendors didn't hound me in Morocco; only a couple of mild-mannered fellows made contact during a week of travel there.

FACTS, TRUTH, AND WRITING STYLE

Travel writing has creative latitude. Travel articles are usually classified as features—lifestyle entertainment stories. Aesthetics—the style you develop as you write—may allow the omission or rearrangement of the sequence of events or compression of detail. After all, the story does have to move along at a readable pace. Including every fact and every aspect of your experience detracts from the construction of a strong travel article. We've touched on this topic in chapter five during the discussion of style and omitting information to allow the reader to make discoveries. Whether you account for every moment of your travel experience in a chronological fashion or roam around disregarding time is a matter of style. I tend to favor telling the story and letting chronology slide, as long as readers aren't misled. Pursuit of style shouldn't cause you to forget the truth. For example, if you start the story at the end of your journey, explain it to the readers. Otherwise you run the danger of confusing them vis á vis geography and transportation routes. The voice in the story needn't go over every connecting detail—you aren't on the witness stand—but it has to hold together. The threads you lay down should connect, but how you connect them has to be intriguing for the reader and effortless to read.

FACTS TO SKIP

A student in a writing workshop asked me to critique a detailed article about her trip to a South Pacific island. Because she wrote about every meal, beverage, taxi ride, and hotel room, I felt like I was plodding through her appointment book or expense log. If a cab driver or a waiter figures in an anecdote, include details about the meal or the cab ride, but generally commonplace experiences should be compressed or omitted in travel articles. Minimal data about hotel rooms, meals, and beverages goes in the sidebar about transportation and costs. Skip commonplace experiences.

BALANCE AND PERSONAL EXPERIENCE

Travel is: freedom, learning, self-exposure, self-knowledge, new people, luxury, trial, difficulty, excitement, challenge, achievement, and endlessly interesting. Travel represents all these things to me. You can make your own list. Every reader of travel articles has a similar collection of words that characterize travel. What a wide, brave spectrum of ideas we travel writers are dealing with! Remarkable, isn't it, that travel can bring both happiness and difficulty, often at the same time. In some ways, it is like an intimate human relationship, evolving as it happens, never stagnant, always kinetic. True travelers are involved in the act of travel to the point that it becomes a state of being. Travel is movement and meditation. Travel is a pleasure but also is charged with attitude, emotion, and experience.

The travel writer plays with the personal point of view to make a story engaging but tries to be balanced in presenting the impression of a place. What travel means to you will determine the experiences you choose to write about and how you present them, both in your journal and in the finished travel article. Watch your choice of descriptive words for attitudes and innuendo.

Sometimes the events we actually observe are so implausible that they seem to be a figment of the imagination and read like fiction. I could hardly believe what I was reading in Spaulding Gray's piece about seeking a psychic healer in the Philippines. A combination of horror fiction, travel narrative and detective thriller, the story ran in the November 1993 issue of *Condé Nast Traveler*. I had the opportunity to ask Spaulding before he died in 2004 about that article and he said he wrote it as he experienced it, but that memory is always a filter. When reality seems preposterous, give the reader enough reference points for verification so the story stays firmly inside the boundaries of nonfiction.

Colin Thubron, an intrepid travel writer with many prizes to his credit, told me during an interview that he worries travel writers prolong myths and clichés. "I really have to check facts out," he said. "People don't mention what they don't see. They miss the things out there that might surprise them. I may do too much analyzing. When I'm obsessed with a subject, I'm thinking how to get people to talk about it, how to describe the next landscape." During the interview, which ran in *The Bloomsbury Review* (January–February 2000), we discussed truth and travel writing, which was a theme at the University of Pennsylvania conference where we both were speaking. I'd noticed an increasing tendency for travel writers, particularly those working under the rubric of adventure, to exaggerate or bend events to suit a stylistic goal and thrill readers. "We expect truth within the form. I take exception when the reader expects truth and the writer purposefully distorts the event," Thubron told me. "A postscript or an editor's foreword alerts readers that the writer is playing with images, but to present all as truth when whole sections are invented, that's wrong. The caveat, of course, is that nothing written is truth. Writers forget; they exclude information all the time, creating a parallel text to what actually happened. When you work from notes, it's the author's choice. No travel book is entirely truth in that sense. But, when reality is so extraordinary, why invent?"

CLICHÉS ARE NOT FACTS

Just because you're heard certain phrases often doesn't mean they're true or worth including in your article. European countries are often depicted as cultural treasure troves where commerce is second to art—a cliché that limits and misrepresents modern Europe. How many times have we read statements in travel articles describing Asian countries as mysterious and secretive, populated by Zen practitioners who value meditation and ancestor worship more than money? Aren't these stereotypical notions clichés? Don't fall into the trap of ignoring contemporary politics, industry, and trade. The southern United States isn't just known for its down-home cooking and warm hospitality. What about its literature, the landscape, its football and commercial poultry?

Word choice can convey hackneyed images. Search for new ways to describe facts. Cultivate simile and metaphor for description in your narrative. An unusual comparison may be more evocative than a string of fancy adjectives. Where the water is sparkling blue, the parks are green and verdant, the sky dotted with luminous clouds, the market bustling, the babies cute or squalling, the women vulnerable but strong, and the men virile but gentle, we have entered the land of Cliché. That's the one country a travel writer avoids.

RESPONSIBILITIES OF A TRAVEL WRITER

People read travel stories for many reasons: to explore ideas for vacations, to travel vicariously, to confirm their own experiences, to learn about the world. A travel writer's work may influence opinions and affect decisions about spending money and time, and that imposes a responsibility to create honest and clear prose.

Travel writing necessarily includes staying at various kinds of lodgings, using public transportation systems, eating in restaurants, and engaging the services of porters, maids, and other attendants. When reporting on conditions at hotels, resorts, cruise ships, restaurants, and other packaged travel and entertainment experiences, it's important to remember that the experience is wedded to a particular time. If your assessment is extreme in either direction—just too wonderful or too awful—consider that you'll have to check your perceptions. Circumstances might well change for the next visitor. Fact finding through judicious questions and research will cover some of the unknowns in order to present a balanced assessment. Balance is necessary in criticism and in praise, so if you, the writer, have a terrible experience, you have a duty to reexamine the facts or redo the experience. On the flip side, do you really believe your three days of paradisiacal splendor at that secluded resort on Maui will be the same for the next visitor?

Even if your experience was sublime, ask probing questions about what could go wrong and how it would be handled. What does the hotel in the tropics do if there is a power outage and the air conditioning fails? Suppose the swimming pool has to be closed; does the hotel offer alternative recreational facilities? If the chicken is undercooked or there are eggshells in the crème brûlée, will the chef offer apologies and a replacement serving? Will the restaurant charge for the spurned plate anyway? If most of the cruise ship population suddenly turns up sick, caught by one of the elusive bugs that flourish in untidy groups in confined spaces, will the company offer refunds and medical care? Like any reviewer, the travel writer explains what happened clearly, not raising specters of failure and predicting consistent problems but displaying a willingness to look at the good and the bad in a given situation. If conditions are truly distasteful, ask a manager for remedies quietly and politely. Take careful notes of names, dates, and conditions. Don't threaten retaliation in your article or review for poor accommodation or service. Professionals don't act that way.

Although free travel is covered in greater detail in chapter nine, now is a good time to mention that a travel writer's credibility depends on balance and honesty in recording the facts. If you are offered a free trip or a cruise, or a free stay at a fine hotel because the managers know you are a travel writer, and nothing goes wrong during your entire trip, consider whether the service and courtesy would be the same for the average traveler. Are room upgrades offered to other guests? Do all cruise passengers receive a welcoming fruit basket and complimentary wine at dinner? There's no reason to go out of your way to find fault just to prove your endorsement can't be bought. Seek the facts that your readers need. Be guided by your responsibility as a communicator of facts, as well as your impressions and observations. Some experiential truths can be nasty. If you've been robbed during your trip and if crime is a problem experienced by many visitors, include a note about being watchful of personal items in the "ways and means" sidebar accompanying the article. Did you fall victim at the market to a scam artist who seemed to sell you a heavy vase but, you later discover, substituted another box with a carefully wrapped rock inside? Let readers know what to expect and how you reacted. Conscientious travel writers share this knowledge so readers can avoid similar problems. Don't forget discretion. Every experience you have may not be appropriate for a travel article. If you've overindulged in the local firewater or mood-altering potion, you might want to spare your readers the details. Instead, include a friendly warning in the article about social interactions with the natives.

TIME AND HONESTY

Travel is all about stopping and starting, yet travel articles present a story as a continuous narrative. Writing style allows latitude for skipping literal physical movements—how you get from here to there—so the story flows in an engaging fashion. Some travel articles and books are composed from experiences gathered during several journeys to the same place. It's up to the writer to explain the sequence of events or whether the information was gathered during different trips. Some travel writers are scrupulous about placing events in an accurate time frame; others present several visits as a continuous journey without an explanation. A traveler who has experienced the rigors of long months away from home in a relatively tough environment might resent this omission. Passing off legs of travel as a continuous experience, implying a personal involvement and dedication to extended travel that apparently didn't occur, leans toward misrepresentation. It's one kind of journey to come and go from difficult regions like western China or Equatorial Africa, with intervals of ease, picking up the narrative thread as you return. It is another kind of journey to stay in country for months or a year—as long as the story takes to unfold.

When your travel article or book is based on several visits to a place, it is politic to say so in an early paragraph. Your work will likely be richer and more detailed when you have several opportunities to explore the destination. Writers who return to a place to examine the effects of time's passage usually explain their purpose in the article, helping the reader understand the special motive, which may be heavy with personal nostalgia. When you've been a resident of the place you are writing about, it adds credence to your travel piece to mention that intimacy, assuming, of course, that the explanation enhances the story.

exercises

EXERCISE 1: Select your facts. Facts should move the story along. Facts that inhibit story flow or stop the reader should be edited or rephrased so they enhance the narrative. Take a copy of your article and, using a highlighter, mark every phrase that contains a fact. Mark sentences that include dates, historical information, names of leaders, etc. The piece shouldn't look like a flood of marker color. If it does, start pruning those facts. Read the sentences before and after each sentence containing a fact. Does the information hang together and relate? Do the facts help propel your story line or hinder the reader?

EXERCISE 2: Animate ordinary facts. These sentences contain the same facts presented in different ways. Be attentive to the visual images that come into your mind as you read the sentences. Which do you enjoy reading?

> Washington, D.C. was a wet lowland between the Potomac and Anacostia Rivers when Pierre Charles L'Enfant, a French architect, started to sketch a plan for the city in 1791 at the request of George Washington and Thomas Jefferson.
>
> In 1791 the French architect Pierre Charles L'Enfant first saw the swampy river delta that he would transform into the new nation's capital city.
>
> The year is 1791. Slapping mosquitoes, the French architect Pierre Charles L'Enfant looked in dismay on the swamp that he was commissioned to transform into a capital city for the new American republic.

> The Villa Borghese in Rome was the private retreat for Cardinal Scipione Borghese, who commissioned the marble building in 1613. It is now a public art gallery.

Rome's Villa Borghese, a marble palace commissioned by Cardinal Scipione Borghese in 1613 as a suburban retreat, now houses an art collection open to the public.

When the aristocratic Cardinal Scipione Borghese commissioned the Villa Borghese in 1613 as a pleasure palace for himself and his retinue, could he possibly foresee that the elegant marble rooms would be open to the art-loving public three centuries later?

Select several facts about the last historic house or landmark you visited. Write a basic declarative sentence or two using the facts. Then manipulate the sentences. Turn the information around so the facts are still present but rework the information until you have sentences that create visible scenes.

EXERCISE 3: There are clever ways of informing readers how you got from here to there, what you ate, and where you stayed. If you've traveled recently, describe an evening during the trip. Tell about traveling to the restaurant, the components of the meal, and what happened throughout the evening. If you haven't a fresh travel memory, describe an evening out in your city or town.

After you've finished writing, use a highlighter to mark all the pronouns at the beginning of sentences (I, we, our, you, he, she, they, it). Wherever you have used pronouns, revise and rewrite the sentences so that verbs, prepositional phrases, or subjunctive clauses lead your sentences. Reread your text and notice the difference. Is the second version more visually interesting than the first one?

EXERCISE 4: Pretend you are a gossip columnist. Write up the same trip or outing using the suggestive language of a "people" column. Be daring! What happens to the text's meaning? What would happen if travel articles were constructed from biased impressions about a place?

TRAVEL PHOTOS

When you page through a magazine, what commands your eye? Ah, of course, the photographs. Brilliant though the writing might be, your eyes gravitate to images. Visuals help readers see the story as it unfolds because dense blocks of text are difficult for recreational readers. Photographs, illustrations, quotes pulled from the story, and other graphic material help improve the visual quality of a printed page.

Images enhance written material and assist the communication process. Writers usually don't have to provide the illustrations for stories for major glossy magazines. Those publications have photo editors and art directors who are responsible for finding and buying photos or assigning photographers or artists to illustrate articles. These editorial graphic specialists handle photo selection and page layout.

Many newspapers and smaller magazines expect the writer to provide photographs with a travel story. During the query phase, clarify what the editor expects. Ask what format the images should be—digital or print. Ask what form the digital file should be and what pixel resolution is needed. If the publication uses slides or prints, clarify preferences.

If you have appropriate photographs, sending them along with the story may improve marketing appeal. The editor can buy the story and photos in one package, saving time and resources. However, be attentive to how you send images. If you are sending material by e-mail, be certain that the editor wants digital image files. No editor will open large files from an unknown person. Consider sending reduced-size images—thumbnails—to give editors an idea of photo options available. Prior to sending files by e-mail, always clarify the number of images and preferred file size (number of pixels) and type (GIF, JPEG, TIFF, etc.) of image file the editor expects.

When the story describes a remote place where photographs would be difficult to acquire, the writer should make an effort to take high-quality photographs while on the journey.

Submitting a story about an unusual destination without photographs might affect an editor's decision adversely.

Photos used in travel pieces should relate to the story line. Generic shots of monuments or beaches won't be as eye-catching as unusual scenes with people in action. Deciding which photos to use is the editor's job, so if you are going to send photos, send lots of them. Include tightly focused shots of crowd scenes, broad shots of the landscape, details of buildings, close-ups of people and animals.

Think of photos as a series of visual stories. For each location you plan to feature in your story, capture a series of photographs. Shoot an opener that sets the scene, details that expand on the ideas, and ending photos that wrap up the "mini-story." To illustrate your entire article, you would have many series of mini-stories that can be grouped. For example, in Curaçao, I noticed teenage boys with elaborate haircuts, designs shaved into a crew cut. I took photographs of the boys sporting these haircuts. But to really explore the visual storytelling possibilities, I should have sought out a barber who does the special designs and taken pictures of boys getting haircuts. Photographs that expand on anecdotes contained in the story are more useful to editors.

Training your visual sensibility to recognize a scene with graphic impact is a lifetime task. Although you are primarily dedicated to writing, cultivating an informed visual sensibility will serve you well, enhancing your ability to see scenes to write about and scenes to photograph. It may be appropriate to take a course in graphic design, art appreciation, or photography. You can also improve your visual and design skills by practicing: Look around when you are walking, driving, standing—anytime you are idle. Notice patterns, figure out where the light is, where shadows fall, and degrees of contrast. Frame scenes by putting your hands around your eyes like a picture frame and stare through the limited space. Study the composition you create; improve it. Visit art and photography galleries. Look at art and photo books. Study photos in online image collections, such as the New York Public Library or the Library of Congress. Take classes in the visual arts.

WHAT KIND OF CAMERA?

With the array of digital and standard SLR (single lens reflex) cameras, point-and-shoot cameras, cell phone cameras, and disposable cameras, you are probably wondering what tools to use for travel photography. If you're not already an accomplished photographer, don't invest in an expensive camera until you've learned how to "see" with visual sophistication. Learn how to take photographs, and then find a camera you can operate easily that produces reproduction-quality images. As with computers, PDAs, and other technical tools, if you can't use the equipment handily, it won't be much help to you. And, if you haven't yet developed your visual sensibility, the camera isn't going to compensate. When you've learned how to focus closely on subjects you photograph, you'll know what type of camera or size lens to buy.

Professional news and travel photographer Christopher J. Williams advises, "The most important thing is to know your gear intimately. It is better to only take one lens and one camera that you understand than to drag a bag full of high-tech wizardry you don't know how to use." Spend money on lenses rather than the camera body. To produce quality images, the lens is more significant than which type of camera. Major camera manufacturers produce entry-grade lenses all the way through professional-quality glass.

Seek the advice of a professional photographer or a reliable camera merchant when you outfit yourself for travel photography.

In workshops, participating writers ask whether they should use slide or print film, or whether digital images are sufficient. I tell them that, as always in this business, it depends on the publication. Digital images are fine for Web-based publications and, with sufficient resolution, useful for newspapers and some magazines. However, there are publications that prefer transparencies or want prints so the in-house photo editor can scan the images. There is no set rule for the preferred format for images, but I'd recommend that a serious travel writer be equipped to provide digital images (either directly from a digital camera or by scanning standard prints) and actual prints or transparencies.

Williams advocates digital camera technology. "I use Nikon digital cameras which can take standard lenses," he says. He equips himself for travel photography with a zoom 300, a regular 20-80 lens, plus a wide-angle lens. That's a lot of hardware to carry around, but serious photographers learn to live with the "lug" factor. "Canon and Pentax are okay too, but if you already have lenses, get the digital body that matches them," Williams advises. Typically, he takes three memory cards (for a total of 561 megabytes of memory) with him for a day shoot, which gives him eighty pictures at highest resolution. With a 256-megabyte memory card, he can store one hundred pictures of lower resolution.

The writer must discuss photos with the editor. Ask about quantity and type of photos that the editor requires. Ask for the publication's preferred digital resolution, file format, and what method of delivery is expected (by e-mail, on CD, in print format).

Ferne Arfin, a freelance travel writer based in London, offers this illustrative lesson: "With so much new technology, publishers and writers are hovering between digital and conventional photography. It's very important that writers and editors are talking the same technology. Recently, my publisher told me she could only use pictures at a resolution of six hundred dpi ("dots per inch" is the term used to express spacial resolution of digital images) and ideally, at twelve hundred dpi. I had spent hours editing my pictures at three hundred dpi. My computer would have taken ages to handle six hundred dpi for each shot. I looked into converting images from film to disc at six hundred dpi; costs varied between twenty-three and forty-five pounds (forty-four and eighty-six dollars) per shot, for at least one hundred shots! Yet all the professional color labs I spoke to had never heard of working at twelve hundred dpi! While talking to the editor again, I deduced that she was talking about laser printer resolution and I was talking digital camera resolution—two very different areas of technology."

Some writers may be undecided about whether to use digital or standard cameras. Others swear by digital photography. "Digital photographs are no longer an option, they're a necessity," says Betsy Malloy, a California travel writer and online editor. "When editors expect authors to provide their own images, they not only want high-resolution digital images to accompany the piece, but the sale is made or broken on the quality of those images. A high-quality digital camera provides the opportunity to ensure your images are good enough on the spot while retakes are still possible," she says.

HOW TO TAKE PHOTOS FOR TRAVEL STORIES

If you are a novice photographer, use a basic digital or point-and-shoot camera with a close-up lens feature. Learn, through trial and error, how to frame images, move in for close-ups, and control image content. With a digital camera, you can practice and learn the camera's range before traveling, without significant expense. No film to buy, no developing or enlarging costs. With some photography experience, equip yourself with a 35mm SLR or digital camera and practice using it before you venture forth on a research trip for an article. Test the various features and settings on the camera. Take pictures with different settings and take lots of photos, close-ups, and long shots of people, buildings, and scenes. Log photos in a notebook so you know what you shot, who is in the picture, the location, and any other details you might need for a caption. When the film is developed or you upload digital images to your computer, notice what worked and which images were over- or underexposed. You don't have to be a photographer, but with modern automatic camera equipment, it's possible to sell your images.

Take many pictures. The first thing to learn about taking photographs to illustrate travel articles is that you can never shoot too many pictures. And no matter how many rolls of film or megabytes you shoot, only a handful of the images will be superb. In other words, a writer who is an adequate photographer will still only produce a few photographs suitable for publication. If you're just starting out in travel photography and decide to work with digital, you can develop skill and speed without the expense of film or processing.

Since photos can be an essential selling point in presenting your manuscript to an editor, travel writers need to be competent photographers. Develop your visual sense, take lots and lots of pictures, and upgrade your picture-taking skills. Look at the types of pictures that illustrate travel magazines or books.

By taking, say, ten times as many photographs as you might usually do if you were simply shooting family snapshots, you should improve the odds of taking photos that are clear enough to appear in a print or online publication. Resist the impulse to take the easiest photos, the obvious scene that first strikes you. Walk around the subject and study all the possibilities; seek engaging angles. Imagine what a scene will look like in print. Look through the camera lens, checking the potential for each scene, or scrutinize the digital screen, moving the camera to find preferential angles. Kneel down and shoot up toward the subject or find a vantage point where the scene can been photographed from above.

Standing and shooting the first scene you see will yield photographs that everyone else has taken; "stop, point, and shoot" rarely produces a fresh image. But making images more complicated doesn't necessarily mean you'll have better photographs. Until you have refined your skills, just take lots of pictures and scrap the images that are blurred, lack contrast, or are too busy. Realize that no matter how many years you've been taking pictures, shooting for publication is quite different. Admit your limitations, difficult as that may be. Accept that you'll probably have to discard many shots. Then loosen up and click.

Another reason for taking many pictures is that you'll develop reflex abilities to quickly grab that one shot that won't happen twice. I remember being in Agra on a busy market street. I was just looking around, perhaps writing down my impressions or sketching. All of a sudden I heard the deep throb of a motorcycle engine. I didn't hesitate, but yanked out my Minox 35mm camera and aimed at the street. Two motorcycles with sidecars were roaring through town. I clicked the shutter and advanced rapidly; of the three pictures I took, one sold.

The motorcycle street action didn't appear in the text of my story, which was about having tea with a rickshaw driver, but it did illustrate the commotion of street markets in Agra, which was a theme in the story. The speeding motorcycles showed the vicissitudes of street life much more vividly than a pretty picture of colorful vegetables at a market or a cloth vendor's stall draped with saris. If your story roars with action, the photographs should complement the text by showing people in motion.

As you travel, think about what scenes illustrate the mood of the place. Take photographs that capture the essence of the location. Is this place serene, bustling, noisy, crowded? Are buildings under construction, decorated with baroque curlicues, or peeling paint, or are they scrubbed and cared for? Do the people in public smile, laugh, scowl, or chatter? Seek photographs that tell a story, people interacting, people watching each other, animals eating, sales transactions, children playing together. Photographs of historic landmarks that feature a caretaker trimming trees, a costumed guide leading a tour, or an artisan at work are more interesting than static shots of a building or statue.

Your own appearance in the travel story and relationship to the story line suggests that photos of yourself would support the narrative. Action photographs of yourself may be useful; posed snapshots are not. Take photographs of yourself or your family involved in an activity featured in the travel article—climbing the mountain, tasting wine, riding the pony, stepping onto the ferry. Photographs shouldn't look posed, with all the people lined up staring at the camera. If you travel alone, learn how to use the remote release feature on your camera. Prop the camera on a bench, wall, or rock to capture yourself in mid-stride against a natural backdrop of a public setting.

Though it's tempting to take photos of yourself next to a distinctive landmark or in the foreground of a stunning landscape, those photos are generally for your personal use. Such pictures look posed and stiff. If you don't have a remote feature, you'll have to ask someone else to take them. Do you really want to hand your camera over to strangers to take pictures of you? The result is usually a fuzzy, overexposed long shot of unidentifiable people dwarfed by a monument or staring starkly at the camera. Rarely do photos of posed people taken by amateur photographers work for publication.

Crowd scenes show the ambience of a place but are difficult to photograph effectively. Photos that work in crowds: close-ups or medium-distance shots with a few human heads. Take vertical frames because you don't know what the layout in the publication will be. A vertical frame will have fewer people in it but still convey the density of the gathering. A horizontal photo with many people in it loses the specifics.

There will be times when you can plan your picture taking in advance. If you know you are going to write about five different landmarks or buildings, you know you should take pictures of them all. Offer an editor options. Take distance shots and close-ups of details. Walk as close as you think is appropriate then move in closer. If the weather is unreliable, take the planned pictures at the first opportunity that you have sufficient light. Late afternoon and early morning offer fine opportunities for well-defined contrast. When the sun is high, the light can be too intense, burning out the image you are striving to photograph. Make several visits to the place, if it is close to home. Photographs don't have to be taken at the same time you actually visit the landmark to gather information for the article.

In addition to planned photographs, you'll need other photographs to illustrate a travel story. Especially prized by editors are photos that evoke spontaneity. Wander around the area detailed in the article you are writing; when a scene catches your eye, take many photographs from different perspectives.

Photos serve a dual purpose. The photos illustrate your article and will also trigger memories as you write about what happened during the trip. Photos supplement your travel journal and help you recapture the scene in exquisite detail. Pursue a particular topic by taking photographs of the subject wherever you go. For example: parked bicycles, haystacks, unusual store windows (watch out for your reflection in the glass), poodles or barbershops. A series of pictures of taxicabs from around the world might be the basis for a travel article or even a photo book someday!

Take photos of road signs, direction markers, and other visual cues that help a reader understand the location. I like to take photos of unusual graffiti. Signs can be the subjects of photographs, especially if they are humorous. Remember to stand close enough to the sign so it fills the viewfinder.

Speaking of the viewfinder—what you see is what you get. Stray hairs, thumbs, waving branches, fluttering leaves will be in the picture if you see them through the lens. Strive to put the focal point of the picture just above or below the center horizontal line and just to the right or left of the center vertical line.

If there are people in the photo, check that background trees or telephone poles aren't growing out of the top of a person's head. When you look through the viewfinder and you aren't pleased by the scene, shift your position or the camera, if you're working with a digital camera, to adjust the perspective. Frame the subject with an arch or wall. Use natural entry points to draw the viewer into the picture. A path, road, or bridge will provide an avenue for the reader's eyes to gravitate toward the center of interest.

People are best shown in a context rather than posed. Tell your human photo subjects to look at each other or what they are doing rather than at the camera. Take photographs of people working or playing—cooking, fishing, weaving, making a bed, gardening, kicking a ball, skating, plucking a harp or bowing a violin. Sometimes, though, an artfully posed group of people tells volumes about a place. For example, the line of villagers staring at the camera suggests their ritual of sitting around near doorways or in cafés passing the time of day. Children are especially sympathetic subjects for illustrating travel articles, clinging together and showing no fear of the camera. However, it is prudent to ask permission before you take anyone's photo.

Think of the photographs you take while traveling as art, not snapshots. Create a composition in your photographs. People who notice the article in print will look at the photos first. By taking the photographs to illustrate your article, you have the opportunity to make visual accessories that enhance the story. The photos should be strong, inviting, and inspire curiosity so potential readers become actual readers.

Think about contrast, the photo editor at *The Washington Post Magazine* told me as I was embarking on a long research trip through Asia. Take verticals and horizontals and move in for close-ups of everything, my editor at National Geographic News online, Sean Markey, told me. To "read" properly in print or on the Web, an image needs to have distinct light and dark tones. Before taking a picture, I learned to imagine the scene as it might appear with the story. Would the subject show up, or was it in shadow? Was the background too busy for the subject to be distinguished? Is the scene generic or can I see a specific focal point for the photo?

For a picture to sell to a newspaper, magazine, or Web site publication, it should have action, movement, and help tell the story. In general, photo editors like to see people in the images. Not a posed photo of your companion leaning against a monument and staring at the camera, but a natural scene with people integrated in the local action. Bear in mind that glossy, nationally circulated magazines will assign professional photographers and have no interest in seeing photos provided by story authors. The exception might be if you are an established professional editorial photographer (sorry, no wedding photographers) and writing travel articles is your sideline.

Though beautiful to behold, seascapes and landscapes don't hold a reader's attention. In some ways, lovely scenes are the visual equivalent of gushy writing. The eye craves people or activity, even a boat on the horizon, to fix humanity in the picture. People want to study pictures that tell a story and editors need them to add dynamic information to text. Select views with people, animals, or buildings to add interest and stimulate curiosity. Even if these particular features aren't mentioned in your story, and they don't have to be, any action in the picture enhances rather than distracts or deflates the story.

There is a temptation to try and show everything in a picture, to squeeze in the whole market, all the folk dancers, the breadth of mountain range. Focus on precise areas rather than the broad sweep: one hill, one tree, a corner of the garden, a niche in the cathedral, the edge of a market stall. Fill the frame. Pictures that are two-thirds sky or sea will have to be cropped anyway—all that light space is deadly for contrast in print—so anticipate the editor's frustration and aim your camera fully at the subject, trimming unnecessary or bland areas before shooting.

You don't have to depict the entire building. Viewers can extend a wall or a porch in their imagination. If the subject of the picture is compelling, the eye will be satisfied with the detail. Your best test when reviewing your proofs or negatives is how your own eye looks at the pictures—are your memories swaying your judgment? Try and look at images objectively. Does the picture tell a story? Are you curious about who is in the picture and what they are doing? Is there anything in the picture to identify it and locate it in time or place? You don't want editors to react by saying, "Oh, that could be anywhere."

Improve your photography skills by enrolling in photography courses at a university, community college, or arts center. Study the works of other photographers, starting with travel magazines and books. Learn from what photo editors at major magazines have chosen to illustrate their pages.

OTHER SOURCES OF TRAVEL PHOTOS

Before sending out photographs, ask yourself: Will these photographs help my writing or hurt the presentation? What do you do when none of the pictures you've taken relate to your story line? Or when the technical quality of the photographs doesn't match your excellent writing? Turn to tourist bureaus, digital image libraries, and other photographers.

When I'm hunting for photographs to illustrate a travel article, I turn first to my own photo files and then to tourist bureaus or to the city's chamber of commerce. These offices are concerned with publicizing the merits of their state, country, city, or unique monument and generally are eager to assist writers and editors find appropriate photographs.

Nearly every foreign country that encourages tourism has a tourist information bureau, generally in New York, Miami, or Los Angeles, or a similar office affiliated with the country's embassy in Washington, D.C. Most maintain Web sites where photos may be viewed and/or downloaded. For example, the Las Vegas Convention and Visitors Bureau offers photos to illustrate travel articles promoting the region. Writers who have a commitment from an editor can request images for publication with travel stories. Typically tourist and visitors bureaus are dedicated to helping travel writers and editors, but be aware of restrictions on photo use (some prohibit use of their images on other Web sites), and all require a credit line attributing ownership of the images.

For photos depicting popular destinations, consult the press relations department of state, provincial, or national tourism or economic development departments, which are usually in the capitol city. Their employees maintain photo collections of scenic and historic landmarks, tourist attractions, and general views of their respective region. If the tourist or convention office doesn't have the photograph you require, ask for suggestions where you might find it. Perhaps you need to contact a local historical society or the management office of a particular institution, park, or landmark.

Photos from tourist bureaus are almost always provided without charge. If the bureau offers prints on loan, you may be asked to sign a receipt promising to return the pictures after publication. Whether you download photos or borrow prints, tourist bureaus and similar institutions always want a credit line to appear with the photograph that identifies its source. If a credit line, which acknowledges the photographer or source of the image, isn't already provided, type the credit line and affix it to the back of the photograph or attach the text to the digital image. You also need to provide the caption, which describes the scene in the photograph. For example, a photograph of the statues of the lions outside the Art Institute of Chicago might have a caption: "Lions guard art treasures inside the Art Institute of Chicago" and a credit line: "Photograph courtesy Art Institute of Chicago, 2005" or "Photograph by Phoebe Shutter, 2005, courtesy Art Institute of Chicago" or, if the city of Chicago's tourist office loaned the photograph to you, the credit line might read "Photograph courtesy City of Chicago, Graphics and Reproduction Center, Photograph by Phoebe Shutter, 2005."

While photo editors or art directors at large publications will be acquiring the images for publication, as a freelance writer, you'll often be responsible for ferreting out photos, especially if you work with small publications, as most of us do when we're starting out. When you're researching images, either through Web-based photo archives or in libraries, determine which department, archive, institution, or park service should be listed in a photo credit line. The specifics of credit lines vary from place to place. When you obtain the photos from an institutional source or a government office, ask for the preferred wording for photo credits. Be sure to send a copy of the published piece to the office that provided the photos and return loaned materials.

Photographs provided by a tourism bureau are generally the product of professional photographers, so the image resolution is high. However, some tourist bureaus tend to keep photos on file for many years, so the scenes may be dated. Before sending out photos with your article, look at them closely. Automobiles and fashions change. Buildings are razed and new construction changes the landscape. That busy street clogged with traffic in the photo may have become a pedestrian walkway; the park entrance may have been redesigned. Always verify that the images you send with your story depict places covered in the text or related to the text.

Bear in mind that some photos contained in tourist bureau files have been used over and over again to illustrate travel articles. These stale images do not enhance your chances of selling a travel story. A travel editor usually wants unique images, photos that relate specifically to the story under consideration. Try to take your own photos or travel with a skilled photographer so you can offer uncommon images with your article.

STOCK PHOTO SERVICES

Usually the photo editor at a large publication will undertake searches for photographs through stock photo agencies. The expense involved usually makes it prohibitive for a freelance writer to use stock services. Charges for research start at one hundred dollars and escalate. Then there is the fee for each photo use. Not to mention the financial responsibility of hundreds of dollars per frame if the photo is lost. Your best bet is to use photos taken during the trip by yourself or another photographer working with you.

Rare is the writer who takes a picture as well as she crafts a paragraph, so a source of free photographs snapped with professional precision is an asset to any writer. Make friends with photographers. If you meet a photographer during your travels, get his name and contact information so you can make contact later if you need photos of the landmarks you've visited.

A popular vision of photojournalist is the adventure-bound intrepid story catcher, cameras slung over khaki or leather jacket, who rafts down roiling rivers, leaps onto helicopters, and glibly talks entry into the inner sanctums of foreign dignitaries. While there are doubtless many weather-beaten photographers capturing the images that inform us of the world's culture, don't confuse news photography, as depicted in popular culture vehicles such as movies and television programs, with travel photography. The tasks are different. Travel photographers capture timeless moments that will illustrate portraits of a place and its people. News photographers seize the action of the moment. Travel photographers also try to take pictures with immediacy and spontaneity evident in the picture, but the emphasis is on representative moments rather than news events.

There's still plenty of adventure for the travel writer who takes photographs. As a travel writer, you'll take photographs for each story, using the images to remind you of scenes when you write the story and to help sell the story. As you progress in your career, you'll create a databank of images for use with future stories. If you really hone your picture-taking skills, you could also try selling photographs from your travels without the stories.

Forget about your clean clothes. Taking pictures from a variety of camera positions compounds interest in all your pictures. Silhouettes, shot from an elevation, may require you to step up on ledges, rocks, and windowsills. Watch your step! Protect your equipment with waterproof cases. Always carry spare film—or storage cards for digital cameras—and batteries. You'll never use your last set of batteries when you're near a store. Remember to recharge your equipment.

Some photos shouldn't be taken. Consider whether the photograph would be an invasion of privacy. Find out what is considered good manners among the people you are visiting. Ask yourself: How would I feel if someone started taking pictures of me? Is your attitude condescending and rude or conciliatory and interested? Friendliness, honesty, and good manners are the principles that should govern photographing people.

There is the matter of legal or political restrictions concerning photographs. Find out in advance if you will need written permission or a license to take photographs in churches, shrines, or archeological sites. You may have to pay a fee to take photographs. Keep the receipt; it's a business expense. It is also wise to remember that at various times and places, some countries regulate the importation or export of unexposed or exposed film, camera equipment, and accessories. Again, if you are unsure what the rules are, research the information before you start traveling. Ask if military structures, natural resources, airports, and official buildings of various types are off-limits to photographers.

WHAT CAN GO WRONG

Most of us worry whether airport security scanners affect film adversely. Take a lead-lined film bag along if you are doubtful about the efficacy the x-ray machines in the region where you will be traveling. In some remote airports, however, security staff might not be familiar with lead bags. During enhanced air travel security, your luggage may be opened and searched or subjected to intense x-ray scrutiny. Don't put film in checked baggage. In most of the industrialized world, the scanning machines will not affect film, but repeated x-ray exposure may cloud unprocessed film. I usually carry exposed film in a clear plastic bag in my jacket pocket or tote bag. At the moment I pass through the metal detector, I pass the bag of film to the attendant along with keys and pocket change and walk through. Usually, I have no problems with this system, but there was the time in Brussels when I was severely chastised by a security guard who insisted all film had to go through the x-ray device. The bottom line is: Heed the instructions of security personnel.

What's the worst that could happen? You could lose all your photos or be in a remote area without a camera. My photo horror story occurred during a trek in Kamchatka, in the Russian Far East across the Bering Sea from Alaska. With my trusty 35mm camera and dozens of rolls of film, I thought myself well equipped for weeks of rafting, trekking, and touring in the wild. Imagine my chagrin when after days of snapping photographs, I realized the shutter wasn't actually moving when I released it. Had a water spray damaged it during the rafting, or steam while I shot pictures of geyser eruptions? Perhaps the camera had been banged around in my daypack.

I never did determine the source of the damage to the shutter mechanism, which was repaired upon my return home. Fortunately, my travel mates, including a filmmaker, offered to share their pictures. I paid for processing duplicate slides and photos and had enough images to illustrate several travel stories. But though their photos were interesting and of high quality, the images weren't my own. The experience has made me more attentive to monitoring the state of my cameras. And yes, it's best to have a couple of cameras with you.

Photographers and tourists are targets of opportunity theft. Instead of stashing your camera in an expensive, professional-style camera bag, use a beat-up duffel bag or a child-size daypack. Be creative. Make a protective liner with bubble wrap and duct tape. Fancy camera bags with brand names plastered on the side invite theft.

LEGAL ISSUES

If you are concerned about legal repercussions, use model releases. In general, for editorial photography such as travel articles, you have the right to take pictures of anybody who is in a public place. You don't have the right to invade someone's privacy by going into his home or other personal space (car, place of worship, front yard) and photographing him without permission. If you plan to sell the image for commercial purposes, such as for use in an advertisement or billboard, it would be prudent to obtain a release. If you're in a place where photographing people is culturally taboo, be especially careful about how you approach people.

The model release form states that the person in the picture knows you are going to take the photo and that you can use it any way you want without compensation. Formats for model releases are available in photo how-to books and on the Internet. Bringing out a model release form might cause some people to ask for money, since they probably hadn't considered that you might be taking the picture and then selling it. I haven't yet paid anyone for taking their picture, and most folks are delighted at the attention. Sometimes I'll get a name and address and send a copy of the photograph after I've returned home, a nice way of thanking someone for helping your travel photojournalism career.

If someone seems hesitant or downright hostile about having her picture taken, I back off. I admit that occasionally, I'll back off and change to a telephoto lens and then take a picture from a distance. Only once was I physically attacked for taking a picture. It was just a few miles from my home when I took a picture of a mother who was shouting and gesturing offensively during a children's soccer match. I also took a photo of her as she flailed her fists at me, but I didn't pursue charges.

STORING PHOTOS

Photographs, negatives, and slides have to be stored carefully to prevent injury or deterioration. Digital photos also should be organized and saved with backup files. Various storage systems are available from photography supply stores or online. Options include plastic storage sleeves punched for insertion in loose-leaf binders for negatives or slides, file boxes with glassine wrappers for negatives and boxes for slides. Whatever system you choose, make sure the materials are archival quality to preserve the photographs. Photo management software will help organize digital files.

When you take photographs, jot down details in a notebook with the frame number. This is extremely important to remember because you will have to write captions for the photos if they are used in publications. After transferring images to your computer or processing the film, write captions and label the images. Many photographers cull bad frames from the digital images right away, so a blurred or overexposed shot won't find its way into a presentation.

Doubtless you'll accumulate photos from other sources—other photographers, tourist bureaus, fee-free digital archives, and public relations firms that represent tourism clients. Verify the caption and credit lines, and date photos in your files. It is surprisingly easy to forget the details, and a photograph you can't identify is no use to you or an editor. Cultivate a habit of labeling images as soon as you get them or upload them from your digital card.

While working on travel stories, consult your photo files to see what resources are available. Once you know what photos you've taken or have on hand, you may tailor some details in the story to correspond to those images.

Digital cameras have created a new storage problem for the traveler, namely what to do when you run out of gigabytes. Julian Cook, a Washington, D.C.-based travel writer and tech equipment reviewer, offers this solution for storing digital images: "Weighing in at a little over five ounces, the Archos Gmini 400 portable hard drive has a twenty-gig storage capacity," says Cook. "After filling up your camera's storage media, transfer digital photos to the hard drive just by plugging it into a slot on the Archos. The storage capacity is 200,000 photos in JPEG format. The appliance also stores music files. The downside is that you do need to recharge the Li-ion batteries occasionally."

THE MECHANICS OF SUBMITTING PHOTOGRAPHS

When you make an exploratory marketing call, have some notes on what photos are available so you can answer intelligently when asked, "Do you have photos?" As you discuss your story ideas with editors, or in your query e-mails and letters, offer to provide photos. Promote your photo skills, especially if the editor expresses interest in the story.

Before submitting photographs with your article, find out what kinds of photographs are expected and what form—color, black and white, slides, negatives, prints, digital, transparencies, contact sheets. If the publication is concerned about writers and photographers taking complimentary press trips, let the editor know if you have taken the photos for the story while on a subsidized trip or have used your own money.

Sending images electronically routinely gives writers and editors fits. A September 2004 discussion on Travelwriters.com (a Web site for travel editors and writers) revealed that writers discover—to their dismay—that attached photo files don't reach editors or can't be opened. The reasons might include security barriers set too high, or the publication may limit download file size or time. Perhaps the ISP (Internet Service Provider) limits the number of attachments per e-mail. Even if the electronic file is received, photo-editing software might not be integrated. Files might be labeled or saved incorrectly on the sender's computer or stored improperly on the receiving computer.

Some writers use an e-mail server that provides server storage space. Or, writers and photographers with their own Web sites create a folder of photos, then advise the editor where to look for photos. The editor goes to the URL, opens the folder, and downloads the desired photos.

Some editors solve the download image problem by requesting images on CD, which brings us back to mailing or overnight delivery. Remember that if you send manuscripts and photographs on an unsolicited basis, you do not have any financial recovery rights if the photos are lost. That means, unless an editor has told you that the publication wants to see your article and photos, either on spec or under contract, you are sending unsolicited material and run the risk of loss. Most reputable publications make a sincere effort to return unsolicited material if a stamped, self-addressed envelope is enclosed. At the minimum, if you are sending unsolicited slides or photos and want them returned, label each photo with your name and address and provide a postage-paid envelope for their safe return.

It's never a good idea to send large image files by e-mail unless you are specifically requested to do so. Always ask an editor or art director exactly how they prefer reviewing or receiving images—on CD, by e-mail (what size image, what kind of file), by hand delivery, express mail, or through a Web site where you store images.

If you're sending prints or slides, your name and address goes on the back of each photograph or on the cardboard holder of each slide. Some photographers use a rubber stamp or address stickers to label photographs. If you aren't the photographer, put the correct name and address on each picture or slide frame. Do equivalent file identification if you send images digitally. Use file names that the editor can recognize with the story name or subject and the author or photographer's name in the file heading.

If you are making simultaneous submissions of your travel articles, sending out photos to many editors can be expensive. That's why many travel writers maintain Web sites with thumbnail versions of images or send very small electronic image files along with the story. If you're working with prints, consider sending a sharp photocopy of the picture so the editor can get an idea of what is available. However, it's far more practical to scan the prints and send them by e-mail (in correct size format) once the editor has requested the images.

If you leave caption writing to the publication, you increase the possibility of errors. Do it yourself and the editor has one less task. Cutlines or captions are inserted with the digital image or, for prints, printed on paper and attached to the photograph. For slides, write captions on a separate piece of paper keyed to numbers that are written on the corresponding slides. As stated above, if an agency or institution provided the photo, the photo credit should acknowledge that fact. Use the wording provided by the photographer, tourist office, or agency or a variation of: "Photo by (name of photographer)" or "Photo courtesy Malaysian Tourist Bureau," etc.

If you've sent images by e-mail and the editor can't find them, verify e-mail addresses, file title, file format, and other attachment parameters. Offer to send the files again or to send the images in print format.

If you sent prints and haven't received the images back, a month or so after publication, call your editor and ask when you can expect the photographs to be returned. Editorial departments are chronically understaffed and overworked; perhaps the photos are on a desk waiting to be sent. Don't assume the editor misplaced your photos. I embarrassed myself in this way once. Two months after publication, I couldn't find the negatives and drawings I'd provided for a story about Indonesia. I self-righteously assumed the illustrations hadn't been returned to me and called the editor to complain. He insisted that all photos had been returned with tear sheets. I doubted, I whined. He suggested that the materials might have been lost in the mail, although that had never happened before, or perhaps they had been lost at my end, i.e., on my desk! An orderly hoarder, I couldn't believe that. A couple of years passed. One day a manuscript page slipped between my desk and the wall so I had to move the desk to retrieve it. You guessed right; in the crevice between desk and wall was an envelope containing the missing negatives along with two copies of the published article. I phoned the editor at once and apologized; we had a good laugh.

Photographs are rarely lost in the mail, but it can happen. If you're working with prints, you may want to take steps to guarantee the safe return of irreplaceable photos. Provide an addressed return envelope and appropriate prepaid express mail envelopes with a note requesting that someone at the publication handle this extra service. Or, open a FedEx account and provide the account number, asking the photo editor that your materials be sent back using express service. In practice, most publications pay for return postage or express mailing fees for photographs or other materials related to articles they'll be printing. Of course, if the editor requires slides or prints, you could send duplicates.

A more common legal problem concerns the copyright for photographs you take. If the negatives or prints aren't returned, or if digital images are stored in the publication's computers without proper attribution, there is always the possibility that the images will be used again, possibly uncredited and unpaid. The chances that a reputable publication will use photos without credit or payment is extremely rare, but it can happen, usually because someone in the editorial or photo department thinks the photos belong to the publication. Again, always attach identifying data to digital images, stamp your name on the back of prints, or write your name on slides so there is no question about who is the copyright owner of the images.

QUALITY CONTROL

What if you don't like the editor's choice of photographs? Perhaps the photo was published reversed or cropped in a way you don't like. Do you have recourse? Not really. If the error misrepresented the article—for example if a photograph was used that doesn't relate to your article in any way—you could ask that a correction be run in the publication that explains that the error was editorial and not the fault of the writer. Such problems are so rare, though, that you shouldn't consider them a real issue.

TIPS FOR TRAVEL PHOTOGRAPHERS

1. Have a definite objective for the photographs. Take pictures that support and illustrate the places you are writing about.

2. Keep equipment in good repair, batteries charged, and carry extra batteries, digital storage cards, film, and whatever other accessories you need. Chose filters and extra lenses with your experience in mind.

3. Patience is important. So is an ability to see the humor in situations and laugh at your mistakes.

4. Learn as much as you can about local customs before you take pictures of people.

5. Take lots of pictures. You'll be lucky if 10 percent of your photographs are visually sharp and contribute to a strong narrative.

6. If you work with film, put in a fresh roll when are approaching a situation where you know you will be taking lots of pic-

tures. How will you feel if you have to stop midway in the ceremony to change film? Let a couple of unshot frames go; film is inexpensive compared to the impossibility of recovering pictures you miss.

7. Switch to digital format and carry extra storage cards.

8. Cushion equipment from bumps and falls. Dust, sand, salty air, extremes of heat and cold, rain, and fog are all difficult for the camera to live through.

9. Check and clean photo equipment before departure and each day during the trip.

10. Carry an extra point-and-shoot camera, especially if you are going to remote areas.

exercises

EXERCISE 1: Using your crisply honed observation skills, take notes about published photos. Page through glossy travel magazines. What do you see? Are the pictures taken from unusual angles or did the photographer use a natural frame such as an arch, trees, or a window around the subject? How many close-ups or distance shots illustrate each article? Can you see what is in the background? Do people in the photo look posed or natural?

EXERCISE 2: Using one of the drafts you wrote for exercises in chapters three and four, evaluate what photographs you will need. Read the piece and highlight subjects that are inherently visual—people doing things, colorful markets, animals, children, close-ups of architectural details. If you have already taken photographs related to the draft, go through them and select a dozen shots that relate to the story, illustrating the character of the place and its residents. Weed out any photos showing people staring stiffly at the camera (unless that's the artistic effect you seek), blurred scenes, or those taken from such a distance that the subject is difficult to see. Are the photos a mixture of close-ups and medium-distance shots, verticals and horizontals? Is there drama or dialogue in the photos—people looking at each other or moving toward something?

EXERCISE 3: With a draft or finished travel article about a place close to home, go out and "shoot the story." Take sufficient film or digital storage cards with you. Concentrate on getting every possible photograph. Even if it's a struggle to find a hundred or more photographs about one travel subject, the exercise will push you to be creative, to watch and wait for unique photo opportunities.

MARKETING TRAVEL ARTICLES

You have a story, or two or three. Perhaps you've constructed a marketing plan and researched publishing options. Like most freelance writers, you're wondering if your article will appeal to editors. With gumption and persistence, you'll find an audience. Bear in mind, though, that marketing travel articles requires preparation and focus. You are selling your work and experience.

Prepare for this enterprise. Do some research before contacting editors or sending out queries. One useful step in marketing your own work is to reread the story and make a list of magazines, Web sites, and newspapers that you believe would be interested in the story. If you aren't sure what publications are available, browse the Internet and search in libraries, writers guidebooks, and periodicals aimed at freelance writers. The marketing list you're creating is not a list of where you wish the story would be published but a realistic summary containing perhaps a dozen publications, including online publications, where a writer at your experience level could expect to be published.

Start the list with the travel or weekend leisure sections of the papers in your hometown or a nearby town. Remember to include some of the free entertainment or community papers that circulate in nearly every locality. If you can't find any small papers that might seek new writers, scour the Internet for travel, outdoors, history, cultural, and special interest publications (online and print) related to the story you are currently selling. Put this prospective marketing list aside to work with later.

Review the types of travel articles detailed in chapter one. Into which category does your piece fit? There's a chance the article may fall into several categories, which will broaden your marketing prospects. Skim the travel section of a current edition of *Writer's Market* or one of the many Web sites dedicated to the needs of freelance writers. Read these guidelines for writers and identify which publications are seeking travel articles in areas your article fits. While in the market research phase, I bookmark interesting Web sites or use stick-on notes to mark publications listed in the market guide that might be interested in particular travel articles I'm ready to send out. Or, make a list with the relevant Web sites or page numbers in the writer's guidebooks for easy reference. While the personal essay or articles featuring your opinions might appeal to you, bear in mind that freelance writing is a commercial product. Analyze whether your favorite themes are what the editor is looking for. Examine what is being published and take your cues from the magazines and newspapers where you want your work to appear. Select publications where it would be realistic for a beginner or novice to be published. If you are already an established writer, search for new places to publish.

WHAT IS YOUR MARKET LEVEL?

Another facet of marketing is selling your past experience. Your strongest tool in marketing your writing is your previously published work, your clips. Copies of published articles show editors that you are capable of writing for their publication. When you market story ideas, you're convincing editors that you have the ability to produce the quality of writing they seek, on deadline and at the requested length.

Beginners have a dilemma. Without clips, they can't prove their ability to an editor, and if their work doesn't get to an editor's eyes, they won't ever be published and get clips. This circular negativity doesn't have to apply, however. Consider this:

Every writer was once a beginner. Every writer started small, with a first acceptance for publication. And that first sale raised pulse levels and expectations. The thrill of the first acceptance letter or phone call ranks as a major life experience for many writers I've talked to.

Though years have passed, the thrill of my first magazine acceptance letter hasn't worn thin. *American Antiques* accepted my query about a special interest destination story featuring Maxfield Parrish's house, Wells Woods, in New Hampshire. The house had been renovated and opened to the public as a bed and breakfast inn. I had stayed there, paid for my lodging, and interviewed the owner, mentioning that I hoped to write a travel piece. At that time, my publication history was slight indeed—a couple of first-person essays published in newspapers and a collection of reviews and sports articles for my university newspaper. The antiques piece was my first magazine sale after I'd decided to make my way as a freelancer. The twenty-five dollars (yes, really!) payment didn't begin to cover expenses, but it created an endless horizon on which I could imagine future successes.

You're a realist; you know your writing is solid, has flashes of flair, and grabs a reader. But your published words have only appeared in newsletters, local periodicals, or weekly papers. You can query a glossy nationally circulated magazine or a newspaper with millions of readers, but be prepared to face repeated rejection. The more sensible approach is to work your way up, publishing in regional travel magazines, special interest magazines, and small circulation newspapers.

Face it, *The New York Times*, *National Geographic*, *Islands*, or *Gourmet* probably aren't going to publish your first travel article. Don't waste their time and yours by pitching story ideas or sending manuscripts to large-circulation glossy magazines and internationally known newspapers until you have achieved a certain level of publishing success in your field. A writer's early sales nearly always appear in small newspapers and regional or local publications or specialty magazines.

A strongly focused, expertly developed, vividly described travel experience that is printed in your hometown weekly with a byline is a worthwhile clip to have in your portfolio. Contribute a short review of a resort hotel to an online travel newsletter. Write for your university alumni magazine or the publication issued by a fraternal society you belong to. In a full-length piece, a range of your writing skills, including interviews with sources, fact-finding, and in-depth reporting will be displayed. In a short review, command of snappy vocabulary will be featured.

You might not be paid for these first few publication credits or the payment will be miniscule. Perhaps the editor will offer you a free subscription to the paper or newsletter. At this point, the goal is to collect a few published clips to serve as leverage into larger circulation, higher paying publications. But don't write for free, beyond your first couple of articles. Ask to be paid if the editor likes your ideas. You are a professional. Strive to amass a variety of publication credits—long and short pieces with your byline on them. Of course, you'll take every assignment or offer of publication you can. Don't underestimate the value of a big display in a local publication.

MOVING UP

Regional travel markets provide an opening for novice travel writers. Creating story ideas and writing about locations close to home offers a couple of advantages—you'll be writing about what you know, always a solid bet, and you'll be developing stories and acquiring published clips at minimum expense. The regional travel market needs writers from the region. Writers from the region have an edge over out-of-town writers that editors appreciate. Your experience and firsthand knowledge will be trusted.

To break into the regional travel market, explore which publications are solvent and inviting submissions. Troll newsstands and local bookstores. Look for scenic magazines that showcase the region. For example, in my area, the regional print travel and lifestyle magazines include *Baltimore, Blue Ridge Country, Fred-*

erick, The Maryland Natural Resource, and *Washingtonian*. Online travel magazines with Mid-Atlantic regional coverage include *Virginia Wind* (www.virginiawind.com), *Road & Travel* (www.road andtravel.com), *Oceana* (www.oceanamagazine.com), *Go World Travel* (www.goworldtravel.com), and *Weekend Guide* (www.week-endguide.com). Obviously, there are dozens more special interest, travel, and lifestyle publications online and in print that serve the region. As the writer in search of publication, you'll have to do the fishing.

Ask the local tourist board, chamber of commerce, or visitors and convention bureau for leads to regional publications. The state economic development bureau or commerce department should be responsive. Tourism is big business everywhere and counties, provinces, states, and cities are eager to promote regional travel. As a travel writer, you facilitate the promotional process, help them do their jobs. Analyze what kind of travel stories are regularly published in these magazines. Are all the travel stories about country inns or bed and breakfast properties? Is family travel the focus, or golfing or outdoor adventure travel? What kinds of advertisements appear in the magazine? How long has it been published? Does the writer provide the photographs?

Bear in mind that some regional magazines—even magazines supported by state offices of economic development—start up and disappear in a year or two. A few years ago, I remember preparing restaurant and country inn reviews for a Baltimore-based regional travel magazine. The editor accepted the story, provided an assignment letter stating that expenses would be reimbursed and gave me a deadline, promising the story would run soon afterwards. As soon as the story was turned in, I headed off on a previously planned research trip and sent a bill for my expenses and the writing fee. Normally, that would be a reliable arrangement, and since the magazine seemed to be healthy, I fully expected the finished product and a check to be in my post office box when I returned. As you may have guessed, the magazine fell on hard times during the three or four months I was traveling and the assignment editor left the publication. The remaining editor was sympathetic but said there was a long line of creditors with larger unpaid bills than mine, such as the printer and the landlord. The magazine soon disappeared. I took that as a lesson never to run up expenses on behalf of a publication, no matter how apparently solvent, and I used the story research in other travel articles.

As beginners or novices, many freelance writers are grateful just to hear an editor say "We like your story" and forget to nail down the details of when or how much they'll be paid. It's always preferable to be paid on acceptance, rather than upon publication. Sometimes writers turn in their story to an interested editor and receive no specific information as to when the story will run or what rights the publication is purchasing.

If you find yourself in such a bind, call the editor and ask: "When will my article be published?" "What rights does this publication purchase?" And the all-important one: "How much do you pay?" It's best to have a number in mind (a realistic number) so if the editor lobs back "How much are you asking?" you're ready. Research in advance what fees comparable publications are offering. Obviously the *Montreal Gazette* isn't paying writers at the same rate as a free local tabloid focused on arts coverage. Local publications often don't pay anything to beginners, but if the publication runs one or two of your stories, insist on payment before providing further story ideas or articles. In general, I recommend not writing for free, but if you are truly a beginner with no clips to your name, follow the time-honored route of writing for token fees or for free a few times in order to establish a publishing track record.

While an editor has your stories under consideration, the publication might change hands, be acquired by another publisher, or the editor might leave. Whenever there is turmoil in an editorial office, you should protect your work by withdrawing it from consideration. It is not productive to leave your work product—your intellectual property—with a sinking publication. The stories may be on hold and still owned by you, but in the editorial office, someone could assume ownership. Send certified letters to the new publishers, withdrawing the stories from consideration. Then market the stories elsewhere.

Is a clip from a publication that no longer exists useful? How can I market my writing skills if all my clips are fifteen or twenty years old? Can I use articles from newsletters that have nothing to do with travel to show my writing skills? If I write public relations papers, legal briefs, and government reports, can I use those work products as writing samples? These are some of the questions I'm routinely asked by former journalists and aspiring freelance writers who are making the transition to travel writing. You can use any published item, if the writing is good, because the writing stands on its merits. The same goes for work that appears in giveaway newspapers, newsletters, and limited-circulation publications. Even if the dateline was years ago, if the writing is solid, your talent will show. But editors have no interest in reading professional writing samples from non-journalism professions. The writing style and diction in science, law, advertising, or management simply doesn't translate to journalism. Editors want to see news and feature writing samples as examples of a writer's skill. If you are resuming a writing career after an interval, it may be prudent to briefly explain time gaps, career changes, and other ellipses in your publishing history.

Many aspiring travel writers start by publishing their stories on travel Web sites, usually without compensation. Obviously, an edited Web site with an established name and readership is preferable to a start-up site. Still, the experience of producing material on deadline, to a specific length, and going through the editing process is useful for those new to the trade. Bear in mind that Web publications, like magazines, come and go. Print out a copy of the story as soon as it appears on the Web site. Push yourself to write for print and continue to seek audited, nationally circulated publications.

Freelance travel writers with a variety of clips and some experience can expand their portfolios by writing brief items for large-circulation publications. While analyzing publications and becoming familiar with magazine formats, you'll notice that most publications have a "front of the book" or "back of the book" section composed of a few pages of short items. Sometimes the sections have bylines after each item. Using the masthead as a guide, determine whether the publication's staff writes these short items or if they are written by contributing editors or by freelancers whose names do not appear on the masthead. If the short items were written by people whose names appear on the masthead, the publication may not be assigning to freelancers, but keep looking. Many magazines routinely cultivate new talent from the freelance pool by offering the short items as a lure. If the writer handles the assignment well, there may be longer stories to come. Can you approach a magazine and simply offer to write blurbs or short items in the offing? No. Approach the editors of these sections with carefully researched ideas that fit the format and the magazine's tone. Remember, the magazine has a fleet of able writers already available; you break in by having clever ideas, researched news, and an ability to ferret odd lore that would appeal to the particular publication's audience. A few magazines also feature a one-page essay written by freelancers that appears on the last page, another opportunity for writers with modest experience in search of publishing venues.

Since there is no space to develop a mood or story line, every sentence in a short piece has to be sharply focused. The items may be short, but a writer puts considerable effort into crafting a chewy paragraph or two. An argument could be made for specializing in short items, because the pay scale is often surprisingly generous for this length, at least in the major travel magazines. Consider, though, that a long piece in a regional publication might be a better clip for your portfolio than a two-inch squib in the roundup travel notes page of a glossy magazine. As you compile and send out examples of your published work to editors, you'll want to include full-length stories as well as short blurbs, because in the short pieces, there is scant opportunity to assess a writer's ability to handle complex story threads.

NETWORKING TO MEET EDITORS

How do you know if your writing is good enough? When are you ready to move up to a new level of publication? Seek advice at writing workshops or courses. If a manuscript critique is offered at the workshop, take advantage of the professional input. Attend writers workshops and conferences where local editors are speaking. Working editors sometimes teach courses at local colleges and universities. You could enroll and improve your writing while initiating professional contacts.

Do you hesitate to approach editors and introduce yourself? They wouldn't be at the conference or teaching a class if they weren't eager to meet writers. Writers err in being too shy or too greedy for the editor's time. No need to tell your life story; just present yourself and ask if the editor is seeking new writers or interested in reading manuscripts. Ask whether the editor will accept e-mail queries. Should you send the finished piece? You might ask for the editor's card; offer your own. Usually editors will remember you if you are brief and organized. Fix your name with the story topic in their minds. Follow up within two weeks. If an e-mail or regular mail query was discussed, send it, along with samples of your published work, URL address, or links to your Internet-based published work. If the editor asked for the completed manuscript, send it off topped with the strongest lead you can muster. Maybe this editor prefers receiving manuscripts in the mail; make sure you enclose an SASE and a cover letter mentioning your meeting during the class or conference. When you send a story by e-mail, ask for an e-mail confirmation that the story was received.

If the piece is rejected, send a query on another topic, and so on. Should you feel that you aren't making headway, try a publication with a smaller circulation and work on your writing skills. Try editors again when you have fresh material to offer.

APPROACHING EDITORS WITH IDEAS

Once you have a dozen or so published credits in small periodicals and papers, start sending out travel article queries to large-circulation publications. Query only after you've read at least two or three copies of the publication. Familiarize yourself with the types of feature articles and what departments appear in every issue. Bear in mind that the online version of a nationally circulated paper or magazine could be a digest version of the print edition.

Read the masthead. Who publishes the magazine? Is this an inflight magazine? If so, take note of the destinations served by the parent airline because those places will be featured in the magazine. One reason for reading several back issues of a magazine, or checking the index to past issues on the publication's Web site, is so you won't propose a travel article idea that appeared in a recent issue.

Another reason for this background research is to cultivate a feeling for the magazine's preferred style—bright and breezy, fact oriented, sophisticated or humorous. Note whether the writers are well-known established authors or freelancers like you. Scan the brief bios at the end of the features for this kind of information. Some magazines include a page that lists contributors near the front. Does your experience parallel that of the freelancers whose work appears in the publication?

If the publication doesn't have a presence on the Internet, and there are many publications that don't, contact the publication by phone or regular mail, asking for editorial guidelines and a sample copy. Call local magazines or newspapers and ask to have the guidelines and a sample issue sent to you. Prepare a phone script with your questions and story ideas, just in case an editor picks up the phone. Even if the editor isn't available, while you are on the phone, extract useful information from editorial assistants. Ask whether they use freelancers, which editor reads articles, if articles held for consideration, and how long. If the person you are talking to is receptive, pitch the idea; you may receive practical advice about how to proceed in your marketing effort. Ask if you should query or send the finished piece. Verify the correct spelling of names and titles.

I recall a participant in a food-writing course at L'Academie de Cuisine in Bethesda a year ago. During the introductions, he explained that he'd never published an article but wanted to develop a sideline career as a freelance writer. He listened carefully to suggestions about how to get started and scribbled dutifully in his notebook. During the open discussion period in a subsequent class, he reported that he'd called a regional outdoors publication with a phone script pitching a food-related travel article, with a couple of other story ideas prepared. It happened that the editor answered. The aspiring food and travel writer talked his way through his first query and by the time the call ended, he had two stories lined up. This won't happen to everyone, but if you don't prepare yourself and you don't try, there's an excellent chance you'll remain unpublished.

Despite the possible success of phoning editors at small publications, I advise against calling editors at well-known magazines, large newspapers, or other national publications unless you've received favorable feedback from a query. While it is useful to have self-confidence and ambition, if you have no published work or writing experience, why would an editor seek your ideas or articles? Select publications that match your experience level. Look to small-circulation, free, or limited-distribution publications for your first few publishing experiences. Build on your initial success and gradually move into regional travel magazines or the weekly leisure section in a newspaper. Then, with a dozen or so published examples, tackle a midsize metropolitan newspaper, and so on.

Be realistic and work your way into the glossy well-known publications; it makes no sense to waste your time and an editor's time proposing story ideas to glossy magazines or nationally circulated newspapers when you have no publishing experience. They just aren't interested! You need experience; writing, like brain surgery, is not a skill you acquire in a couple of weeks. If you aim too high on the publishing scale and only receive rejections, you'll soon be discouraged and give up your publishing dream.

Send queries outlining your well-defined story ideas to local and regional publications to build your publication track record. You can always rework those story ideas for a big-name magazine later when your credentials are established. When you have attained a certain level of experience (a few years of freelance publishing and a stable track record of publication credits, an article every month or every other month if you're writing part time), then you can contact editors by phone and they'll welcome your e-mails. We'll cover how to nurture relationships with editors in chapter nine.

TIPS ON HOW TO WRITE QUERIES

This brief, bright letter presents an idea to an editor and asks if the editor is interested in reading the finished manuscript. Most editors prefer queries. E-mail or letter queries save time and allow the editor to see if you can present an idea succinctly in writing. As the editor reads the query, he will hear whether you have a voice. If the tone of the query letter is flat and lacks personality, what will spark an editor's enthusiasm?

Communicate the story idea and how you plan to develop the focus. Select vocabulary and use diction to demonstrate that you are a confident writer, not a show-off. The editor may respond with a version of "go ahead, we'll look at it on spec," which means you can go ahead and write the piece and the editor will at least read it. "On spec" is not a contract or an offer to buy your story. On speculation simply means the editor likes the idea and will look at the article if you send it to her. There is no commitment. If you send in the article, and the editor pays you, your freelance travel writing career is launched.

Working editors have neither the time nor the inclination to offer critiques of unsolicited material. Cover letters asking for advice or begging for corrections or critiques generally herald the insecure and amateur writer. It would be a waste of time for an editor to read further with a pitch like that. But, once in a while, a query letter or unsolicited manuscript captures an editor's interest and attention. Perhaps, if it strikes a chord, the writer will be called and asked to rework the piece for publication. Put your best work forward and hope that you hit the editor's desk on an easy day when he's in the mood for prospecting new talent.

My advice: Never copy another writer's query letter format. Use your own voice, your own style. But so many participants in writing classes have begged to see a sample query letter that I now offer one, as long as they promise never to use it as a model. The point in including this fake query letter is to show correct business letter or e-mail format and to demonstrate the points that a query should cover. Use your own diction, vocabulary, and style. You will do yourself no favors by copying this letter; it is simply a model.

---

5 March 2006

David M. Uneeda, Editor
Far East Adventure Traveler
2-91-47 Nishki-Azabuzon
Minataur-ku 10635
Tokyo, Japan

Dear Mr. Uneeda:

Let me introduce myself: I am a freelance features writer interested in contributing to *Far East Adventure Traveler*. My work appears in publications such as *Travel & Leisure, Japan Times* and *Departures*.

I understand that Singapore and Malaysia will be featured in an upcoming issue of *Far East Adventure Traveler*. Perhaps you would be interested in considering an article on Penang nature walks or the gardens of Singapore.

Currently, I also have stories in progress featuring caving in New Zealand and volcano climbing in Java. Perhaps you will be focusing on these destinations in future issues. Please let me know if these stories interest you.

I can offer first rights to the Penang nature walks article at 1,200 words, available immediately. The Singapore parks story is 900 words, and I'm offering second rights. A longer version of the Singapore parks story appeared in a U.S. newspaper a few years ago. I've fully updated the fact box and other details.

Though you may have your own photo resources, I do have a selection of digital images for both travel stories. I'll need to know your preferred photo file format. I've included URL addresses to a couple of recent clips for your review. I hope to hear from you soon.

Best regards,
Freelance Writer's Name
E-mail
Tel and Fax
Street Address

The general pattern with freelancers is to write for a publication for a while and as their writing style improves, they move on to higher profile publications. This creates a window for other aspiring writers. Editors have told me that budget constraints cause them to reject good stories; they can't buy every story that comes along. However, a writer who continues to send out well-written work will eventually find a place to publish. "Send me a good story," Michael Shoup, travel editor of *The Philadelphia Inquirer*, told me. "If it is, I'll recognize it and put it in the paper."

PRESENTING YOURSELF ON PAPER OR BY E-MAIL

During my years at various departments in *The Washington Post* newsroom, I opened thousands of letters with manuscripts. A remarkable number of the letters announced that the story attached is the "greatest piece of writing you'll ever read," "a perfect solution to the nation's problems," or that the article is "exactly right for your publication." Confidence is a useful quality, but those types of statements are silly. No need to explain why your article works; editors will read a few paragraphs and know right away whether the story is right for their newspaper, magazine, Web site, or radio station.

Correct business manners in e-mail and other communications are noticed. Braggadocio and extreme informality may adversely affect an editor's reaction to your e-mail or letter. Stick-on notes, index cards, and scribbled lines on scrap paper are not query letters. Sending photographs of yourself, brochures describing your achievements in another field, letters of endorsement from former employers, and other material unrelated to the manuscript you are selling does not enhance your professional image as a writer.

Presentation is important. The successful query e-mail is well written and brief. Format an e-mail query just like a business letter with your contact information, date, and a correct business closing. Though e-mail encourages informality, your first communication with an editor should be straightforward, clear and correct. If you are sending the query in the mail, use plain white or ivory paper. Forget about arty notepaper or greeting cards. Bright colored paper or fancy letterhead will not compensate for bad writing.

What impression does an editor get from informal e-mails with misspellings, no contact information, or lax sentence structure? Unless you've met the editor, addressing a stranger by first name could be considered presumptuous. Always include contact information in the communication. Depending on "reply" functions for e-mail isn't a secure or professional way to establish long-term contact. Include your full contact information in all queries sent by e-mail and regular mail. If editors want to call you, will they be able to reach you?

Check spelling and grammar. Computer spell checking functions do the job, up to a point. You still need to review the spelling of proper names and place names, as well as read the letter once again before sending just in case grammatical errors were retained in the piece after revision. Computer spell checking functions routinely make errors—passing over correctly spelled words that don't belong in the text. Are you absolutely certain you have the correct spelling of the editor's name and the current editor?

Use the established business correspondence format. If you are unsure of how a business letter is constructed, consult business letter templates online or in a reference book. Briefly, this is the format: Put your entire return address in the upper right hand corner, if you aren't using printed letterhead, which isn't necessary and doesn't really impress anyone. Type your phone numbers with area codes just under the return address and include your e-mail address and Web site information if you have one. The inside address goes on the left side of the letter and includes the name of the editor, the name of the publication, and address. Under the inside address, type the salutation such as Dear Mr. or Ms. (name). The body of the letter follows. On the right-hand side or flush left, type the complimentary close, such as Sincerely, or Cordially, leave a few blank lines for your signature, and type your name underneath. Don't forget to sign the letter.

Would you believe that freelance writers send queries by e-mail and fax without a return address or even a telephone number? I've seen letters arrive by mail without the writer's signature, and e-mail queries with no surname. If you are sending out multiple queries, and you use a mail merge function of a word processing program, read each letter over before mailing. What message does it send when a letter is properly addressed on the envelope but the text of the letter is directed to another publication? Then there was the hapless writer who left the last rejection letter paper clipped to his manuscript. Imagine the chagrin when he opens the envelope to find two rejection slips—ours and the one from the last magazine he sent the article to.

These kinds of errors signal that the freelancer is sending out simultaneous queries or submissions, which is fine if that information is stated in the letter or e-mail. When a query e-mail or letter has a grammatical or spelling error in the first line, do you think an editor reads further? Mistakes like these show carelessness.

Other errors freelancers make in their query and cover letters include: offering to change the article before the editor has even read it (the writer lacks self-confidence); suggesting the editor can revise the article (of course they will; that's what editors do!); asking for a job and pitching story ideas in same letter (don't confuse the issue; seduce an editor with your ideas before asking for a job or a regular column); over-explaining expertise and credentials (the writing should stand on its own); sending a draft of an article and offering to fix it if the editor is interested (take pride in your work; send out finished work); presenting manuscripts or story ideas that are similar to what the magazine or paper printed recently (once a travel topic has been addressed in its pages, publications usually wait several years before featuring the same idea or place again); sending a marked-up copy or an improperly saved file that the editor can't open or read because of single-space formatting, an odd font (Times New Roman, Courier or Arial are standard), or insufficient margins (editors don't open strange computer files or look at manuscripts that are difficult to read).

Some writers enclose a list of all the magazines and newspapers where they have been previously published, but a list doesn't tell an editor how you write nor the length or substance of the stories. Better than a list of publications are samples of your published work or links to URLs where your work appears on the Internet. Present them with pride and style. Rather than sending original copies, send clear photocopies of previously published work. Or scan the articles and include as e-mail attachments with the query, explaining that the attachments are samples of your prior work. This presumes, of course, that the editor invites e-mail queries and will accept an e-mail with an attachment. Always include the publication name and dateline with the scanned or photocopied article. If your story was on the front page of a section, fit the masthead into your photocopy by using reduction keys on the copier or scanner. Don't reduce the print so it becomes too small to read.

Every editor I've talked to or worked with has told me they prefer to read print materials because they already spend far too much time in front of a computer. Even in this totally digital age, I suggest that on the first approach writers send easy-to-read copies, stapling the pages of each story together and paper clipping them all with a cover letter and using the mail or an express delivery service. After you've established a working relationship with an editor, you can easily send file attachments by e-mail. The editor will read the article during the editing process, on screen. It's really only in the beginning, when an editor needs to focus on the writing and story line, learning your writing style, that print copies are preferred.

So, how do you ensure your e-mail query or the cover letter with a manuscript is actually read? Be brief. Use the crisp lead from your finished story as the opening in your letter. Offer the completed story to the editor, state how long the article is and whether you have photos. If you've already had contact with the editor, mention that you'd previously run the idea past the editor, who had expressed interest.

PREPARING THE MANUSCRIPT FOR SUBMISSION

For newspapers, you'll probably be presenting the travel article as a complete package ready for an editor to buy and print. Is the manuscript proofread? Is the format a standard typeface in twelve-point pica with double-spacing and wide margins? If you've secured permission to send the story by e-mail, send in a rich text format or document file—whatever the editor has requested. Many editors prefer to receive the completed story in hard copy from writers they don't know. In that case, send the manuscript unfolded in a large envelope to travel editors at as many newspapers as you care to approach in noncompeting circulation areas. Include a self-addressed stamped envelope for response. Before sending prints or slides by mail, ask if that is the preferred format. Many publications prefer digital image files. Review chapter seven on issues concerning images.

Include your name, street address, telephone numbers, and e-mail with the manuscript. Some publications prefer a completed invoice with Social Security number to facilitate payment. If you are concerned about sharing this information, bear in mind that if you want to be paid, you'll have to provide a Social Security number at some point. Discuss the payment process with the editor when the article is accepted. Some freelance writers include contact and payment information on the first page of the manuscript, just in case the e-mail or letter is separated from the manuscript.

Always number pages; refrain from exotic formatting such as boldface or excessive italics and quotes. Publications with in-house software programs could convert formatting codes into some entirely different symbol. Avoid problems by using consistent, simple fonts. Let the copyeditors insert bold or italic font and other distinguishing marks.

Some writers type their name and a word describing the story (the slug) in the top right-hand corner of each manuscript page. For example, if I were to send out a story about wood carving in Bali, I would write "O'Neil/BaliWood" at the top, right side.

The travel story length that is most saleable falls in the 800- to 1,200-word range. Even if writers guidelines state that articles of 1,000 words are acceptable, many publications prefer shorter material. Learn how to write tightly and keep articles in the 900-word range. Each publication has its own guidelines about word length, and a travel writer who knows an editor's preferred story length demonstrates research ability and an understanding of the editorial process. Only a certain number of column inches of each page are devoted to text, photos, headlines, and other filler.

The rest is earmarked for advertising, usually established well in advance. That is one reason why editors are confined to predetermined story lengths. The other is that today's average reader has a low tolerance for lengthy articles, no matter how fine the writing. Internet publications prefer even shorter stories; 400 words are standard, which is a squib, not really an article. If you can't show your story briefly, match your garrulous style to a publication that uses longer articles.

To make your own estimate of standard word length, you could scan the document into a Word document file and then use the word count feature in the tools menu. If you don't have a scanner, count the number of words in one inch of a column of printed text in the body of the article. Then measure the number of inches of columns that are the same width throughout the article. Each publication has its own design signature, which may mean larger or smaller typefaces and nonstandard column widths. Often, the opening page of a magazine story will have very large type for the first few words, or the words may string across the whole page. Count these words individually, then add to the word estimate derived from measured text. Don't include photographs, headlines or large-typeface quotes (pull quotes) or other filler material when counting total word length. Multiply the number of words in one inch by the full length to get the approximate number of words in the piece.

When you start researching markets for stories you've written, confirm your estimate of preferred story length with someone on the editorial staff by saying something like, "Seems to me most of the travel articles are 900 words. Do you ever accept destination stories at the 1,400-word length? Do you have flexibility with length?" While discussing the details of editorial needs, always establish whether the sidebar (a box or column of travel information on costs, addresses, and other dry information that interrupts narrative flow) is part of the total word count or extra. Occasionally, a sidebar can be sold separately to accompany other related articles, so if your piece is turned down, offer the sidebar, if substantial, on its own.

Recheck the article for grammatical errors or misspelled words. Proofread, spell check, and fact check your manuscript. Are the numbers transposed? Software spell check programs do not always discriminate in matters of grammar. If you are weak in antonyms and homonyms, make it a point to read your story again after using the spell check function. Words may be spelled perfectly but used incorrectly. Proofread manuscripts and cover letters twice.

Small magazines and newspapers welcome a finished story with photos. Keep your stories short and focus on topics that showcase the region. Sniff out the hard-to-find historical landmarks, the factories that offer tours, the special inns, or the unusual food festivals.

SIMULTANEOUS SUBMISSIONS

Submitting your travel story to several editors at once is acceptable as long as the circulation areas of the publications don't overlap. Submit the same story to a paper in different urban areas, and tailor flight information to each location. On the manuscript, or in the e-mail or cover letter, include this information: "This is a multiple submission, to noncompeting circulation zones." The cover letter or e-mail for this mass-marketing effort should be short and to the point. Avoid cute openings like "hi" or "good morning." Put the story lead in the paragraph of the letter to pique the editor's interest. Add a few words about the subject of the travel article and mention any hook for that particular publication, any special connection to that paper's readership.

If you are mass-marketing the article (also called self-syndication), send the articles to several newspapers at a time. If you receive a rejection letter, read it carefully. Sometimes publications change editorial needs and what was rejected today may be used at a later date. Take note when the publication's form letter indicates they aren't considering any freelance material. You'll want to update your records and strike that publication from your mailing list.

After an article has been published you usually have the right to resell the work to other markets if the reprint rights revert to you. Before every sale, clarify what rights the publication is buying. First rights means the publication "rents" the story for the duration of the publication date—twenty-four hours for a newspaper, a week for a weekly, and so on. Some publications that pay grand fees might be purchasing the rights for six months. You'll only know what rights you are selling if you ask the editor or have a contract or letter of agreement to study.

Look carefully for clauses governing electronic rights, digital rights, worldwide rights, or republication in other media. If digital rights are included in the first sale, you won't be able to resell the story to a Web publication, for example. Think carefully before agreeing to any contract, verbal or written, that specifies "all rights." For that, you should receive a handsome fee.

Before reselling a story that has been published, clarify what rights the first publication purchased and keep notes on what rights you sell to each subsequent publication. Generally, monthly magazines reassign the rights to the writer a few months after publication. If you have a contract, read it. If not, and you are in doubt about who holds the copyright, check with the publication that bought the story first. Chances are that you own the rights and can market the story again and again. Recycling and reselling travel articles is discussed more fully in chapter nine.

COMMUNICATING WITH EDITORS

As stated elsewhere in this chapter, I do not advise contacting travel editors by phone—I would fear for my kneecaps if any editor discovered that I urged beginners and novices to make queries by phone. But it's only natural for confident, experienced writers to seek immediate answers. I know there will be readers of this book who consider themselves ready to approach editors directly, people who overestimate their abilities and relish the personal connection of a phone call over the slower pace of a query letter. If you must call to make a query, I suggest sending an e-mail and asking when you could call.

Believe it or not, editors are human. They are crankiest around deadline and in the late afternoon when they'd rather be heading home. Find out what days are busiest and whether a call is even an option. Many editors just don't have the time to take phone calls from writers. If you are an established writer with dozens of publishing credits in national magazines and big-city newspapers (Chicago, Toronto, Los Angeles, Seattle, Houston, London, Miami, etc.), go ahead and call. If you are a newcomer and have a few published clips from local publications, write a query by letter or e-mail or send the complete story by regular mail. Of course anyone can try and contact an editor by phone, but be warned that editors don't like interruptions. The phone call query may even harm your chances for acceptance. Editors like to review written queries and proposals so they can evaluate writing skill. If you are willing to risk a call, target your marketing calls to editors likely to be interested in your work. Don't ruin your budding travel writing career by intruding on a busy editor at a publication far beyond your experience level.

Christopher J. Williams, a board member of the International Food, Wine & Travel Writers Association who has freelanced from overseas, advises, "At the beginning of your travel writing career, search for smaller or unusual publications to sell to. The country—and the world—is full of regional newspaper travel sections and smaller magazines. Everyone submits to *Condé Nast* and *National Geographic Traveler* magazines and usually gets rejected. Sell to the small places and get yourself published before you approach *The New York Times*. Both your ego and the editors will appreciate it."

If you are cold-calling a small publication, find out the name of the assignment editor for the type of article you are proposing. Before you launch into your pitch, ask if the editor has a minute for you to present a story idea, and a few minutes is all you can expect. Brevity will help your case. You've written out the story idea already and have selling points to repeat if the conversation evolves. If the editor is busy, ask if you may call at another time. Don't call on deadline. I can't think of any editor who would accept a call from a freelancer during deadline time. So find out beforehand when the crunch comes at the publication you are contacting. Obviously, a weekly travel section is under tighter time constraints than a bimonthly nature magazine. First thing Monday morning or the last hour of Friday night doesn't make much sense either. Time your calls for hours when people are relaxed—late morning or early afternoon.

Although you are just one of hundreds or thousands of freelancers who approach a given publication in a year, there are two kinds of freelancers who are remembered vividly by editors—the professionals and the pests. You can be a novice and still demonstrate professional qualities by your neutral but friendly language and voice tone, your considerate attitude, and your concise presentation. Your awareness of editorial needs shows that you've done your research. Listen to what the editor says and ask specific questions about editorial deadlines and time constraints. The pest, on the other hand, questions an editor's judgment, boasts, is coy about story ideas because the editor might "steal them," exaggerates past experience, and rambles. The pest refuses to believe that the editor has actually rejected the idea. Then calls back again and again.

In constructing the points for the query conversation, for example, if I'm pitching a travel story about biking in Florida, I might cite recent statistics about bike tourism, and I'll have the names of a few restaurants, hotels, and attractions near long-distance bikeways. If there is a centennial date for the invention of the bicycle or the inauguration of a Florida bike trail, I'll have it ready. In short, my phone pitch will be swift because I have the important sales information ready. The research will be useful anyway for the article.

If the editor isn't interested but seems willing to talk for a minute, turn the call into an informational interview. Ask for direction: What does the editor need? Find out what subjects are submitted too often, what they have on file. Ask if you may send story ideas in the future. Don't get flustered and fold your cards just because your first idea met rejection. You've met your goal by getting an editor or an assistant on the phone. You'll reap information that will be useful in future queries.

Remember, each time you talk to someone inside the publishing industry, you gain experience, confidence, and information. Before you call any editorial office, make a realistic assessment of your level of achievement, and be prepared to present your background and ideas succinctly. You'll be asked which publications you've written for. You may be asked for specific editor's names, as a reference.

Keep in mind that the publication's budget year plays a role in freelance assignments. Editors rarely have money left in their freelance budget at the end of the year. But they might be interested in assigning articles early in the following budget year. Be prepared to let your story sit on an editor's desk or hard drive until money becomes available and the story can run.

Consult the editorial calendar that you've requested from the publications you plan to write for. Holiday and seasonal pieces are lined up well in advance. Winter destinations are sold in late summer and fall. Approach newspaper editors about summer destinations in late winter and early spring. Get a jump on other writers by pitching your travel story ideas early, or send the completed manuscript.

WORKING THROUGH REJECTION

One benefit of working on assignment with a contract is the kill fee. If your piece is completed according to contract but ultimately doesn't run, you could receive a kill fee, which is a percentage of the total contract amount. Most freelance assignments are on spec, though, which means kill fees are fairly rare. Whether you get a kill fee or not, you still have to think about marketing the story elsewhere. One thing to remember about rejection—it gets easier as your experience grows. What might feel devastating the first few times eventually won't affect you at all.

How a writer reacts to manuscript rejection ranges from remaining calm (it didn't sell here, so it can sell elsewhere) to a competitive stance (now I'll have to try harder) to weakened self-esteem (must be something wrong with me or my work). Try not to take manuscript rejection personally; every writer has had a manuscript turned down.

If you've received several rejections for a manuscript you considered a sure sale, it may be time for a serious reevaluation. Let rejection of your manuscript send you into editor mode. Reread your piece and ask yourself if the writing is fresh and enticing. If comments were noted on the manuscript or in the rejection letter, heed them. Have a friend or colleague read the piece and offer a critique. Consider joining a writers workshop and work on the piece in a group setting. Consider setting the manuscript aside for a while and work on something else with a clear mind. You'll return to the rejected piece later and be able to breathe new energy into the prose, or rework the idea into a different angle.

An article may be rejected for myriad reasons. Reasons that may be related to the writing, or to the publication's editorial plans, or the story focus. There may be mitigating factors that neither the editor nor the writer knew when the idea was originally proposed.

If the writing itself is the problem, perhaps the tone was off. Too cute, too snide, too scholarly, full of insider's jargon, or just plain ordinary. The diction and syntax might not meet editorial standards. The vocabulary may have been too common or too pompous or affected. The length could have been a factor. There are so many reasons why an article doesn't meet the editorial mark, and though some stories can be reworked, usually editors decide not to put in the effort.

Assuming you researched the market and were confident that the publication showed interest in the subject matter, and even assuming that an editor had given you the go-ahead to write the piece on spec, articles still may not be accepted. Perhaps the piece read too much like an article already in the works at that publication or was similar to a story that recently appeared in its pages. Perhaps the publication changed its editorial image or redesigned its format, changing story lengths and putting an emphasis on images. Maybe there were staff changes. Finally, though you may not like to admit it, maybe the writing just didn't make the grade.

If you didn't research the market and just sent the piece out blindly, it's very possible that your piece fell outside the scope of the publication. Market research is never a waste of time.

Working through rejection means staying focused on your goals. You still have to find a publisher for your article. Use *Writer's Market*; consult the marketing list that you've drawn up and seek new publications. Cast your marketing net a little wider.

Getting past rejection should also propel you to the manuscript. Comb the piece for a fresh slant that may make it attractive to another publication. Check your prose for zing. Does your voice shine through the text? Will the reader learn something, be surprised, have an emotional response? The worst thing a rejection letter can do is stop you in your tracks. Don't quit writing and don't lose momentum. Get together with a writer friend and have an editorial jam session. Critiques can be done by e-mail or in person. Sometimes we writers are too close to the piece and can't see stylistic problems or content omissions.

Here's a handy motivator to keep on the marketing path. During the market research phase, create a spreadsheet or write down on an index card the dozen or so places you plan to send your piece. Pre-address mailing labels, if you are so inclined. Note the date when you send out the story to the first choice, second, and so on. In the spreadsheet, note dates when stories are purchased or returned and any comments from editors. If you are meticulous about expenses, record postage and photocopy charges related to each submission. When the manuscript comes back (IF it is returned) note the date and send it back out at once, bearing in mind seasonal needs. If you use the mail rather than e-mail for submissions, ensure each manuscript looks fresh. By keeping the article in circulation you maximize success and keep yourself motivated. Eventually, the acceptance date for each article will occur with a minimum number of submissions. Soon the first place you send the article will accept it!

MARKET RESEARCH AND TRAVEL TRENDS

Before selling a product, the salesperson has to know what it is. Same theory applies to marketing travel stories. Decide which category the travel article is before attempting to identify the markets to tackle. See chapter one on types of travel articles for ideas. Sometimes a story fits more than one type of travel piece—weekend escape and outdoor adventure, holiday peg and family outing.

Clarify for yourself what makes the article unique. Check online or in electronic databases or the print guide to periodical literature to see what other publications have printed similar stories, and when. Identify the particular slant or hook that makes your article timely. Perhaps a recent news event relates to your article. For example, early in 2005, archeologists in Mexico City announced the discovery of the remains of ten people, one dating back to 1,300 B.C.E., indicating pre-Hispanic cultures lived in the area. An enterprising travel writer would use that discovery reported by the Associated Press as a news hook to sell a travel article about exploring the ruins in and around Mexico City.

Next, line up all the publications you plan to contact. And within each magazine or newspaper, target which editor would be interested in your article. Many newspapers and magazines have several sections dealing with lifestyle and travel. I've seen travel articles in design, food, financial, and weekend entertainment sections. Look beyond the travel sections of newspapers and explore publications dedicated to subjects other than travel.

During your online and library research, you may read about a publication that seems appropriate to contact. Try to locate an online archive for the publication, but if you can't find it online or at a newsstand, you should contact the publication and ask for a sample copy. Some publications offer free samples; others charge a nominal fee for the magazine plus postage and handling. A friend or colleague may alert you to a publication, but before sending a query or the finished story, verify that it is in print. Countless publications fold, and information online or in various publications' directories may be stale. Check online resources first, since that's easy, and also consult *Writer's Market* or other reference guide to magazines and newspapers for address information for hard-to-find publications. If available, obtain the publication's address, phone number, Web site address, and e-mail of a current editor.

Broaden your search for potential markets. While the annual *Writer's Market* is useful, every other freelancer is using it. I troll for information about new publications online and in the annual directories to magazines and newsletters published by firms such as R.R. Bowker or Gale. You can buy a CD of these directories or an online subscription to their database online, if you're willing to pay the rather high fees ($1,630 for a CD of the *Gale Directory of Publications and Broadcast Media*, for example). I consult these directories in the public library where there's no charge.

These massive multivolume directories are standard tools in the reference section of any public or university library. Look under the heading of *Travel & Tourism* to see what kind of publications are listed. Chances are you've never seen these publications on the local newsstand. Some are trade publications, others are limited circulation or promotional. Look upon all of them as potential markets, especially for a writer looking to enter the travel writing business. Other headings to check include *Transportation, Leisure, Recreation, Hobby*, etc. Just paging through these directories should give you ideas about selling various travel pieces. Refer to the appendix of this book for more information on periodical directories.

NICHE MARKETING

Not a cigar smoker? Then you might not know about *Cigar* magazine, a thriving glossy magazine with apparently lush advertising contracts and thus many pages of editorial content to fill. There are only so many column inches an editor can dedicate to photos and stats about cigars, leaving you opportunities to sell him features about the history of tobacco, tobacco farms, cigar factories, tobacco growers, and cigar-shopping venues.

Travel newsletters are a potential market. Many are completely written and edited by one or two people whose names are on the masthead. However, newsletter publisher-editors have many rainmaking duties, looking for advertisers or promotional deals, and they may well need freelance editorial assistance. With the thousands of specialty newsletters available—travel, hobby and sport, regional groups, ethnic heritage associations, arts and languages—there are many possibilities for selling travel-related articles.

Experienced researchers know the standardized subject headings, so they can look up these topics in any reference volume. Most libraries use Library of Congress subject headings. During your market research phase, you'll consult a variety of directories in search of publications to buy your work. And you'll be searching online using popular search engines. Look beyond the categories of "travel" and "hospitality industry." Note subject headings for further reference—for example, if "transportation" doesn't yield any potential magazines for your travel articles, try "transport" or "transit systems." If you locate a good travel book, check to see what subject headings are listed on the copyright page. Those same headings might be useful in online, database, or directory searches locating categories of magazines or other books related to the travel industry.

Follow trends in leisure travel by talking to other travelers, travel agents, guides, and your sources at the tourist boards. What attractions are people visiting? Is regional weekend travel or educational travel increasing? Study the advertisements in newspaper travel sections. Notice what package tours are featured. Stay abreast of business trends in the tourism and hospitality industry. If three no-frills airlines are offering discount fares from Chicago to Florida, wouldn't that tell you that a travel article about budget travel in Florida would be on top of a trend? When *The Wall Street Journal* reports that a major auto rental company is inaugurating a super-luxury car class, there just might be a travel story in the making.

Travel trends also relate to news. After a hurricane has demolished the coastline of a Caribbean island, it's hardly likely that an editor will seek a travel story featuring that place. Tourism has probably fallen sharply. When a year or two has passed, and the island has rebuilt its hotels to prepare for tourist visits, think about selling a story on the rebirth of tourism.

WHAT DO EDITORS WANT?

This applies to magazine articles and book proposals. In your query, show them why your story is different. Give the editor a reason to say yes. The best way to do that is to show them the unique qualities of the story idea, why it appeals to a certain demographic, and why you're the only person to write the story.

- Construct your ideas in a letter that reads with zip.
- Use vigorous language that shows personal enthusiasm.
- Make the writing as clever as you possibly can.
- Demonstrate you've done some research on the topic.
- Entice the editor to agree that she must read the story.
- Show your knowledge of the market and the audience.
- Advance the concept in brilliant, zesty language.

Bob Jenkins, travel editor at the *St. Petersburg Times*, advises, "Find a day job. Everyone I talk to, both among my newspaper colleagues and among the freelancers I use with some regularity, says the markets are drying up, fees barely meeting inflation, publishers demanding universal rights. An option many of the clever ones have turned to is selling to the niche publications, such as magazines marketed just to doctors and dentists or selling to Web publications."

While that sounds grim, the travel industry is cyclical, and in 2010 travel writers may be enjoying lush times. Meanwhile, prudent freelance travel writers diversify, researching special interest, food, outdoors, family, and other lifestyle publications, as well as niche areas such as business newsletters, customer magazines for corporations and service organizations, and non-U.S.-based publications for opportunities.

Even controversial topics can be used for travel articles. We all know about war, terrorism, transportation strikes, mass illness on cruise ships, exceedingly bad weather—these events are continuing problems. Writers need to keep the "bad news" in mind when they construct story ideas, but don't shy away from a region or topic because you think editors only publish stories that encourage people to travel. It's how you slant your idea about the controversial topics that will make it appeal to an editor.

Rosemary Brown has edited magazines for overseas development and environmental nongovernmental organizations in America and the United Kingdom. A freelance travel writer, she is currently a journalist/editor for the Rainforest Foundation in London, England. "Writing for publications connected to not-for-profit or nongovernmental organizations (NGOs) can offer a win-win opportunity. Your travels can be enhanced by unique experiences and insights in the field, and you'll be writing about causes close to you heart. You'll need that reward because the fees will be modest," says Brown.

Groups dealing with global issues like Save the Children, World Wide Fund for Nature, and the International Committee of the Red Cross fund overseas projects and publish regularly. They could be potential markets for globetrotters adept at grasping and communicating global complexities in the nonprofit world. "Nongovernmental organizations use their publications to communicate their mission, objectives, and successes to their donors, supporters, and policy makers," says Brown. "Their publications aim to raise awareness of the issues they are tackling—whether it's poverty, injustice, human rights, etc.—and to raise funds to support their work. Find out where their projects are located and see if they match up with any of your travel itineraries. Query the appropriate editor with your clips, noting that you have plans to be in the region." The editorial lineup for the publication and the editor's confidence in your ability to communicate the NGO's "messages" will determine the reply.

Tom Swick, travel editor of the *Sun-Sentinel*, says, "My advice to freelancers is to read a publication before sending it something—now easily done online—to see what kind of writing it publishes. I'm always getting submissions of consumer articles when I buy mostly armchair stories."

Sean Markey, an editor at *National Geographic News* online, offers these tips to travel writers:

- Send good clips. Show me you can write, and you've got my interest. Even if I don't want the story you sent on spec, I might be interested in you. I look at clips first and résumés second. Don't be shy about sending samples from the *Sticksville Daily Bugle*. Most of us started out writing for the little guys, too.

- Know your audience. Who are you pitching? A magazine? A newspaper? A Web site? What's their average word length? Do they publish narrative, or more just-the-facts-ma'am journalism? Editors know what they're looking for. It helps if you do, too. If you're really serious, become a serious reader of the publication you hope to crack into. Study its style and story selection.

- Don't make me work. Remember, editors are busy people, just like you. Sending your clips and résumé via e-mail? Cut and paste them into the body of your message. That way I can scroll down and read them straight away. Sure, you can attach PDF or Word versions, too. But then you're assuming I have the time to click, drag, and open them. Maybe I don't.

- Don't make me gamble. Synthesize tips one through three, and send me clips and story pitches that fit the style, subject matter, and word length of the articles I publish. It helps take the guesswork out of that most basic question we editors ask: Is the writer up to the job?

- Stay positive. If it were easy, everybody would be a travel writer. Just keep writing and pitching. Things will gel sooner or later. Whatever you do, don't wait for someone else's permission to write. Start now, and you'll give yourself the greatest gift of all.

Mary Gallagher, who edits and produces the Web travel site GallaghersTravels.com, as well as television and radio travel programs, works with thirty contributing journalists. In a travel writing discussion on Travelwriters.com she wrote: "My complaints are: not enough photos, poor writing, not running spell check, not enough or no sources, using the same word over twice in every paragraph. Read your story aloud a few times—is it interesting? Different?"

Bob Jenkins, travel editor at the *St. Petersburg Times*, told me he receives manuscripts from beginners. "And from lots of writers who probably don't think they are beginners but no one has taken them aside and told them they need help. Overwhelmingly, there's too much first-person writing of commonplace experience," says Jenkins. The writer should compress the narrative to pass along information and save individual perspective for personal experiences that fit in the travel narrative, he adds.

Another weakness Jenkins sees in freelance manuscripts is "gushy writing—'Oh what a beautiful sunset.' As William Zinsser says, 'If you write correctly you won't need adjectives. The right word will be there.' Writers tend to rave on and on about the buildings and the mountains, but I think we need to focus on the people."

Jenkins decides how much to pay based on how much work he has to put into the piece. "We don't have readers' time for long, maybe thirty minutes, and there are a couple of hundred headlines in a daily paper, so your writing beneath the headline better be pretty good."

PROTECTING YOUR IDEAS

Over the years, I've spoken with many freelance writers who are ready to market their story ideas. When I ask a writer to tell me more, to evaluate whether it is appropriate for a newspaper or a magazine, or which section might be interested in the query, occasionally a writer will demur, suggesting that the editor might use the idea without crediting the originator. Some aspiring writers even go so far to say, oh, someone there might steal my idea. Do they really think a publication with staff writers and experienced editors might be so short of ideas that they have to steal from freelancers? Paranoia like this is nonsense. If you can't express the idea, how can an editor respond? Professional editors and staff writers generate more than enough ideas to keep everybody busy. They aren't in business to steal from freelancers.

There are times when several people come up with the same idea—the world is full of coincidence. Publications run stories that resemble material that freelancers have submitted months before. Deciding that the idea was "stolen" based on such scanty information is risky. Magazines routinely assign stories many months in advance. Your freelance submission or e-mail query may cross the editor's desk after the story was assigned to someone else but before the finished manuscript sees print. To you it looks like your idea was taken and assigned to someone else; if you complain to an editor, you could look like a paranoid neophyte who doesn't have a clue about lead times. But if you are certain that a publication used your ideas, images, or written material improperly, strive to negotiate a reasonable resolution. In chapter nine, there is more information on how to resolve difficult editorial situations without animosity.

HOW TO ENTER THE GUIDEBOOK MARKET

Writing a guidebook takes more time and effort than travel articles. You could consider the time commitment for a guidebook like producing thirty to fifty travel articles. The rewards are longer life for your work and, perhaps, a wider audience. If the guidebook endures through several editions, you might think the royalties will build your freelance income. Yet guidebook writers tell me that they routinely sign contracts for flat fees with no royalties involved. Guidebook writing will not make you rich or famous. The key to a successful travel guidebook is discovering a particular special interest niche that you can fill.

Whether you plan to write a regional guidebook about Southern country inns that serve tea or beach resorts that accommodate pets, the first step in your project is to establish that your book is needed. Take the time to survey the appropriate categories in the library card catalog (Travel, Tourism, Pets, Recreation, etc.) and in bookstores. Check the latest edition of *Books in Print*, available in any library reference section or on the Internet for a fee. Are there fifty guidebooks to the region you plan to write about? None that explores your special topic on country inns that serve tea? What other special topics do the existing Southern states guidebooks address? For example, do you see titles like: *Southern States for Wheelchair Users, Free Museums in Memphis, Vegetarian Restaurants East of the Mississippi*? If your topic is already overdone, use the *Books in Print* listing for possible ideas to restructure the topic.

Decide whether your guidebook concept has been done already. If not, you know it's at least worth your time to pursue the topic to the book proposal stage. Of course, there may well be books in the works that resemble your proposed idea. But if there is one book, two on the same topic will find an audience as long as they are promoted effectively. Sometimes publishers follow each other's lead; if one publishing house commissions a book on a certain topic, another will at least consider a similar topic more seriously. As the idea forms, take the time to write every aspect of the travel guidebook that is floating around in your mind. Or tape record your thoughts and transcribe them. Remember that nothing will happen until your ideas are on paper and organized in a way that can be understood by others. That's the book proposal writing process.

Arrange the material in a logical sequence. Construct an outline—including a table of contents, an orientation or overview, specifics about the place, expansion on the specifics that develop the topic, other aspects of the topic, closure. Rearrange the text you've written thus far so it is coherent within the structure of a beginning, middle, and end. The draft outline should be three to five pages double-spaced. If you have more material than that, extract the essence to write the outline and save the explanations by grouping related thoughts under headings so you can go back and use or reorganize as needed.

Next, write a statement of purpose. Why is the book needed? Who is the audience? Why should you write it? What special knowledge or experience qualifies you to write the guidebook? Where does the book fit in the travel guidebook arena? When you are satisfied that you have a coherent outline, you'll need to write a marketing plan. Go back online or to the library and research prospective travel book publishers. Who will publish this book? What publishing houses are handling travel guidebooks, especially in the region? Why would each be interested (or not) in this guidebook? Who will buy the book and why? Where could it be sold? What is the competition? How is your project different (photos, first-person stories, historical timelines, illustrations) from similar books? Are there multiple markets? For example, a guidebook to Southern country inns that serve tea may have several potential audiences—food lovers, regional travelers, Anglophiles.

Contact the editors you have targeted through market research. Ask if they would like to see the proposal. Find out what materials the editor or editorial board needs to review in addition to a proposal. Depending on the publisher, you could be asked to send one or more copies of a résumé, list of prior publications, samples of your work, a completed chapter or two for the proposed book, a table of contents, a book outline, and other materials. Package the book proposal neatly, typed, double-spaced with wide margins. Send to one publisher at a time. If you haven't received a response within a month, inquire about the status of your book proposal. Perhaps the first publisher will make a commitment to your project and offer a contract. Perhaps not. Continue sending the proposal package to publishers that you have identified as potentially interested in this travel guidebook topic.

Quite often, one person does not write series guidebooks. Editors commission several writers to handle different aspects of a place and an in-house or contract editor completes the project to give it a unified tone. Helpful books about travel endure—how to pack, travel with children or pets, travel options for the visually impaired, shopping for antiques, turn your travel into an import–export business, etc.

Guidebooks age rapidly. Every year or so, a publisher needs a new edition. Generally, the freelance team that produced the last edition will be contracted again. However, if you have developed a travel specialty and notice that the guidebook series omits that special aspect of travel, approach the series editor and discuss the possibility of contributing to the next edition of a particular guidebook about a place you know well. For example, a city guidebook series for a general audience might need information on activities for children in each guide. Contact the publisher and ask the series editor if they would consider adding a chapter on travel with children to the whole guidebook series, or to just one specific guidebook on a trial basis. Explain that you've developed a professional specialty about travel with children, have the published articles to back up your claims and furthermore, you know the specifics of this location. Ask if the editor would consider your proposal. If the idea works in one guidebook, chances are the series editor will expand the program. Revisit guidebook publishers' Web sites; often publishers recruit travel writers for specific upcoming projects.

Margaret and Allison Engel, twins and writing partners, wrote *Food Finds*, a mail-order and visitors guide to America's best local foods, published by HarperCollins. "We had no contacts with the New York publishing world when we started," says Margaret Engel. "We just wrote what we thought was a killer two-page letter and spent a lot of time making it appealing and attractive. We looked at the food and travel books on the shelves in bookstores and picked out the ones we liked, about five publishers. We called them up and got the food and travel editors' names."

The Engels mentioned two or three other similar books. They pointed out what was different. "Size up the competition, show them why it would sell. Give them a reason to say yes to your book," advises Margaret. "The best way to do that is to show them the market, the audience and why people would logically pay fifteen or twenty dollars for this book. Plus, put it in a letter that has a lot of zip and zing in the language. We made it as clever as we possibly could." Of the five proposal letters the Engels sent, three publishers responded immediately. "We never had to get an agent until we got into serious negotiations." Margaret points out that the proposal letter could be sent to agents, one at a time, who would then turn around and use the proposal to approach publishers on behalf of the writers.

With several food and travel books to her credit, including a nationwide travel guide to attractions for baseball lovers written with Bruce Adams, Margaret has tips to share about writing guidebooks. "I wish I could have known you can ask publishers for money for photographs, that it can be separate from your advance. We ended up paying out of pocket and it was expensive. I wish I would have understood that you don't make money on the sale of the books, that it comes from the advance. Writers have to understand that you don't make money. You have to do it because you want to do it anyway.

"After you publish, writers go into depression when they see how the marketplace treats published works. Just getting it done is an achievement. Publishers are overworked and underpaid. Editors do not have time to be marketers. The publicity departments in publishing houses are so underfunded and understaffed that the most obvious steps are never taken," says Engel. She recommends hiring a private company to do the publicity. "Go to the heartland and get a small industrious company."

Jamie Rosen, who worked on the *Let's Go* guidebooks published by Harvard University, thinks writing travel guides is easier than travel articles. "Guidebooks are just tons of research. Lots of people traveling probably say to themselves, gee, I could do better myself. It helps if you are as clueless as the person who will be using the book. People who speak the language and know the culture might breeze past situations that people reading the guidebook might need to be led through. If you are writing a travel guide about Germany for people who don't know German, it's not a handicap if you don't speak the language. For example, if you're looking for particular bus, you have to get explicit instructions, not just ask someone when you know the language."

On the mechanics of researching travel guides, Rosen advises, "At the time I worked as a *Let's Go* writer, I used notebooks and wrote things down. I've never had experience working with a laptop, but if you are spending time in cities, it might be easier. But if it gets stolen, there goes your book."

CHECKLIST FOR MARKETING

1. You can't write for it if you haven't read it. Go to the local library or newsstand and seek out the publications you are going to sell to. Read several issues.

2. No one starts at the top. Find your own level, work in it, then work up out of it.

3. Start with local newspapers and magazines, small publications, regional travel magazines, and publications with a small editorial staff. Write for your high school or college paper, the alumni magazine, a community newspaper. Use the experience to tackle more complex writing projects for broader publications.

4. Don't give your work away. If the publication doesn't offer a fee, ask for a subscription, free advertising, or printing services in exchange for your articles. No matter how small the honorarium or in-kind service, you'll feel better if you receive something for your work and you'll be respected for your professionalism.

exercises

EXERCISE 1: Write a short query e-mail or letter for the travel article you've been working on. Figure out a way to use the story lead in the first paragraph to attract attention.

EXERCISE 2: Write a phone script for one of the travel article ideas you created for the exercise in chapter one.

EXERCISE 3: Dream a little. Write three guidebook topics that you would enjoy researching and writing. Analyze why these books should be written. Could you test the merits of these topics by writing travel articles first? Where would you sell the travel articles if you decide to proceed on these ideas?

EXERCISE 4: Assess your personal goals. Write about what is important to you about travel writing—getting your thoughts on paper and writing a story, sharing the stories with friends, writing for a broad audience, the quality of the publication where the articles appear, the pay, a byline, where the publication positions your article, a wide readership, owning reprint rights and selling the article to many publications, or some other aspect of writing or publishing.

EXERCISE 5: Develop a marketing plan. For each of your finished travel articles, identify ten markets that are not travel magazines or travel sections in newspapers. Take your list of story ideas and under each, write the names of publications where the finished article would possibly fit.

EXERCISE 6: By now you've examined several publications and have identified likely markets for your story idea. You've read several issues—online and print. Some online versions of publications use different content than the print editions. You know what slants the editor favors and the demographic group that reads the publication. You know whether articles are in first (I, we), second (you), or third (a visitor, the traveler) person. You've determined length and are sure that the publication hasn't run a similar story within the past two years. Now, find three other places where that same story concept can be published, perhaps with a slightly different slant. The other journals or newspapers should be in different circulation areas to broaden your exposure. For example, what publications that are not specifically about travel would be interested in printing stories about:

- a visit to a 1910 carousel with restored painted wooden horses
- an article on finding kinfolks in Germany or Vietnam
- experiences during a two-week painting residency course in the North Carolina mountains
- a fishing and rafting tour to a remote Canadian outpost
- an incident in Vatican City when vagrant children steal a traveler's wallet and subsequent interactions with the local police

THE PROFESSIONAL
TRAVEL WRITER

A re you a travel writer? At a certain point, you'll feel like you are a professional travel writer and have the experience to back up the claim. You'll be past the point of trying to be a travel writer. How will you know?

Here are a few characteristics of a travel writer: passionate about travel; motivated; confident; friendly; curious; professional attitude; research ability; self-sufficient; organized; has foreign language skills; knowledge of geography, natural sciences, history, and cultures; writing ability; photographic skill; willingness to learn; humility; stable health; physical stamina; psychological Flexibility; emotional balance. Not every travel writer displays all these characteristics all the time, but most of us have some of them.

As you grow and improve—and in every activity, skill, or profession, if you keep working at it, you will improve—take the time to reassess your goals. "Developing your written voice and becoming a productive writer requires simply a commitment to exercise," says Jennifer Dargan, a freelance writer in Virginia. "The best way to improve is to write daily at some regular interval—even if only in short bursts. Just keep doing it," she recommends.

After a few years of freelance writing for print or Web sites, you may want to make a lateral move such as writing for radio or switching from travel editorial to travel advertising. You may decide to lead tour groups or lecture about your travels. Keep your own counsel, but don't be shy about self-promotion. Remember to slip away from those who steal your time talking about their fantastic trips and suggest you'd like to write about their experiences rather than your own—comments that are silly and insulting. Often, non-writers have ridiculous ideas about a travel writer's life—"If you travel so often you must be rich." I've heard social chatterers claim that "anybody can do travel writing; all you have to do is travel." Yet they've never set pen to paper or fingers to keyboard. I suggest saving your enthusiasm and energy for the written word and promoting your work. Yes, travel writing can be fun, but good writing rarely comes without effort, and rewarding travel experiences with encounters worth telling depend on a well-honed mix of curiosity and personal charm. Travel experiences worth writing about require a delicate mix of engineering and serendipity.

So what do you tell people who ask what you're up to on those trips? While there is no reward in being completely shy about what you're doing, I've found it helpful to downplay my role. I find myself saying, "Oh, I write the occasional travel article" or "I've sold a few travel articles" or "I like to travel so much that I write about it when I can." That way, privacy and a certain distance are retained, which permits your observer and reporter mode to continue unimpeded.

The alternative, if you talk about yourself too much, may lead to time-consuming questions, unsolicited rambling stories, and a drain on personal energy and enthusiasm. Peter Mikelbank, a writer and television producer based in Paris, told me years ago not to talk about my travels until I'd written up the notes, to save the best thoughts and impressions for the story. I could dine out on the anecdotes later, after the story appeared.

There is a balance between shutting up bores who consume precious time and missing that special conversation that arises from an unexpected encounter. You'll have to be the judge. If you thrive on obsequious chatter about the travel writer's lifestyle, go for it. Writers tend to keep their noses to the page and their ears to the truth. As Tom Swick, travel editor of the *Sun-Sentinel*, says, concerning researching a travel story, "The best way to write about a place is to go alone, anonymously, and talk to nobodies."

Keep in mind the joy of travel in travel writing. You are a connecting link in a long line of people who love travel and recognize the magic of a place and its people. You are sharing in a mystery, the secrets of the world, and you are sharing those secrets with other people by writing. There may be places you won't write about because you want to preserve the memory for yourself rather than share with an audience. Perhaps you'll recognize that there are places in the world that can't handle the impact of mass tourism and you'll refrain from writing about them. It's possible you'll visit places you cannot bring yourself to write about because you've been so affected and humbled, that you can't relegate the experience to the confinement of words.

As David Yeadon, an adventure travel writer, said during his lecture at the National Geographic Society in 1994, "The joy of travel writing is celebrating the richness of the now, but more, all the themes underlying these mysteries. Everything resonates with power and depths you know. The lost worlds—even unlost worlds—are telling you so much, giving so much. Celebration of the unknowable is the joy of travel."

Find ways to challenge yourself in daily life so that when adversities happen on the road you'll have the resources to meet situations without Flinching. Pretend you are traveling every day. Use different routes to get to work. Walk two miles in the rain. Eat at ethnic lunch counters that don't take credit cards. Ask directions at a bar instead of a gas station. Vary your mealtimes and other daily routines. Talk to shopkeepers, street musicians, and bus drivers. Take notes on what you did each day. Make every transaction or encounter a lesson in thoroughness. Ask the questions you know you'll want answered later. Encourage people to explain things to you. Practice saying, "Can you think of anything else I need to know?"

ON THE ROAD

When the flow of events isn't going your way, it might be best to lose small and head to another locale. On the other hand, if circumstances are ideal, perhaps the best course of action is to stay longer than you planned. Some days just don't go as projected, we all know that. And some days seem worse, stacked against us. Transportation delays, non-operational phones, unexpected public holidays, bad weather, closed roads, lost reservations, gasoline shortages, wildcat strikes, traffic gridlock, elections, even revolution. If you are going to be out in the world experiencing, what the world dishes up may not always be tasty.

It is a skill to know whether the judicious course of action is to beat a hasty retreat or hole up and lay low, even though your itinerary says move on. Consider whether you'd be happier remaining, even though it might mean passing up another experience. Continue the research you've started, explore a back corner you just learned about, and you just might turn up an unusual story. Sticking with an itinerary worked out in advance would be folly if you miss a superb experience and a great story that you could pursue with a change of plans.

What about those reservations and appointments that will be affected by a change of plans? Well, with a telephone or e-mail, most changes can be arranged. If you're so far off the main path that no telephone or e-mail is available, delays or postponements are probably expected. In most places, assuming there are sufficient resources, people interpret a visitor's desire to stay longer as flattery. On prearranged travel writer's junkets, it may be difficult to arrange an impromptu extension. Flexibility usually belongs to those who pay their own way. If an area is particularly attractive, advise people who are arranging your trip well in advance that you might want to stay on longer. Whatever the situation, state your needs politely and stay flexible.

Lynn Remly, a travel writer based in the Greater Cleveland area, comments, "It's important not to burden yourself when on a trip, particularly a strenuous one. You may find yourself making choices based on the amount of stuff you have to drag along (laptop, camera equipment, and so on) rather than the value of a view or event to your article. Can you imagine not visiting the Potala Palace because you didn't want to carry your laptop up the steep walkway?" Remly says she carries "a simple pocket-sized notebook and a couple of pens to write down facts or impressions as the day unwinds; then I transcribe my notes in the evening at the hotel or in the train."

Knowing yourself and your personal needs will serve you in every aspect of travel and travel writing. If you've been on the go for weeks and the opportunity arises to relax in solitude, would you turn it down to pursue some prearranged itinerary or appointment? The shuffle of reservations and appointments may seem like a burden, but in the long run, your own comfort and energy reserves are at stake. If you luck into a wonderful situation, enjoy it as long as you can.

FINANCING THE FREELANCE LIFE

Yes, there are writers who earn a reasonable income by freelancing. And you can, too. How much you earn depends on the energy you put into marketing your skills and your writing. Whether the annual income from freelancing will support you depends on where you live and how much you spend. If your plan is to support yourself completely from travel writing, I recommend seeking markets in corporate magazines, trade journals, advertorials, and incentive travel. Or write for better-paying markets such as health care or finance, and view the travel writing as personal fulfillment. A novice freelancer who relies solely on sales to newspapers and magazines will starve.

Freelance writers don't have to live in expensive urban centers. While writers may crave the stimulation and the networking opportunities of big-city life, settling in a rural area or small town can cut expenses and increase a writer's focus. A writer's residence doesn't determine skill, and a travel writer works in the field anyway. Proximity to a well-served airport might be the location factor to consider first. With sophisticated portable electronic tools, wireless or high-speed Internet access, and a flexible calling plan, today's freelance travel writer can work the world from the hinterland. Figure out what it takes to cover expenses. Find a way to cover that amount with steady contract work or what artists and musicians call the "day job." Eventually, you'll amass clients to cover your needs and perhaps quit the regular job if you want. Don't forget to factor in the subsidized health insurance, pension plans, paid vacations, and other benefits associated with being an employee. As a freelance writer, you'll cover all your costs.

Few writers are able to find full-time work in the travel field. Magazines and newspapers have few full-time staff writers. Travel trade magazines may hire news writers, and the online travel industry offers marketing and promotional work. But if writing is your goal, you might not be pleased to be writing one-sentence promotional blurbs for discount vacations selling online. Most travel writers I know undertake writing opportunities in several disciplines while maintaining a job, either full or part time. A punishing schedule of full-time work, travel for research purposes, and freelance travel writing demands stamina. You'll need an understanding family and a flexible workplace.

Which brings us to negotiating time for travel. Personal and work commitments may impinge on a fledgling travel writer's freedom. At the beginning of your career, concentrate professional travel writing activities during vacations and weekends. Write about places close to home that don't require extensive and expensive travel.

Extracting yourself from your partner, family, work, and other commitments requires compromises and communication. Other members of the family or work colleagues may have to shoulder the tasks you normally handle during your absences.

On the work front, you'll have to persuade team leaders that they can get along without you for a few days, weeks, or months. Your case will sound better if you already have a substitute identified and trained. Whether or not you are paid during your leave depends on company leave policy. If you're planning on coming back to the same job, find and train replacement staff who can take over your duties so colleagues aren't burdened during your absence. Convince the decision makers that you need the time for legitimate professional development or educational advancement. Fortunately, management attitudes concerning personal and professional development have evolved. Management and human resources realize that talented staff members are easier to retain if they're able to pursue self-actualizing projects. Employers and supervisors are more likely to understand and agree to your proposal for extended leave if you focus the discussion on professional development.

The word "vacation" has no place in such a discussion. Let me say it again: Travel writing research is not a vacation. You'll be working harder for longer stretches of time than during a typical workday. Obviously, we're not automatically entitled to more time off work than the other staff, so even unpaid leave should be treated as a benefit to be cherished. Resentment from co-workers is a possibility, but if it is clear that you are furthering your career rather than just "taking another vacation" perhaps you can win them on your side. Involve your work colleagues with your publishing successes by sharing stories and photos with them.

With permission for time off granted, at least in theory, plan the financing. Will you be able to afford living without an income? If the trip is just a few days, perhaps annual leave can be used, but for longer sojourns, you may have to consider leave without pay.

When I started researching and writing travel articles, I would work a temporary job for six to eighteen months and save enough money so I could travel for several months. Temporary work can be found in most cities, even during times of economic downturns. Such a plan requires self-discipline and austerity. Financial windfalls and all-expenses-paid high-end assignments remain a rarity for most travel writers. You'll still have to save your money and travel for the sheer pleasure of being on the road. And you'll sell your stories several times over to recoup expenses, or perhaps realize a profit.

NETWORKING IN THE TRAVEL INDUSTRY

Gather and nurture the connections you make. On press trips, you'll meet travel editors and other writers. All those public relations representatives, hotel publicists, airline executives, and tourist board managers are players in the travel writer's world. Who you know is as important as what you know, so collect business cards, develop a firm handshake, a direct smile, and a memory for names and affiliations. Stay current on developments in domestic tourism and global travel. Subscribing to consumer travel magazines is one way to watch travel trends, but reading industry publications online gives you a jump. Check out the many travel trade and promotional Web sites, as well as print publications. If a nearby college or university offers diplomas in tourism management or the hospitality industry, make contact with the instructors and students.

Move even further back on the food chain of information and you'll put your name on a few e-mail lists from state and international tourist boards, transportation companies, hotels, travel brokers, adventure travel packagers and other industry entities. Be careful, though, or you may be deluged with press releases announcing airline routes, hotel renovations, or holiday vacation travel packages. What you do with this information is up to you, but a travel writer with marketing ability could figure out interesting angles for articles that transform the travel industry's publicity into articles for travel consumers—your readers.

MAXIMUM MARKETING

You've read the chapter on marketing and editors. Perhaps you've sold several articles. Maybe you are in a slump and think you aren't getting through to editors. Or you just want to move ahead faster. Shift your perspective. Broaden your marketing base. Don't just focus on newspaper travel sections or travel magazines. Expand marketing research beyond the travel Web sites and print publications.

Tourism is one of the world's greatest economic generators; indeed some countries rely on tourism for their gross national product. Cyclical shifts occur, but tourism isn't going to vanish. Cook up a food angle for your travel article and rewrite it appropriately. Recently I read a travel article in a masonry business trade publication. The author had traveled the globe visiting sites where fine buildings were constructed of brick, and over the years he'd accumulated material for a book. An engaging travel vignette evolved from one of the author's hunts for brick buildings dating back to the earliest ruins of civilized settlements. Could you develop an article with a travel focus for the business journal of your trade or profession?

Incentive travel, business travel, and the ease of international travel have made the world accessible to a broader range of people, from elementary school students to golden agers. Adventure tours and educational travel are expanding markets.

OUR RESPONSIBILITIES AS TRAVEL WRITERS

Apart from business necessity, traveling is a discretionary purchase. Both time and money are being voluntarily spent and we travel writers influence how people spend that money. This is a responsibility and a challenge.

Another type of responsibility arises from your relationship to the location and the people you visit. Are you telling the truth about the place and its residents? Will your travel article help that small Yukon village prosper or will it pervert their traditional lifestyle? Consider what might happen when a tour operator from Minneapolis decides to organize "Ski and See" tours to the snow-bound northern Inuit village you visited alone and wrote about. The tour operator brings busloads of visitors who spend token cash on souvenirs, but the bulk of the fees aren't invested in the village. Tourists overrun the village and drain resources (food, heat, water, electricity, space) without building sustainable programs. Pay attention to outcomes. Be a travel writer who helps heal the world and its people.

Don't be greedy in your own travel choices. Adhere to a code of ethics for sustainable, responsible travel. Even though you may travel alone or in a small group, be aware of what your presence does to the place you visit. Are water and energy resources adversely affected by the presence of visitors? Select travel options that minimize pollution and wasted resources. Be part of the solution. Ask questions and investigate. Who is making money from tourism? Who is prospering or suffering?

THE TOOLS OF THE TRADE

You are the most important resource, the most valuable asset, for this trade of travel writing! Learn how to take care of yourself before you travel extensively. How you respond to the act of travel will affect your performance as an observer and writer. Travel can be stressful, which may adversely affect the immune system. Experiences and situations will unfold depending on your own physical and emotional balance. The way you interact with the world and its people directly relates to how you feel. Be aware of what you require to sustain health and well-being. Know your physical priorities—rest, nourishment, quiet, cleanliness, and companionship. Know what emotional boosts you need to maintain your equilibrium and a neutral perspective. It's tough to be interested in strange places and talk to people if you're not happy. Cultivate your curiosity and reward yourself. Self-knowledge on a primal level is an extremely important aspect of the travel experience. Be honest now: When you are out of your element, away from home, how do you fare?

What kinds of feelings and memories arise when you think of past travel experiences? Do you tend to be optimistic or negative? Are you paranoid and suspicious, fearful and hostile? Are you overly trusting and always smiling? Analyze your reaction to travel and how you react to difficult circumstances.

Successful traveling is a process. Once you recognize that your personal travel needs are just as important as electricity for the computer or a charged battery for the digital camera, you will understand how keeping yourself in harmony will make or break the trip—and the resulting story. Meet the world you see with awareness and curiosity and you will have one kind of trip. Meet the world with discontent and obsession and you will have quite another.

Rejection of your writing affects morale. It can be discouraging to know that many people without talent get published. But a writer with talent and marketing savvy has an unlimited future as a travel writer. Handle rejection by seeking new markets for your work. There are endless places to publish around the world; the only hurdle is pushing yourself to send your work out.

SETTING UP YOUR WORKSPACE

We discussed the travel journal in chapter three. After you get home and start transcribing your material, you'll need a place to write.

A computer and Internet access are indispensable tools for a productive travel writer. The time saved in producing stories will pay for the computer within its tax-depreciable life. Do we need to mention the advantage a computer gives in the task of reshaping and structuring articles for resale? Or for writing query letters, conducting research online, interviewing by e-mail, and printing copies of your work? If you want to advance your travel writing career rapidly, invest in a notebook computer, one that's lightweight and has a long battery life. Alternatively, buy a PDA or communications device (Treo, BlackBerry, etc.) with lots of memory and a full-size folding keyboard. Many writers also depend on hefty desktop computers with all the accessories.

Consider what you are going to do with the computer—crunch numbers for corporate deals, publish a Web-based travel letter, or write words? If you plan to use online databases, electronic library catalogs, and the Internet for research, you might want a broadband or cable connection rather than dial-up access to the Internet. Remember that laptop and notebook computers are totally portable and owning one permits you to write on the road or while enjoying the summer shade on the backyard patio. Just try doing that with a desktop computer.

Adjustable office furniture is imperative. Typing for extended periods at a poorly arranged work station that strains your hands and arms may lead to repetitive stress injury in the hands, wrists, elbows, and shoulders. Consult an ergonomics expert or appropriate Web site or book to determine the appropriate distances and angles for your chair, keyboard, desktop, lamp and monitor. If you're working with a notebook computer, vary your typing posture. Rest and exercise your hands and arms; they are precious tools.

TIME MANAGEMENT

Show up at the computer, writing teachers admonish. Show up and you'll get the writing done. Eventually. But getting to the computer can be a problem for busy, traveling writers. Finding blocks of time for extended writing sessions sounds like luxury to me. Most freelancers have learned to carve time out of other commitments. They work on drafts while commuting (dictating while driving or scribbling during subway rides or during lunch). Use the morning hours and write for an hour before leaving for work. Stop watching television or DVDs completely (yes, really!) and you've found, on average, the equivalent of two or three days of writing time per week. Forego gabbing with friends, postpone shopping, hire a teenager to do your household chores. A ruthless analysis of how you spend your time will always yield at least an hour a day that could be spent writing—and usually more. Even parents with small children can find the time, although it might be in fifteen-minute gaps between the demands of that job.

Think about your story when you are driving and idling in traffic. Even if you can't write down what you're thinking immediately, the exercise of working your brain over the story will help advance the process when you do sit down at the keyboard. Quit the compulsive checks of phone, text, and e-mail messages. Go on a data and news fast—no newspaper reading, no television news, forego e-mail for a week, quit browsing the Web: Just write. The point is to find time for focusing on the writing, not the business of freelancing or research preparation. Show up at the computer or pull out pen and paper and jostle words around. If you can't get to your desk, carry a notebook, like reporters and writers have been doing for centuries. That would be a notebook you write in, powered by a pen or pencil, not one that needs a battery, wi-fi, or electrical outlet.

Like painting a room, writing is mostly prep work—research, legwork, lining up the quotes and people to question, finding images, verifying facts. Then you need to find the time to push onward to locate the contacts with callbacks or e-mails soliciting information and to nail down the interview appointments. The writing seems the easiest part to me!

CONTACTS

Okay, I confess. I've been updating a computer-based database of my contacts and mailing list for the past seven years and I'm still not done. It's far easier to use existing e-mail address lists and the two huge Rolodexes that are my workday friends. The cards are faster to access and have the advantage of covering decades of people and institutions that I've contacted over the years.

Develop your own file system for names, addresses, e-mail information, and telephone numbers. When you get a new contact name at a magazine, public relations firm, or tourist office, record it in your contacts database or on a new index card, or whatever system you prefer. I use a contact database for information obtained from e-mail and the Internet, supplemented with business cards stapled on Rolodex cards. I sometimes file contacts by location (country, state, city, region) or function (hotel publicist, photographer, tourism promoter) rather than individual names. You can also file contacts by category, such as airlines, hotels, resorts, outfitters, or tour companies. Usually I create one contact entry for the publication and save editors' names and direct phone, fax, and e-mail information as I acquire them. Once I've worked with an editor, I'll create a separate contact entry or index card under the editor's last name. My personal information filing system is idiosyncratic and flexible; yours should reflect your personal research and retrieval needs. Construct a contact system—in a PDA, computer database, spreadsheet, or on paper—that suits your own needs and preferences.

REFERENCE BOOKS

Even in the Internet era, every writer I know amasses a personal set of reference books. The reference books closest to my desk include the *Oxford English Dictionary*, the Bible, a classical dictionary, Eric Partridge's *Usage and Abusage*, Strunk and White's *The Elements of Style*, the *Prentice Hall Handbook for Writers*, several language dictionaries (Spanish, German, Italian, French, Russian, Japanese, Latin), *A Dictionary of Literary Terms*, *Larousse Gastronomique*, *The Associated Press Stylebook*, several atlases, *The Columbia-Viking Desk Encyclopedia*, *The World Book Dictionary*, a dictionary of English synonyms, *Roget's Thesaurus*, and *Bartlett's Familiar Quotations*.

It may seem faster to look up words in the dictionary or thesaurus that comes with word processing software, but I tend to seek words with more complexity than the paltry collection offered by Microsoft's products. The Internet is a wonderful research tool, but it isn't the only tool you need to be a competent writer and researcher. My library includes hundreds of literary travel books, antique guidebooks, recent travel guides, pamphlets on specific historical landmarks, photo books about places, and lots of maps. Of course I verify current information on the relevant Web sites, but I'd rather have a range of research sources available than the relatively narrow spectrum of duplicative Web-based travel information.

RECORDER

To capture the sound of the call to prayer at dawn, cathedral bells, children at play, or street hawkers, you'll need a recorder or other electronic tool that stores sound. When you are writing, aural reminders—music, people talking or street noise—will help you remember to describe sound in the article. Mood is effectively created through sound. Stimulate your creative experience by listening to sound that reminds you of the place. Record interviews, your impressions, and ambient sound while you travel.

EXPENSE RECORDS

Contracts for travel writers sometimes include a clause concerning expenses. A figure may be listed and all expenses up to that amount will be reimbursed. Some publications routinely agree to reimburse reasonable expenses related to the writing project. Other publications rely on a written agreement to cover mileage, long-distance calls, and other modest expenses. Before you incur expenses on an assigned writing project, find out what will be reimbursed. If you are writing on spec, ask the editor if you'll be reimbursed for expenses and to what extent, assuming the article is accepted for publication. Be specific. Ask if you can take your source out for a meal. Ask if your personal travel, lodging, and meals will be reimbursed. Many publications expect the author to cover personal expenses or arrange their own transport and lodging. Unless you know the editor and are confident of the reputation of the publication, obtain agreements about expenses in writing or e-mail and save them. After you have worked with the editor and the publication, you can be less compulsive about securing written agreements.

During the beginning phase of your travel writing career, expenses will probably exceed writing income. Keep a meticulous written log of mileage related to researching and producing articles for sale. Leave the mileage notebook in the car so it is always available to note brief trips to the post office or library. Ask for receipts for any expenditure related to travel writing and save these receipts, writing on the back what it was for.

Some freelancers use a PDA or notebook devoted entirely to travel writing expenses. They tally cab fares, newspapers and magazines bought for research, office supplies, Internet café charges, express delivery fees, etc. Other writers bundle the receipts in an envelope and save them with a copy of the published story. While that may appear excessive, bear in mind that if you are faced with an inquiry from the tax collectors, evidence of claimed expenses (paper receipts, credit card statements, etc.) and copies of your work products (published articles) will support your claims.

Here's what I do. During each writing research trip, I save all receipts. Shortly after returning home, I sort the receipts and total the categories—transport, hotel, personal meals, entry fees, business meals with contacts and sources, local transportation, etc. Later I'll add the relevant credit card charges with foreign exchange costs. The receipts are clipped together and stored in an envelope and the category totals are summarized for tax reporting. I also keep a mileage logbook in the car, reporting mileage for trips related to freelance writing. When April fifteenth looms and it's time to provide the income and expense numbers to the accountant, I have an easier time of totaling the year's expenses. Other writers record their business-related expenditures on a PDA or use expense-tracking software. Some writers toss every receipt in a shoebox, waiting until tax return season to deal with expenses, or they hire a professional to sort out the mess.

What about the expenses of a companion who goes along on your travels? As long as the travel companion has a business purpose—taking pictures, gathering research, translating—expenses could be part of producing articles for sale. An effective way to handle a companion's expenses is to work as a team, sharing a byline. Each freelance writer's tax situation is different, so before amassing significant expenses related to your travel writing career, read the guidelines that the IRS provides for Schedule C income reporting. Consult a professional tax advisor about what expenses you can deduct and how to handle freelance income.

FREE TRIPS

As far as free travel goes, be picky. If you decide to take complimentary trips that are offered to you, be careful about where you sell the resulting story. In today's marketplace, the travel writer who relies exclusively on subsidized or free travel offered by the travel industry risks stamping her career with the "industry shill" and "hack" brands. The received wisdom is that a travel writer who accepts free travel can't maintain an unbiased perspective. What do you think? There are a few articles archived on the Internet on this subject, and every so often the debate crops up in the discussion areas of Web sites aimed at travel writers and aspiring travel writers. Almost all of the big-name glossy magazines and reputable newspapers won't even consider articles that arise from subsidized or free travel.

I've also heard people who earn their living from travel writing brag that they've never paid a cent for travel and have never had to write a negative word about a place. Bombastic talk perpetuating the public myth that travel writers always travel for free, get the best deals, and don't have the same travel experiences as everyone else doesn't enhance the professional image of travel writers. Establish your own ethical standards. If what you experience and see isn't acceptable, you shouldn't let the absence of a bill shape your opinions. Writers who see no fault, ever, in the places that offer unpaid accommodations, meals, or transport are really working for the places that offer the free travel.

Accepting junkets and familiarization ("fam") trips carries ethical responsibilities. The tourist office, resort, or public relations firm representing a state or country that invites you expects to see a published article. Yet there are times when you write the article, send it to an interested editor at a publication that has no rules barring articles from press junkets or fam tours, and for one reason or another, the article doesn't get published. You've done your part, but the agency that offered you the trip may not understand why the article wasn't published. They may ask you to try and publish it elsewhere and indeed, since you put so much time and effort into the piece, you'll go ahead and try to market the story elsewhere. Don't forget to send thank-you notes to the people who organized the trip or contributed to your travel research. And when the article is published, send copies to those who helped make the trip possible.

The free trip issue is really quite simple. Accept invitations for free trips you want to take and write about only when you can place a story in a publication without compromising your reputation. Submit such stories to editors at publications that don't mind subsidized travel. Don't try to fool an editor who has a policy against articles arising from free trips; you will damage your credibility. Don't make promises that you can't deliver to companies or tourist boards that invite you on junkets. Be honest and clear in your research and writing, too.

CONTRACTS

After you have a track record (a dozen or more clips), magazine editors may provide a contract with details about expense coverage, kill fee, rights purchased for publication, and duration of those rights purchased.

Usually, you'll receive expenses and a fee for a magazine travel article. Typically the rights purchased are first North American for thirty, sixty, or ninety days. Sometimes, the rights are held for six months or a year. That means you can't sell the article again until the rights revert back to you after the hold has expired. Some contracts stipulate that all rights are being purchased. This might not be a good idea for you unless the fee is generous. Read article contracts carefully. Ask questions. Don't be afraid of showing your inexperience. Realize that a contract, particularly for small start-up magazines, may be dishonored even when it is authentic and signed by a representative of the publication. Publishers file for bankruptcy or go out of business, leaving the writers unpaid. The value of the money owed you may not be worth a small claims action or lawsuit. Your best protection is to deal with well-established publishers.

If you are approaching a guidebook publisher with a proposal or responding to an advertisement for a guidebook writer, insist on a contract or letter of agreement if your application or proposal is successful.

For book contracts, pay close attention to language dealing with revisions and translations. Look for the royalty percentage, if that is part of your deal. Many guidebook publishers pay with a flat fee and no royalties. You may have to estimate what is preferable for you based on past sales of this guidebook series.

Keep copies of all correspondence and conversations related to publishing business, rights, and permissions. If you don't understand the language, ask questions. Engage an attorney or contract specialist to read the contract language. If you don't agree with an element in the contract, don't hesitate to discuss it with the publisher. For example, if the contract says you'll receive twelve free copies of the book and states you'll have to purchase any other copies at the usual trade discount rate, object. You can usually negotiate for more free copies and a more preferable discount for purchase.

During the contract negotiation, aim to retain the copyright, if at all possible. It's true that most guidebook publishers purchase the work outright. If you can negotiate royalties, good for you! Ask an attorney to review the contract. Author's organizations such as the Writer's Union offer a contract review service to their members.

GUIDEBOOKS

I can't emphasize this too often: A guidebook project will take more time than you anticipate and no matter how fast you think you can write, the money will never be adequate compensation. Much of the guidebook writing process involves checking addresses and contact information. Guidebook authorship isn't going to impress anybody, except perhaps your family and colleagues at your day job. Indeed, magazine and newspaper editors might pigeonhole you as a fact checker rather than a writer, since guidebooks typically aren't works of literary merit.

All that said, if the guidebook authoring credit is an element you consider important to your overall career, go ahead and do it. For many travel writers, the guidebook will be a first book credit, providing an enduring example of personal achievement. Shane Christensen, a guidebook author based in Cambridge, Massachusetts, says, "I have had a wonderful opportunity to live international relations firsthand through travel writing, having taken on guidebook assignments in the United States, Latin America, and Europe. And although I've made no great fortune through travel writing, I can think of no better immersion into new destinations."

Often, guidebook publishers seek local residents to write and/or revise previous editions of the guidebook. You may know the city or the region, but you'll still have to spend hours, days, and weeks checking addresses, prices, Web sites, and more tedious details. Unless you enjoy detail work, this process might be thoroughly discouraging.

Writers have told me that guidebook writing is incredibly time consuming and that the pay could work out to be less than a dollar an hour. On the other hand, writers who self-publish their guidebooks and are adept at book distribution and marketing seem to derive financial and professional satisfaction. Be particularly careful if the contract involves revising someone else's work in a previous edition of the guidebook. Will you receive author credit or just receive a flat fee for the research effort? Agents and authors agree that all writers should ask for the biggest advance possible. Royalties are fine, but the size of the advance often dictates the publisher's commitment to the project.

JOINING ORGANIZATIONS

For a novice writer, an organization dedicated to helping writers with their craft can be extraordinarily helpful. And a full-time freelance writer may want the professional identification that a writers organization offers. Some groups provide health insurance, job listings, legal assistance and other services needed by freelancers.

However, mentioning membership in an organization rarely impresses editors. Fine writing impresses editors. Joining an organization with the expectation of improving your publication record is unrealistic. You might meet an editor at one of the group's events, but you'll still have to produce a competently written piece. If you are confident about your writing, meetings, workshops, and other gatherings may enhance networking opportunities and improve specific skills. You might need the organization to develop editorial contacts, to move your name and work around the marketplace. For networking purposes, the organization might be a good first stop on the road to successful freelancing. Writers organizations usually schedule workshops or seminars with editors. "Network, network, network. Contact everyone you know to see who they know. An introduction of any kind can help get your foot in door more easily than a cold query," says Joanne Cronrath Bamberger, who freelances in the Washington, D.C. area. "Don't be afraid to occasionally write on spec. I know the conventional wisdom is not to do this. But I got my first clip in *The Washington Post* by agreeing to do that, and got paid, too."

You can expect to meet other writers through a membership organization and they might share tips on what material various publications are buying. They might even pass along work or opportunities for collaboration might emerge. Writer's organizations sometimes hold book fairs, marketing seminars, or meet-the-agents-and-editors gatherings. Such programs may be open to the general public so you don't need to be a member to attend.

Before joining an organization find out all the benefits available to members. Each organization has its own focus and resources; benefits vary but may include a business center and library, a newsletter that accepts articles from members, referrals to literary agents or editors, bookstore discounts, access to computers and desktop publishing software, manuscript reading and analysis.

Small groups of working writers who provide support for each other when the writing or marketing isn't going well are useful for beginning writers. These focus groups may be under the wing of a larger arts or authors organization, or simply be a group of sympathetic, dedicated writers who meet regularly and discuss their work. If you can't find such a group in your immediate area, place some feelers in online arenas, inquire at the nearest college English or Journalism department, or ask the state or regional arts council for assistance in locating like-minded writers.

One way to start accumulating published clips is to write for the organization's newsletter. Payment probably isn't an issue with this kind of publication, but you should receive extra copies and a byline. Read the print or online newsletter for two or three months before approaching the editor with your idea. Volunteering to help with production is a way to gain publication experience.

HOW TO RECYCLE AND RESELL WORK

After an article has been published, you may have the right to re-sell it to other publications. Clarify your legal rights before offering any previously published material for sale. If you have written under contract, the terms of sale will be described in the contract. Often, a publication will purchase first rights or exclusive rights for a period of time during which the publication has the right to resell the article. At some point, reprint rights usually revert to the author. If there is no contract between you and the publication, ask the editor. When you sell frequently to one publication, editors may forget to send a contract for each sale unless the terms have changed. You needn't insist on a contract for each sale if you have a trusting editorial relationship, but keep records of what you sell and whether the date of purchase is keyed to acceptance, publication, or payment. Then, if you've sold exclusive first rights for six months from the date of publication, you'll know you can re-sell the piece six months afterwards.

Review the terms of your contract carefully. Before you sign, understand what rights you are selling and for how long. Is the publisher buying online and other downstream electronic rights to your article (online databases, pay-per-use research services, CD sales, educational sales)? Contracts vary—sometime magazines purchase worldwide exclusive rights for a period of time, say six months or a year, then the reprint rights revert to the writer. Newspapers may purchase one-time publication rights and electronic reprint rights, which means articles that appear in print are stored electronically and the publisher leases the information to customers. The National Writers Union has successfully established that publications that retain electronic rights must provide extra payment to freelance writers. Remember to clarify; the onus is on the writer to specify terms of sale.

If the original story appeared in a national magazine or newspaper, it's unlikely that a competing publication would purchase the same piece. You can offer travel articles to noncompeting newspapers on a simultaneous basis; for example, you can sell the same story to papers in Chicago, New Orleans, and Seattle. Advise editors that you are submitting an article that has appeared in print. Of course, if your article is published on the Internet, there might not be any interest in the same story because of content saturation. The story is no longer new.

When sending out the same article to many different papers, comment at the top of the first page, "Offered for one-time second rights, exclusive in this circulation area or market." Editors then know that you aren't sending the same article to a competing paper in the same circulation area.

Before reselling your work, make appropriate changes to update the material. When selling your work a second or third time, you may have to make revisions for each sale. Let's say you want to sell the same story to a newspaper in a different city. The "how to" sidebar should reflect transportation details related to the place where the article will appear in print. Dates and seasonal activities may need to be updated. In the query, advise that the story is a second sale, exclusive in that paper's circulation area.

A basic guideline is to seek a resale market where the original piece did not penetrate. If the article appeared in a weekly limited-circulation paper, step up to a daily newspaper in a different circulation zone or a different country. If the piece first appeared in a special interest magazine, try selling it to an online news service. There are several syndicates online that invite writers to post their articles for sale to interested editors. The syndicate receives a percentage of the sale, but this passive method of circulating your work, especially for the resale market, can yield modest income.

Finding your resale path takes time. My formula is to sell to the highest paying top-market publication first, then work down to more obscure publications. Usually, I revise the story sufficiently for each resale so every version of the article is unique.

WEB SITES, BLOGS, AND E-ZINES

Do you have the time and skills to set up your own online travel newsletter? Some writers have found this a rewarding route to attract attention to their work. You could showcase your own writing and solicit articles from other freelancers. Be prepared for lots of work if you follow this path!

Some writers say that the successful online e-letter or e-zine (short for magazine) deals with local topics rather than a broad scope. For example, in my hometown, there are e-letters dedicated to reviews of local restaurants and gourmet stores, outdoor excursions in the area, and a calendar of upcoming dance classes and events with profiles of local dance instructors.

Serious freelance travel writers and photographers may want to establish a Web site that showcases their work. You could register your own name or a business name with Network Solutions or one of the many other domain registration entities. You or someone you hire would create the Web pages that present samples of your work, a biography, and contact information.

Travel blog (online logs or journals) sites offer travelers an opportunity to post narratives tracking their travels. This may be a fun way to keep in touch with family and friends as you travel and a useful way to keep your notes for compilation in articles later on. For example, a travel blog series of weekend getaways could then become the basis of a print guidebook about travel in the region. Travel blogs are unedited Web sites created by the participants, which is different than an online publication refereed by editors.

Combine your special interests and travel writing by creating a regular travel column for online or print distribution. Determine the special interests in which you have expertise and write three to five sample columns highlighting various aspects. Then make a presentation to several online or print editors in the special interest field. For example, if you are a kayaker, you've probably already written several travel pieces about this favorite recreation. Quite likely, those articles could be transformed into a package of sample travel columns. The sample columns might net you a regular space on kayaking for an outdoors magazine or environmental newsletter. The column format is shorter, more personalized, and focuses on a particular incident or subject that has wide appeal.

In the same way, turn any one of your interests or areas of expertise into regular work. Think in terms of a hobby or recreational activity and write about it with a travel focus. Topics such as medieval music, Civil War artifacts, herb gardening, go-kart racing, doll collecting, and chocolate making all have individual publications. After you've written many columns on a particular special interest topic, consider collecting them in a guidebook.

SELF-PROMOTION

Are you uncomfortable with promoting yourself? I am. Although you might wonder how I can make that claim while producing a book about my experiences as a travel writer, I have left most of my career path to chance. I have no brochure describing my travel writing workshops, no letterhead, no advertisements except my Web site. While I can think of dozens of ways that I could be promoting my expertise, thus streamlining my work so it would be more lucrative, I am loath to initiate a public relations campaign. The pop psychology books would suggest I may be afraid of success. I just think that time devoted to promotion doesn't leave much for writing and traveling!

Experienced writers do send out short promotional e-mails to introduce themselves to editors in markets that are well within their level of expertise. They'll include URL links to published articles. Or do the same thing by mail, including copies of published articles and a letter of introduction. You may have to force yourself, but go ahead and introduce yourself to editors at conferences, book expos, or workshops. The introduction may lead to a discussion of what you've written, where it has been published, and where you are next traveling. More often than not, the editor will ask that you summarize your story ideas in writing and send the proposal so the editor can "take a look." An editor who says he'll take a look is not making a commitment to buy the story, but at least the story will be read. If you're prompt about sending him the packet of published clips along with the finished manuscript, there's a chance the conversation will still be in the forefront of the editor's memory. Always clarify whether the editor wants you to send the materials by e-mail or regular mail.

The goal is to separate yourself from the pack. Distinguish yourself in an editor's mind through your articulate presentation and appropriate story ideas. Then continue the self-promotion effort by presenting examples of your sharpest writing along with a letter that reiterates the story ideas or a completed manuscript in which the editor expressed interest. Send by e-mail if the editor has indicated that's acceptable and ensure that attachment files are perfectly formatted. Test by sending a friend the same attachments by e-mail to verify the files can be opened easily.

Establish yourself as a professional writer by acting like one. Self-promoting editorial conversations lead to assignments when you stay tuned to the process, stay flexible, and respond appropriately to each stage of the negotiation. If the editor tells you she's interested, respond immediately with the query or manuscript. If the editor says your experience level isn't up to the standards of that magazine, ask politely for suggestions where you might meet with success. After you've sent in your work and the editor rejects the story, ask where the story might fit in some other publication. If the relationship seems to be cordial, continue the dialogue by asking if you can pitch other ideas; don't stay fixed on the last story. The process by which an idea gets into print can be complex and lengthy, often going a circuitous route that the writer never envisions at the beginning. The manuscript may languish for years and then be rewritten for immediate online publication. Or it may be rejected by one magazine only to find a more receptive berth at another magazine. For a writer with an emotional investment in the manuscript, this process can be harrowing. Look upon your manuscripts as works in progress and each encounter with an editor as an opportunity to refine and improve both the specific story and your own skills.

Networking and self-promotion is an individual effort. You are always your own best promoter. Don't think you can't do it and don't think someone else would do it better. Any writer can promote her work. In my experience, the primary focus is: Remember that you have nothing to lose and everything to gain. Wait until you are relaxed and confident before making calls or approaching editors or agents at conferences. You wouldn't want to leave the impression that you are insecure, struggling to express yourself, or sound choked up and nervous. If your ideas are sound and your product is reliable, editors will want to hear from you. And don't forget to follow up.

The most forceful sales point in your writer's quiver is your portfolio of published work. Get a copy of every piece of your writing that is published. That means everything—newsletters, small hometown papers, college newspapers, daily newspapers, letters to the editor, magazines, business writing, etc. When you are written about, make sure you get a copy of the article. Even if you think that the mention that appeared in your employee newsletter isn't important, you can't predict future needs. Store the original clips in acid-free file folders or archival quality plastic pocket holders, or scan and save digital versions. Don't paste or staple your clips into scrapbooks. Over time most glue destroys paper. There may come a day when you only have one copy of a favorite article left and you'll need to make a photocopy of that clip. You may want to have a record of your work to pass on to family members.

Ideally, you'll get two or more original copies of print published articles. Most publications send out these contributors' copies or tear sheets shortly after the date of publication. If you don't get yours, inquire immediately. If time lapses between publication date and your request for the issue in which your work appeared, there may not be remaining issues available. Similarly, print any articles that appear online as soon as you can. Often, newspapers archive online articles after a week or two and you'll have to pay to obtain a print copy. Also save the URL of the archived article so you can refer prospective editors to an online version of your story. Many writers create Web pages with links to their articles that have appeared online. Then you'd refer the editor to the Web page to browse examples of your writing. Don't do this until you've checked and rechecked every link, however. You don't want to send an editor to a dead-end 404 page.

I keep a large album of examples of published work—the "show and tell" book. Extra copies go in a file folder for each year I've been freelancing. I also make photocopies of the best articles and keep them ready in a "Clips to Send Out" file to use when editors ask for samples. You could also scan copies of the published articles to a CD and send that out to editors, but most editors prefer to read material in print. In a three-ring binder filled with plastic sleeves, I store newsletter articles in which I'm mentioned, announcements of readings or workshops, and any other material related to publicizing my writing career. Along with this, I maintain a Web site related to travel writing and occasionally add Web links to new work as it is published.

Remember to "police your byline" by doing a Web search of your name, the name you use as a byline, pen names, etc. If your work is being posted on other Web sites, you'll want to keep watch and complain if there's copyright abuse. If you're quoted, you'll want to add that to your publicity portfolio.

For your own records, maintain a chronological list of your publications in a standard citation form. Include the title of the article, name of the publication, volume, issue, date, and pages. Maintain the list so if an editor asks for a summary of your publications, you can send a copy of the whole list or extract appropriate titles. The day may come when you apply for writers residencies, workshops, or grants. Almost every application of this type requires a list of published credits. Once you've published a travel guidebook or if your work is included in an anthology, include the reference at the top of the list of publishing credits.

When your experience broadens and professional credits accumulate, you'll need a brief biography. In about 100 carefully chosen words, state the facts concerning your education, employment, and achievements related to writing and place of residence. Cute descriptions of pets, spouses, children, hobbies, habits, and hopes are best omitted. If an editor asks for a description to put at the end of an article—the ending bio—concoct a sentence or two. Some publications prefer that the short descriptions be humorous. Read the publication to find out how other freelance writers describe themselves. If you are unsure what the editor expects for the short ending bio, ask for details.

Do you have a writer's résumé? Even if you aren't planning to apply for writing jobs, the exercise is worthwhile. Focus on your professional writing experience—jobs where you were hired to write or edit, contract writing work that isn't covered in the list of publications, writing projects you directed, any teaching, writing workshops you attended, prizes, awards, grants, etc. Do your diplomas or academic degrees relate to language or writing? Have you contributed to the community with volunteer work related to writing?

Letterhead and business cards are useful to have, but if you can't afford them, refrain from spending money on business accessories you can do without, especially when most communication will be handled by e-mail and phone once you've made contact with an interested editor. Business cards are more important than fancy stationery. When you travel, give a contact or new friend a card with your name and address. Plain white bond paper is perfectly acceptable for writing business letters.

You will have to decide the comfort level of self-promotion. Spend too much time on self-promotion and I'll bet you don't get much writing done. Ignore the promotion angle and you'll see sources of work dry up. A skilled financial manager strives to augment the capital as well as earn money on the money. In managing your writing capital, you need to expand the places where you can write even as you continue to write. Think about a spreading pool of water. You don't want to spread yourself so thin that it dries up in places, but you do need to keep pushing your work to new areas. Self-promotion can be advanced by networking through friends and business contacts. You needn't boast, but telling people what you are working on, where you are traveling next, and where your work has been published recently keeps you in the habit of communicating. All the people you talk to may mention your successes to their friends and an informal promotional network begins.

There are writers who maintain detailed blogs of their current activities—readings, book signings, and notable publications. Photocopy news clippings that mention your activities or copy your articles and send to friends who are interested in your successes and will help you in the promotional effort. If you win a writing award, take self-promotion one step further and send out press releases to your alumni magazine, club newsletter, or in-house company newsletter. Should you advise the general media? It's up to you, but only a modest-sized local paper would devote space to personal achievements such as prizes and awards. Perhaps your home-town paper would interview you after you won a writing prize, and certainly a local paper would announce an upcoming workshop you are leading. Keep in mind your goal for self-promotion. Are you trying to generate more writing assignments? Attract students to your workshops or classes? Sell more copies of your guidebook?

SUSTAINING RELATIONSHIPS WITH EDITORS

During the time I have been freelancing, many of the editors I have worked with have moved to other publications. I tend to view this as a plus for my marketing plans because it gives me entry at two points—the publication where I have already made a successful sale and the magazine where the editor now works. Keeping track of editors requires some networking. Whenever I talk to other writers, I ask what they are currently working on and which editors they've worked with lately. Another way to gather fresh information about editorial changes is to scan mastheads or simply e-mail or call the editorial assistant or receptionist and ask questions.

Many writers make the mistake of thinking that if they don't hear from an editor, the editor doesn't want to work with them anymore. Usually, this is not the case. Editors are busy people, focused on the future. Writers are focused on their unpublished article. A writer's promptness at deadline time is appreciated, but once an article is "dumped" into type, it's out of the editor's sight and mind.

Alas, the writer is, too. Writers grouse that that's why we don't get paid promptly—editors have simply forgotten we exist once the article is typeset or uploaded.

Celeste McCall, food and travel writer based in Washington, D.C., says, "First of all, for obvious reasons, the travel writing field is extremely popular and competition is fierce. Unless you are well established or have visited a remote island off Antarctica, don't bother contacting an editor cold; it is almost essential to know someone connected with the publication beforehand.

"There's a fine line between being persistent and a nuisance," says McCall. "Generally, if I don't hear back from an editor right away, I wait a couple of weeks and contact him or her again. [E-mail and regular mail does get lost and sometimes editors get fired.] Don't overwhelm an editor with writing samples unless specifically requested. Don't give up. If one editor says no repeatedly, try someone else!"

MOVING UP

Look at the stories you've sold for clues to what editors like about your work and are buying. If you are looking at your list of unpublished articles, make an effort to match your topics to special interest magazines. Writers who aren't getting results from their queries may need to freshen up the tone. Could be the writing doesn't grab a certain kind of editor. My experience (and those of most writers I know) is that it takes a while (five to ten years) to establish yourself, and there's no set route. No travel writer can "make" success simply happen, and maybe that energy of pushing puts editors off. Freelancers need to show that they are relaxed, cool, can write the story for editor x, or editor y, or maybe that other editor over in Australia.

Sometimes it helps to go to New York or London and meet the editors in person, that is, if they'll give you, or any freelancer, the time of day. Getting an appointment with a features editor takes a certain level of prior success. A portfolio made of a few newspaper stories and Web site work usually doesn't have enough traction.

A freelancer with Web site credentials could turn that into a meeting with other Web publishers. If the newspaper articles appeared in only one newspaper, angle into another more notable newspaper. Deal with the strongest experience card.

In the newspaper business, for example, people work eight to twelve years at smaller papers and have some kind of stellar experience, such as awards, a breaking story, or enterprise reporting, before the national papers will even look at their résumé and clips. Big magazines have similar attitudes. A few newspaper clips won't open the door to nationally circulated glossies (big-paying markets). A freelancer hoping to raise her professional profile could focus on the really well-known publications—*The Wall Street Journal, The New York Times, Los Angeles Times, The Washington Post, Financial Times* or *The Economist*—or approach the online versions of those publications.

When travel advertising is flatlining because of business downturns, branch out. Do interviews, profiles, investigative stories, business stories, fishing stories. Use each editorial contact to leverage your next assignments. The process of pushing your career forward can take several years. It's not unusual for a beginning freelance writer to publish in no-name Web sites, newsletters, and giveaway papers for three or four years or many more before hitting nationally known publications.

It also never hurts to notice when an editor deserves recognition. When the editor changes jobs, express the appropriate congratulations. Perhaps the magazine has been redesigned or you've enjoyed a recent story; pass on your thoughts to the editor. When you are planning an important trip, let the editors you've worked with before know your itinerary, because they just might have a story assignment for you. Assuming you've already established your skills and credibility with an editor, offer to scout newly opened hotels or restaurants. This kind of informal networking is almost always done with editors who know your work.

If the networking call is to communicate story ideas, have a few notes and a large blank sheet of paper ready. I can't tell you how many times I've been chatting with editors and the ideas and information are flying as fast as I can jot them down. Then the scrap of paper runs out and I can't read all the one-word ideas afterwards. Here's a tip: Ask editors what they are working on. Many of them are writers too, and just like you, they enjoy talking about travel. You'll pick up useful information about choice destinations, trends, and changes in the magazine industry. Here's another tip: Be brief, be first to conclude the conversation, ask intelligent questions, and ask if you can call or e-mail again with more story ideas.

We writers have to be vigilant about reminding editors we've worked with in the past about our successes and our sparkling ideas. Do this with a brief phone call or e-mail update. Or send an especially wonderful story of yours that has appeared in print and attach a note. Have a point to your communication; pitch a story idea and ask for an assignment. Mention your other recent significant writing assignments and achievements.

Sometimes the networking call or note is more effective than a formal query letter because the pressure is off; you aren't selling a story and can talk about your travel plans in a relaxed manner.

PUBLICATION ERRORS

If you think there has been an error or improper use of your material, approach the publication, find out which editor handled the story in question, and gently point out the odd coincidence that material you sent in recently for consideration has just appeared in print under someone else's name. Review the facts from your perspective and from the publication's perspective. Keep your tone neutral, your attitude focused on clearing up a misunderstanding. Get the editor on your side.

When it appears that your work was used without credit, or even if you feel nearly certain that a publication used your material improperly, remember that humor and a sense of proportion goes further than accusations and threats of legal action. What may look like plagiarism or improper use of your writing might simply be another writer covering the same ground. It may be difficult to believe, especially for a novice who hasn't worked in a newsroom, but the ideas you pitch and the stories you send in may have already been assigned. If you have a good idea, rest assured some other freelancer, staff writer, or editor may have had a similar idea. Professionals know this happens fairly often. Similarly, freelancers troll publications for story ideas and often rework stories written by others. Once your work is out in the marketplace, there is nothing to prevent someone else from doing a fresh version of essentially the same story and selling it, perhaps at a higher fee, to a competing publication.

I recall one incident when a freelancer pitched a story idea and included recent clips from a small local paper. The editor didn't react to the story idea and therefore didn't look very closely at the accompanying clips. A few weeks later another freelancer pitched a story that just happened to be based on one of the first writer's accompanying clips. The editor didn't notice the connection and bought the second writer's story. When it was published, the first freelancer thought the editor had purloined her story and slapped someone else's name on it. In fact, the editor was nonplussed when the freelancer threatened legal action. The only error in professionalism was the second freelancer not informing the editor that she had gotten the idea from a previously published story, even though she did her own reporting.

You may feel injured, but desperation and threats put editors on the defensive. It may be true that the editor erred or failed to notice that your story languishing as an attachment to some forgotten e-mail or under a stack of unsolicited articles on a desk was essentially the same as a story some other writer sent in, but pointing out the humor of the situation will go further for you. Keep the issue in perspective—in the scheme of things, how important is one misappropriated idea? Do you only have one idea? Consider that the editor's embarrassment may yield a small assignment or at least an adequate hearing when you have story proposals in the future. Threats rarely achieve the effect intended by the angry writer and such unprofessional behavior will nearly guarantee you will not receive assignments in the future. Who said the free-lancer's life was fair?

LECTURES AND WORKSHOPS

Experienced writers know they have to branch out to reach new audiences. Opportunities come through tangential work—teaching, leading workshops at travel expos, readings, and guest appearances on discussion panels. You can speed the process through self-promotion. Seek affiliation with a travel agency and host a travel discussion forum. Share your love of travel and your unique experiences and encourage the audience to participate. Find a sponsoring organization for courses in special interest travel—how to travel alone, travel happily with children or pets, environmental travel programs, grandparent-grandchildren travel, opportunities for handicapped travelers.

Travel is a popular topic for gatherings at community and recreation centers, senior citizen residences, and in schools. Show slides and talk about your travel experiences and build an audience for your writing. Approach local libraries and bookstores for sponsorship of an open house or travel program. Your payment for such events may be miniscule or nonexistent. The reason for pursuing these opportunities is to broaden your audience and stay in touch with what the traveling and reading public is doing. It also helps to establish your professional presence in the travel industry.

Publicity for a workshop, class, or reading generally is the responsibility of the teacher or speaker—you. Draw up a small public relations campaign plan and write down the interests of the various participants. Enlist the assistance of the organizations you are working with—the workshop sponsor, bookstore, or travel agency where you are holding your event. Remember that early and often are the watchwords of successful publicity.

Send out your press release to the media and follow up with a phone call. Personal contact is usually more successful than e-mail publicity to the press. Be sure you've sent the announcement with sufficient lead time for the publication to list your reading or workshop in the events calendar. For weekly publications, this can mean the announcement needs to be sent out as much as a month in advance, for dailies, up to three weeks in advance. Use radio announcements, flyers, and posters. If the organization has a mailing list, send out registration forms or e-mails and postcards announcing the event. Tell all your friends and colleagues. Be prepared for a full house, but to avoid disappointment, expect a small audience.

Once you have a specialty, or feel that you have developed knowledge and understanding of a particular country or region, you can bill yourself as an expert. Remember, though, that even experts don't have all the answers and if you don't know the answer to a question, say so.

DEVELOP A SPECIALTY

Etch your professional profile by defining a specialty interest. Not just a travel writer, but also one specializing in the Caribbean, outdoors adventure, or family travel. Develop a travel column in that specialty. The fact that you have one and have produced regular clips means something to editors. Will the column be well edited at an online newsletter or a small print newspaper? Possibly not, but if a writer waits for the "right" venue, he may never produce. Embrace each opportunity as it comes up and when you find the next option, quit and take the new one. When you're building your portfolio of published work, say yes to as many opportunities as you can.

Deborah McLaren, a travel writer who specializes in responsible tourism, describes herself as an alternative tourism travel writer with a focus on what communities are doing. "Ecotourism isn't just going to a lodge in the jungle, it is working with communities. I love to travel and it gives me an opportunity to become more involved with the local communities. My travel writing emerged from working in the responsible tourism movement."

Never having written for publication before, McLaren was surprised at the response—a three-part series in an educational travel magazine and an essay in a national women's magazine. In addition to travel writing, McLaren works with communities to develop marketable tours that generate involvement, support, and funds for preservation. She also lectures, leads workshops, and helps colleges plan study travel programs, always with a goal to educate new audiences. "I want to show people a way to make choices about the impact of their travel. Travel agents need information about community-designed tourism, so write for the travel industry publications."

THE FUTURE OF TRAVEL

A few years ago, a correspondent with *Newsweek* magazine asked my thoughts on travel in 2020. Here's what I predicted:

> Lots of people will stay in their homes and live out the scenario that Ray Bradbury wrote a short story about many years ago—the Bradbury fictional family had a simulated/virtual reality jungle/safari projected on the walls of the kids' rooms. I think the kids ended up staying in the virtual world all the time.
>
> In terms of real travel, I suspect people will go to where the greatest sensual experiences can still be had—good food, wine, spas, swimming, sunning, mountaineering, kayaking, etc. Extremes of cold and hot will likely be of interest—people will yearn for any kind of body-based experience.
>
> I predict that "day with a king" type travel will be offered. Tourists will pay hefty sums to visit foreign countries and hang out with the head of state or richest mandarin duchess and in exchange, the country will improve its balance of payments. Space travel is already an option for the "exclusive" travel offerings we see today.
>
> On the other end of the spectrum, folks will pay to experience difficult conditions—as they do now—to mingle, for a short time, with people who live in abject poverty. Perhaps the "volunteer vacation" has good motives at heart, but the downside of these temporary visits by rich-world do-gooders isn't discussed enough.

For myself, in 2020 I'll be seventy, and if my family genes are any indication, I'll be striding along Central Asian mountain ranges at just the same pace as I do now, perhaps with a companion mammal to carry the heavier loads.

TEN STEPS TO GET STARTED

Now that you've read this book and sampled the writing exercises, the world is wide open for you to embark on the path of writing about your travels. Perhaps you've even sold an article or two after absorbing the information on marketing and editorial networking. Right now is the time to step forward and make a place for yourself as a travel writer. I wish you every success in creating a rewarding career.

1. Write as often as you can, and at least twice a week. Set realistic goals: The urge to write every day will come in time.

2. Read a variety of strong writers. Seek works by contemporary and classic authors. Explore different styles and subjects—essays, fiction, nonfiction, humor and, of course, travel writing.

3. Research travel markets by visiting Web sites, newsstands, and libraries at least once or twice a month. Scrutinize the travel magazines. Check out other magazines and assess whether travel pieces appear in them.

4. Collect maps, atlases, and history books to find interesting landmarks, sites, and towns. Start with your home region.

5. Study the travel sections of large circulation daily newspapers—*The New York Times, Los Angeles Times, The Washington Post, The Globe & Mail, Telegraph, The Boston Globe*. Develop a sense of what style and subjects are featured in travel stories.

6. Cultivate your senses—try different foods and beverages, scents, and music. Note your moods and reactions to adversity, change, transition, solitude, and crowds.

7. Develop visual resources—go to art galleries or look at books with reproductions of art, collections of photographs, sculpture,

architecture. Spend time outdoors, in natural settings or wilderness, if you can find it. Think how you would describe what you see.

8. Have fun—break your routines, get lost, encourage an appreciation for the absurd, talk to strangers, ask directions.

9. Prepare. Be ready to write anywhere. Stock pens and notepads in your car, briefcase, purse, or coat pocket. Pack a small case of travel essentials to simplify departure. Acquire quick-dry clothes that pack easily. Organize your desk and filing system. Study languages.

10. Travel. Take every journey you can—short, long, near, or far. Seek pleasure and personal satisfaction. Be self-oriented and follow your dreams. Your happiness will make others happy wherever you go.

TRAVEL LIKE A TRAVEL WRITER

1. Ask locals about the region, its history and people. Talk to the waitress, bartender, ranger, cabbie, desk clerk, or florist. Ask where they eat dinner or breakfast, not where they think a visitor (you) should eat.

2. Always look at the room before registering. Try out the mattress, bed pillows, bedside light, shower faucet, towels, screens, and noise level—whatever matters to you. Avoid paying in advance. Even highly recommended places may have flaws and if you've already paid for the night, you may not receive a refund even if you leave right after checking in to the room.

3. Speak up if a quoted price seems high. The proprietor may have a room that wouldn't usually be rented (broken door, no bath or difficult access). Mention discounts, memberships, etc.; many of those programs require advance reservation for the best rate.

4. Don't dither and waste time. Gather information, make a plan, phone ahead, stick to it until it goes wrong, and then change if necessary. "What if" speculation can drive you nuts, plus you'll never write the article.

5. Smile, be quiet, listen. Even if you don't know the language, listen.

6. Study maps in advance and while you're on the go. Read the local papers.

7. Walk; you can't learn a place from the car. Take local transport. You'll meet the locals and see how they live; get help from bus or ferry drivers.

8. Don't do too much in a day. Don't "overeat" attractions or food. The all-you-can-eat approach to tourism is pointless and tiring.

9. Ask about the food. Don't be afraid to ask the price of the daily specials or the beverages described but not priced. Define what you want. Your idea of roast turkey might not be what turns up on the plate. If you don't know the language, point out the food you want.

10. Maintain your health. Rest and drink lots of fluids wherever you are. Avoid buffets, tepid food left out for people to serve themselves, and anything that isn't prepared fresh, preferably in front of you. In hot countries, eat hot cooked food. Carry your own water and snacks.

This appendix features useful publications, organizations, and Web sites for travel writers. These resources are a starting point for delving into the field. Many of the databases and marketing directories are offered online for an expensive annual fee, so many writers consult the print versions of these resource tools in libraries. Bear in mind, this list of resources is not exhaustive and is presented with the understanding that URL addresses, prices, and availability may have changed since compilation and checking in 2005.

BOOKS

The Associated Press Stylebook
The Associated Press
450 West Thirty-Third Street
New York, NY 10001
www.ap.org/pages/product/order.html
Handbook of standard journalism style.

The Chicago Manual of Style
The University of Chicago Press
1427 East Sixtieth Street
Chicago, IL 60637
www.press.uchicago.edu/Misc/Chicago/cmosfaq/cmosfaq.html
Grammar authority for academic and professional writing style.

Writer's Market
F+W Publications, Inc.
4700 East Galbraith Road
Cincinnati, OH 45236
www.writersmarket.com
Annual directory of markets for writers.

PERIODICALS AND NEWSLETTERS

Publishers Weekly
Reed Business Information
360 Park Avenue South
New York, NY 10010

www.publishersweekly.com
Trade magazine for the publishing business.

Travelwriter Marketletter

P.O. Box 1782
Springfield, VA 22151
www.travelwriterml.com

A monthly paid subscription newsletter—available in hard copy and on-line versions—that gives travel writers and photographers up-to-date information on markets for their work. TM serves a market of experienced and aspiring freelance travel journalists worldwide.

The Writer

Kalmbach Publishing Co.
21027 Crossroads Circle
P.O. Box 1612
Waukesha, WI 53187-1612
www.writermag.com

Monthly magazine for freelance writers.

Writer's Digest

F+W Publications
4700 East Galbraith Road
Cincinnati, OH 45236
www.writersdigest.com

Monthly magazine for writers.

ORGANIZATIONS

American Society of Journalists and Authors

1501 Broadway, Suite 302
New York, NY 10036
www.asja.org

Professional organization for freelance writers.

American Society of Media Photographers

150 North Second Street
Philadelphia, PA 19106
www.asmp.org

Professional organization for photographers in publication.

British Guild of Travel Writers

BGTW Secretariat
51b Askew Crescent

London W12 9DN
www.bgtw.metronet.co.uk

The British Guild of Travel Writers, founded in 1960, includes writers, editors, photographers, producers, and radio and television presenters in its membership.

Canadian Authors Association

Box 419
Campbellford, Ontario K0L 1L0
www.canauthors.org

National writing association founded in 1921, offering support and contacts for Canadian writers.

International Food, Wine & Travel Writers Association

1142 South Diamond Bar Boulevard #177
Diamond Bar, CA 91765-2203
www.ifwtwa.org

Professional association open to writers and photojournalists who publish at least ten articles per year relating to food, wine, or travel.

Midwest Travel Writers Association

P.O. Box 83542
Lincoln, NE 68501-3542
www.mtwa.org/index.html

Organization for professional travel writers in the Midwestern United States.

National Writers Union

113 University Place, Sixth Floor
New York, NY 10003
http://nwu.org

The union that represents freelance writers. For a discussion of freelance writers' reprint rights, visit www.freelancerights.com.

North American Snowsports Journalists Association

www.nasja.org

Association for ski and snowboard writers.

North American Travel Journalists Association

531 Main Street #902
El Segundo, CA 90245
www.natja.org

Professional association of writers, editors, and photographers dedicated to the hospitality industry.

Outdoor Writers Association of America
121 Hickory Street, Suite 1
Missoula, MT 59801
www.owaa.org

Organization for outdoor writers and photographers.

Pacific Asia Travel Association
www.pata.org

Travel industry association for Pacific and Asian destinations.

Society of American Travel Writers
1500 Sunday Drive, Suite 102
Raleigh, NC 27607
www.satw.org

Membership organization for writers with substantial contributions to the field of travel journalism.

Travel and Tourism Research Association
P.O. Box 2133
Boise, ID 83701
www.ttra.com

International association of travel research and marketing professionals. Provides data on tourism to universities and government agencies.

Travel Industry Association of America
1100 New York Avenue NW, Suite 450
Washington, DC 20005-3934
www.tia.org

TIA represents the U.S. travel and tourism industry to promote travel to and in the United States.

Travel Journalists Guild
P.O. Box 10643
Chicago, IL 60610
www.tjgonline.com

Membership organization for experienced freelance travel journalists.

Travelwriters.com
Marco Polo Publications, Inc.
695 Central Avenue, Suite 200A

St. Petersburg, FL 33701
www.travelwriters.com

This network links travel writers, tour companies, public relations agencies, and travelers.

PRIZES AND AWARDS

MediaGuardianUK Student Writing Awards
http://media.guardian.co.uk/studentmediaawards

The Guardian is looking for informative, entertaining travel writing that encapsulates the atmosphere and diversity of a destination.

The Thomas Cook Travel Book Award
www.thomascookpublishing.com/travelbookawards.htm

The Travel Book Award originated as an initiative of The Thomas Cook Group in 1980, with the aim of encouraging and rewarding the art of literary travel writing.

MARKETING REFERENCE SOURCES

Editor & Publisher International Year Book
Editor & Publisher
770 Broadway
New York, NY 10003-9595
www.editorandpublisher.com/eandp/resources/yearbook.jsp

Annual directory of daily and weekly newspapers throughout the world. Lists individual editor names and titles and includes information on syndicates. Listings are by city and state or city and country.

Gale Directory of Publications and Broadcast Media
Thomson Gale
P.O. Box 9187
Farmington Hills, MI 48333-9187
www.gale.com

Annual guide to publications and media organizations.

Hudson's Directories
P.O. Box 311
Rhinebeck, NY 12572
www.hudsonsdirectory.com

Publishes directories of newsletters, magazines, foreign media, Washington D.C. news media, and other categories.

The International Directory of Little Magazines & Small Presses

Dustbooks
P.O. Box 100
Paradise, CA 95967
www.dustbooks.com/lilmag.htm

Annual directory of small publishers and limited circulation magazines.

Literary Market Place

Information Today, Inc.
143 Old Marlton Pike
Medford, NJ 08055-8750
www.literarymarketplace.com/lmp/us/index_us.asp

Annual directory of the American and Canadian book publishing industries, including publishers, agents, editorial services, book manufacturers, associations, awards. Also publishes an international directory.

News Media Yellow Book

Leadership Directories, Inc.
104 Fifth Avenue
New York, NY 10011
www.leadershipdirectories.com/nmyb.htm

Comprehensive directory of news media personnel.

The Standard Periodical Directory

Oxbridge Communications
Thomson Gale
P.O. Box 9187
Farmington Hills, MI 48333-9187
www.gale.com

Annual directory of over 75,000 periodicals in the United States and Canada.

Ulrich's Periodicals Directory

R.R. Bowker LLC
630 Central Avenue
New Providence, NJ 07974
www.bowker.com/catalog/000055.htm

Annual directory of magazines and other periodicals. Also publishes an international periodicals directory.

Willings Press Guide

Chess House
34 Germain Street

Chesham, Bucks HP5 1SJ
England
www.willingspress.com

Directory of publications in the United Kingdom and British Commonwealth.

The Writer's Handbook

Kalmbach Publishing Co.
21027 Crossroads Circle
P.O. Box 1612
Waukesha, WI 53187-1612
www.writermag.com

Annual guide to magazine markets for freelance writers.

Writer's Market

F+W Publications
4700 East Galbraith Road
Cincinnati, OH 45236
www.writersdigest.com

Annual guide to markets for freelance writers.

USEFUL RESOURCES

American Youth Hotels

Hostelling International USA
8401 Colesville Road, Suite 600
Silver Spring, MD 20910
www.hiusa.org

The American affiliate of the Hostelling International network of more than five thousand hostels in over sixty countries.

Chase's Calendar of Events

McGraw-Hill Professional Books
1221 Avenue of the Americas
New York, NY 10020-1095
http://books.mcgraw-hill.com/landingpage.php?template=chases

Calendar of holidays, special events, anniversaries, etc.

The International Ecotourism Society

733 Fifteenth Street, NW, Suite 1000
Washington, DC 20005
www.ecotourism.org

International nonprofit organization dedicated to implementing the principles of minimal impact, sustainable tourism worldwide. Sponsors conferences and publications.

Magellan's

110 West Sola Street
Santa Barbara, CA 93101
www.magellans.com

Retail supplier of equipment and accessories for travelers.

National Park Service

U.S. Department of the Interior
1849 C Street, NW
Washington, DC 20240
www.nps.gov

*Useful source for maps, guides, and information about national parks in
the United States and its territories.*

The Official Travel Industry eDirectory

Advanstar, Inc.
One Park Avenue
New York, NY 10016
www.otid.com

Travel industry reference source.

Sister Cities International

1301 Pennsylvania Avenue, NW, Suite 850
Washington, DC 20004
www.sister-cities.org

*This organization sponsors sister cities by connecting cities in different
countries for cultural and commercial exchange.*

United States Servas, Inc.

11 John St., Room 505
New York, NY 10038
www.usservas.org and www.servas.org

*International nongovernmental membership organization promoting glob-
al peace and communication.*

World Chamber of Commerce Directory

www.chamberofcommerce.com

Reference source for chambers of commerce.

WEB SITES OF INTEREST TO TRAVEL WRITERS

Author-Network

www.author-network.com/travel.html

Links to travel writing sites and online travel magazines.

The Library of Congress
http://loc.gov

Lonely Planet Guidebooks
www.lonelyplanet.com/help/guide.htm

Mediabistro.com
www.mediabistro.com

Home to the Freelance Marketplace, a searchable resource for writers, editors, and other media professionals to get freelance assignments; news, articles, career information, and courses.

Mondo Times
www.mondotimes.com/1/world/ca/61/3042/7615

Online news directory.

NICS - Web Style Guide
www.nics.gov.uk/acc/styleandtone/publishing/editing2.html

Fact checking and editing.

Project Gutenberg
www.gutenberg.org

Library of eBooks.

USC Annenberg Online Journalism Review
www.ojr.org/ojr/wiki/ethics

A guide about ethics for writers.

Transitions Abroad
www.transitionsabroad.com/information/writers/index.shtml

Educational travel resource.

Travel News Daily
www.travelnewsdaily.com

Travel news.

Travel Takes
www.fontayne.com/takes.html

Online newsletter published by public relations firm, The Fontayne Group.

Travelers' Tales
www.travelerstales.com/contact.html

Travel publisher.

U.S. Copyright Office
www.copyright.gov

Copyright information.

Wikipedia
www.wikipedia.org

The free encyclopedia.

Wired Style
http://hotwired.wired.com/hardwired/wiredstyle/toc/index.html

A guide to online style by the publishers of Wired magazine.

WriteNet
www.writenet.org/index.html

A resource for writers and teachers.

The Writer's Life
www.thewriterslife.homestead.com/home.html

An interactive online writing resource.

Writers Resources Style Guide
www.ability.org.uk/writers_resources_style_guides.html

Links to resources on grammar, word choice, and American/British usage.

Writers Weekly
www.writersweekly.com

Marketing information for freelance writers.

adventure story - a travel story that focuses on physical challenges and outdoor thrills

advertorial - a special travel supplement or advertisement section with travel articles paid for by a special interest group such as a national tourist office, a cruise line, airline, or destination resort

all rights - a writer sells the copyright to the material forever

assignment - an editor commissions a writer to prepare an article for a specified price by a certain date

bimonthly - published every two months

biweekly - published every two weeks

boldface - extra-dark typeface useful for titles and subheads

byline - the writer's name, usually printed at the top under the title or at the end for shorter items (some articles do not carry a byline)

caption - a description of the scene in a photograph

circulation - the number of copies distributed for a given publication

clips - copies of previously published work

column inch - the type contained in one inch of a typeset column; column width varies as does type size

contract - a legal document signed by parties to mutually agreeable terms

contributor's copies - free copies given to the writer sometimes in lieu of payment

copy or **hard copy -** a manuscript in typewritten form before it is typeset or posted to the Internet

copyediting - editing for grammar, punctuation, and typographical style

copyright - the protection of a printed work

correspondent - a writer in the field who regularly provides stories for a publication

cover letter - a letter of introduction submitted by the writer with finished manuscript or clips submitted for consideration

credit line - the name of the photographer or source of an image

dateline - the date and place where subject of article took place; runs at the start of the first paragraph

destination story - a travel article about a specific resort, location, site of interest

exclusive market - a noncompeting publication in different circulation areas

first-person voice - the article is written from the author's point of view

first rights - the writer sells the publication the right to publish the article the first time (known as first serial rights and first North American serial rights); the exclusive right to publish the material in Canada and the United States; copyright reverts to the author after publication, unless otherwise specified

free sample copy - editors will send a free copy of the publication if requested

freelance writer - a writer not affiliated with a particular publication who has the right to sell articles to any publication that will buy them

honorarium - a small payment for speaking, teaching, or participating in a panel discussion

justification - spacing type to a specific width so the right-hand margin is uniform

kill fee - money paid to the writer when the publication cancels the contracted work, usually less than the full fee and rarely paid unless the writer and publication have signed a contract in advance

model release - printed consent form to be signed by a person featured in a photograph intended for publication

monthly - a publication issued once a month

ms. - abbreviation for a manuscript

one-time rights - a publication buys the right to print photos or a story once

payment on acceptance - the writer is paid when the piece is accepted, before publication

payment on publication - the writer is paid after the article is published

pen name - use of a name other than legal name (many publications are wary of writers who use pen names)

pixel depth or **bits per pixel (BPP) -** the number of bits used to represent the pixel value in a digital image; determines the image quality and density

press release - announcements issued to the press by public relations agencies, corporate and government communications departments

proof or **page proofs -** the printed edition of an article or book prior to final printing, used for examination and final corrections

quarterly - a publication that comes out four times a year

query - a letter or e-mail proposing an article idea to an editor

regional publication - a magazine or paper dedicated to a limited geographic area

rejection - a letter or e-mail from an editor stating that a manuscript or a query doesn't suit the publication's needs (usually a form letter)

reporting time - the length of time it takes an editor to respond to a writer concerning a query or manuscript

reprint fees - payment to the writer when a magazine or paper uses work that has been printed elsewhere

SASE - a self-addressed stamped envelope

second serial rights - a publication purchases the rights to print material that has appeared elsewhere

semimonthly - a publication that comes out twice a month

semiweekly - a publication that comes out twice a week

sidebar - a small column, box, or paragraph with useful information about costs, addresses, weather, etc.; a news report that accompanies a longer article with specific information on one aspect of the story

simultaneous submission - the same article is offered to several publications at the same time (writers should advise editors when making a simultaneous submission)

slant - a writer's approach to the material so it fits with a specific magazine or paper

small press publication - a limited-circulation magazine that publishes literary content such as essays, reviews, short fiction, poetry, and opinion pieces

speculation or **"on spec" -** an editor does not commit to buy an article but agrees to consider it when the writer submits the work

stringer - a writer with a continuing relationship with a publication; generally, a stringer is a steady and regular contributor

tear sheet - all the pages from a print or web-based publication that make up an entire article; like contributors copies, they are usually sent to the writer shortly after publication (if from a Web-based publication, author must print out personal copies and save the URL link)

unsolicited or **"over the transom" manuscript -** an article that was not requested by an editor

work for hire - the writer receives a set fee for the writing project and surrenders copyright

writers guidelines - specifications for writers created by each print or Web-based publication; guidelines for writers may be posted on the publication's Web site or may be requested by the writer

index

More great ideas from
WRITER'S DIGEST BOOKS!

GETTING THE WORDS RIGHT

by Theodore Rees Cheney

Rewrite, revise, and refine your writing with the book that has helped more than 80,000 writers produce their best work. Theodore Rees Chaney offers 39 targeted ways to improve your existing work through revision and tighter writing.

ISBN-10: 1-58297-358-X, ISBN-13: 9-781582-973586, paperback, 256 pages, #10989

SOME WRITERS DESERVE TO STARVE

by Elaura Niles

Face the hard facts involved in getting your work published by understanding just how the industry works. Written to better your odds of writing success, Elaura Niles offers no-nonsense facts and a dash of wit to help you pitch your work and get it published!

ISBN-10: 1-58297-354-7, ISBN-13: 9-781582-973548, paperback 240 pages, #10985

A WRITER'S PARIS

by Eric Maisel

Plan an actual writing sojourn to Paris or just imagine a getaway in your mind. This stunningly beautiful book written by Eric Maisel, a renowned author and creativity expert, will help you discover fresh ideas and new visions about the art and craft of writing.

ISBN-10: 1-58297-359-8, ISBN-13: 9-781582-973593, flexibind linen, 256 pages, #10990

These and other fine books from Writer's Digest are available at your local bookstore or online supplier.